PLAIN
and
not
so
PLAIN
ACADEMY

A simpler approach to home based schooling

Fifth Grade

Basic Skills

Curriculum

To the home educator,

I am very happy that you have chosen to purchase our products. We believe that our world is way too complex and that it can be simplified to avoid the chaos and confusion. Learning at home should be an enjoyable time between you and your child. Not something that they dread because they have hundreds of repetition problems to do over and over again. Plain and not so Plain Academy's approach to schooling is to concentrate on the basics and then fill in with real life learning. This approach to schooling is meant to take the stress and fear out of teaching your child at home. Your child's entire elementary schooling is going to be one big repetition, year after year. We take all the extra complexities out of schooling and get back to the basics of reading, writing, and arithmetic. By approaching schooling this way, your child will be more confident as they work through the worksheets. This allows extra time to pursue other areas of interest.

If you find that your child is struggling with a particular concept in Plain and not so Plain's curriculum, do some extra problems until they understand it. Make it fun. If they struggle with getting each worksheet done all at one time, have them do part of it and then take a break. No stress.

This 5th grade basic skills curriculum is enough to do 36 weeks of school four times per week. I would recommend doing four days of "worksheet schooling" and then one day of real life schooling. That would give you 180 days worth of record-keeping schooling. Do four pages each day. Also included are 25 weeks of vocabulary words every 5th grader should know. Instructions are included as how to implement these into their week. Also math speed drills in addition, subtraction, multiplication, and division are included in the back section.

This year focus on reading books. If they don't enjoy reading themselves, have a read aloud time and do it everyday. If you are not able to designate a time to do that each day, look into audio books. This will help instill a love of reading.

If needed, an answer key is provided on my blog under the homeschooling section. I was unable to put it in this book due to the size.

Be blessed,

Amy Maryon

founder and owner of www.plainandnotsoplain.com a simpler lifestyle in our complex world

Uncopyrighted

week 1 copy your words

amaze

anyway

basic

brace

braid

daisy

daydream

delay

dismay

essay

faint

hasten

matriarch

nature

place

raisin

wage

rate

Count aloud: Count by tens from 10 to 100. Count by hundreds from 100 to 1000.

Mental math:

- 3+3
- 30+30
- 300+300
- 40+50
- 200+600
- 50¢ +50¢
- 20¢+20¢+20¢

Finding Patterns

You learn counting early on in life. When we count by 1's we say 1,2,3,4,5...

When we count by 2's we say, 2,4,6,8,10, ...

An ordered list of numbers form a sequence. We can study a sequence to discover its counting pattern or rule.

What are the next three terms in this counting sequence:

3,6,9,12,_____,_____,_____

as you can see they are counting by 3's. The next three numbers would be 15,18,21

Your turn:

6,8,10,_____,____,_____

7,14,21,_____,_____,_____

45,40,35,_____,_____,_____

There are ten digits in our number system. They are 0,1,2,3,4,5,6,7,8,9. The number 254 has three digits. The last digit is 4.

Your turn:

How many digits are in each number:

175,000_____   322,342,222_____   221_____

Common Nouns

Common nouns name people, places, and things. They are general nouns. (not specific).

person- police officer   A police officer helps to keep us safe.

place--- park   We love to take the children to play at the park.

thing- coat   Don't forget to grab your coat before we leave.

_____

Fill in the following blanks with common nouns.

1. The _flowers_ look pretty in the vase.
2. My _Alarm clock_ woke me up by buzzing loudly.
3. My _family_ is visiting from Michigan.
4. The _Post office_ sells stamps.
5. The _cat_ scratched my leg.
6. My _blanket_ is nice and soft.
7. My _car_ feels very hot.
8. You can find many _fish_ in the water.
9. We have a lot of _food_.
10. Go find the _toy_ that you lost last week.

_____

Circle the common nouns in the paragraph below. (9 of them)

In that case, go home and pack a suitcase. Take your list and grab your shoes. Then catch a steamship bound for Europe. When you arrive, go to the nearest restaurant and order a soda. Make sure to be polite to the waitress. When you are finished eating, go to the hotel and rest for the evening.

_____

Write a short paragraph telling about a place that you visited. Use at least 6 common nouns.

In the morning we went in the car and went to Walmart to get clothes and glasses and curtins too. Then we went to bobevens and had food. (ATE) RESTAURANT.

Your other task for the day is to read. You can look online at www.plainandnotsoplain.com for book recommendations that we enjoyed reading or do an online search to find something that you are interested in. You should read for a minimum of one hour per day.

Write down the title of the book you are reading and how long you read for today.

Diary of a wimpy kid
    Hand luck

30 min

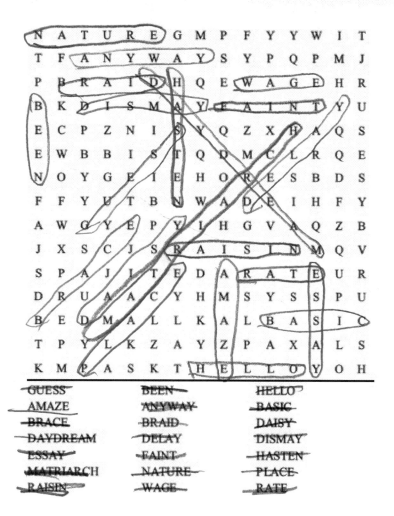

N A T U R E G M P F Y Y W I T
T F A N Y W A Y S Y P Q P M J
P B R A I D H Q E W A G E H R
B K D I S M A Y F A I N T Y U
E C P Z N I S Y Q Z X H A Q S
E W B B I S T Q D M C L R Q E
N O Y G E I E H O R E S B D S
F F Y U T B N W A D E I H F Y
A W G Y E P Y I H G V A Q Z B
J X S C J S R A I S I N M Q V
S P A J I T E D A R A T E U R
D R U A A C Y H M S Y S S P U
B E D M A L L K A L B A S I C
T P Y L K Z A Y Z P A X A L S
K M P A S K T H E L L O Y O H

GUESS   BEEN   HELLO
AMAZE   ANYWAY   BASIC
BRACE   BRAID   DAISY
DAYDREAM   DELAY   DISMAY
ESSAY   FAINT   HASTEN
MATRIARCH   NATURE   PLACE
RAISIN   WAGE   RATE

Count aloud: count up and down by tens between 10 and 100. Count up and down by hundreds between 100 and 1000.

Mental math:

- 6+6
- 60+60
- 600+600
- 60 seconds+70 seconds
- 70 seconds+80 seconds
- 300+300+300
- 90+90
- 50¢+50¢+50¢

  Even and odd numbers. When numbers have a pair we say they are even. To tell whether a large number is even, the last digit has to be 0,2,4,6,8 (we say 0 because 10 ends in 0) If it ends in any other number, it is odd.

  Your turn:

  Circle the numbers that are even

  3577   7644   87   66

  1234   20,001   391,048

Half of an even number is a whole number. We can take 4 apples and split them in half and give each person 2. When we have an odd number and have to split it in half then we will end up with some halves.

counting numbers	1	2	3	4	5	6	7	8	9	10
half of number	½	1	1 ½	2	2 ½	3	3 ½	4	4 ½	5

What is half of 5?_____

What is half of 8?_____

Common nouns

Fill in the following chart with the correct common nouns:

boy	bat	veterinarian	truck	restaurant	park
library	tree	town	police officer	car	
parent	country	student	crayon		

Person	Place	Thing
boy	restaurant	bat
veterinarian	park	truck
police officer	library	tree
parent	town	car
student	country	crayon

Fill in the blanks with common nouns.

1. A _Veterinarian_ is a doctor who helps animals.
2. My family likes to swim at the ___park___.
3. Will you grab the _crayon_ to help spread the jam?
4. You need a glove and a __bat__ to play baseball.
5. Please go hang up your __truck__.

Write me a short paragraph telling me about your favorite animal. Use at least 5 common nouns.

My favorite animal is a dog

Your other task for the day is to read. You can look online at www.plainandnotsoplain.com for book recommendations that we enjoyed reading or do an online search to find something that you are interested in. You should read for a minimum of one hour per day.

Write down the title of the book you are reading and how long you read for today.

Diary of a wimpy kid

30 min

write sentences with your words

count aloud: count up and down by tens between 10 and 200. Count up and down by hundreds between 100 and 2000.

mental math:

- 20+300
- 320+20
- 340+200
- 250+40
- 250+400
- 120 seconds +60 seconds
- 600+120
- 30¢+70¢

Each digit in a number has a place value. The value of a digit depends on its place, or position in the number. We identify the value of the digits in a number when we want to write the number in expanded form. Expanded form is a way of writing a number that shows the value of a digit.

In the number 542, write it in expanded form. It is made up of 500+40+2

Your turn:

Use digits to write the number five hundreds plus seven tens plus eight ones.

In 560, which digit shows the number of tens

The number 80 means "eight tens". The number 800 means eight what?

How much money is half of $10

What number equals five tens

Write the expanded notation of 678

Common nouns

Fill in the chart with 5 common nouns.

Person	Place	Thing
Boy	Restaurant	Dog
Girl	Town	Cat
~~Doctor~~ ranger	Citty	table
Doctor	Cuntry	tree
Teacher	Vilige	Tool

Find and circle the common noun

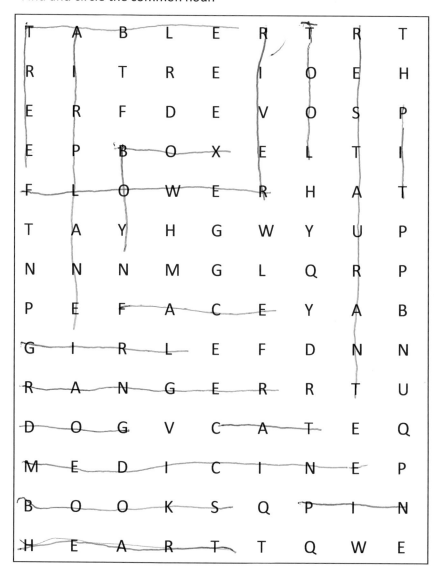

Word bank

~~MEDICINE~~
~~RANGER~~
~~TABLE~~
~~TREE~~
~~RIVER~~
~~TOOL~~
~~AIRPLANE~~
~~RESTAURANT~~
~~BOX~~
~~FLOWER~~
~~PIT~~
~~BOY~~
~~CAT~~
~~CAT~~
~~BOOKS~~
~~FACE~~
~~GIRL~~
~~PIN~~
~~HEART~~

Your other task for the day is to read. You can look online at www.plainandnotsoplain.com for book recommendations that we enjoyed reading or do an online search to find something that you are interested in. You should read for a minimum of one hour per day.

Write down the title of the book you are reading and how long you read for today.

DiAry of a wimpy Kid.

_____

30min

_____

Quiz

Comparing numbers

When we compare numbers we use the < less than and the >greater than symbol. We also can use the = equal symbol. When writing, the large opening points towards the bigger number and the smaller (point) aims toward the smaller number.

Compare with < > or =

51_____21   8_____8   3_____9

Write out four is less than ten

Write out fifteen is greater than twelve

Which digit in 987 is in the ones place

Circle the odd numbers

355,322   35,121   6,784,321

Write the following numbers in order from least to greatest:

435   354   523

20,24,28,_____,_____,_____

106,104,102,_____,_____,_____

What number equals 9 tens

What number equals 11 tens

What number is half of 9

Proper nouns

Proper nouns name SPECIFIC people, places, and things. In a sentence, the noun is the person, place, or thing that can act or be talked about.

Dr. Clark----a specific person

California----a specific place

Empire State Building----a specific thing

Write the correct words from the box to complete the journal entry. Use ONLY proper nouns.

Uncle Jeff	Principal Sam	my principal	planet
my school	Grand Canyon	book	tomorrow
Venus	Saturday	the playground	Flat Rock park
The Shaggy Cat	national park	my uncle	Mountain Top School

I love ___Saturday___ mornings. I go to ___Flat rock park___ to walk the trails and read my book, ___Grand canyon___. Later Aunt Sue and ___My uncle___ come to my house. We plan our trip to the ___national park___. We use the telescope to look at ___Venus___ when it gets dark. On Monday, it's back to ___my School___. I like ___my principal___. He is a good principal. But I still look forward to the weekend.

REMEMBER PROPER NOUNS ALWAYS BEGIN WITH A CAPITAL LETTER!

Grab your book that you are reading and copy ten proper nouns from the pages.

1. Mr. Sandoval
2. Rowley
3. mingo kids
4. _____
5. _____
6. _____
7. _____
8. _____
9. _____
10. _____

Your other task for the day is to read. You can look online at www.plainandnotsoplain.com for book recommendations that we enjoyed reading or do an online search to find something that you are interested in. You should read for a minimum of one hour per day.

Write down the title of the book you are reading and how long you read for today.

Diary of a wimpy Kid

2 chapters

Begin memorizing these common prepositions. It is one of those things like math facts that if you know them, it will make your future in grammar so much easier. This week take the first column and memorize.

about	before	down	like	past	until
above	behind	during	near	since	up
across	below	except	of	through	upon
after	beneath	for	off	to	with
against	beside	from	on	toward	within
along	between	in	onto	under	without
around	beyond	inside	outside	underneath	
at	but	into	over		
	by				
	concerning				

week 2 spelling words

breathe

breeze

crease

delight

donkey

eager

hockey

kidney

lease

plead

queen

recent

respond

screech

sleeve

squeak

steam

zebra

count aloud: count up and down by tens between 0 and 200. count up and down by hundreds between 0 and 2000

count aloud:

- 200+60+300
- 20+600+30
- 250 cm+250 cm
- 640+250
- 260+260

Use digits to write two hundred forty-five

Use digits to write five hundred three dollars and fifty cents

Use digits to write four hundred twenty

Use words to name $623.15

Arrange these numbers in order from least to greatest

462   624   246   426

Circle the even numbers

353,234   321,242   653,111

0,9,18,_____,_____,_____

25,30,35,_____,_____,_____

Proper nouns

Fill in the following chart with proper nouns. Remember proper nouns are to be capitalized.

Person	Place	Thing
Toni	taco bell	catfish
MiA	burgerking	huscky
LeiA	Mcdonolds	tuncky
SArA	Kroger	dog
Crissy	Walmant	bunny

Circle the Proper nouns in the following paragraph. (13 proper nouns)

My favorite place to go for the day is to Hendersonville. I like to go on a Saturday morning when it is bustling with people. My favorite place to eat is at Soly Luna's. I love their fajitas. Made with real Mexican tortillas. I then walk down Main Street and look for Sam my friend. He is usually found playing his guitar in front of the Hands on Museum. He loves his Gibson guitar and can play very well. After we have had a full morning of food and shopping we like to go relax on his boat, The Sailing Seas. I love Lake Summit, it is such a relaxing lake to boat on. We can usually fish and catch some Rainbow Trout to eat. He prepares the fish on a Coleman campfire stove. I love fresh fish. Saturday's are my favorite day of the week!

Your other task for the day is to read. You can look online at www.plainandnotsoplain.com for book recommendations that we enjoyed reading or do an online search to find something that you are interested in. You should read for a minimum of one hour per day.

Write down the title of the book you are reading and how long you read for today.

DiARy of a wimpy Kid

_____

1 chapter

_____

```
E  O  A  Y  Y  H  W  G  Z  C  A  E  N  J  R
I  B  S  H  W  C  Z  L  W  P  T  Q  V  E  T
C  K  C  P  Z  P  L  E  A  D  Z  L  G  R  K
U  G  R  Z  C  B  B  Z  J  K  W  A  R  A  G
C  R  E  A  S  E  I  P  E  A  E  Q  E  O  S
L  M  E  Q  D  O  N  K  E  Y  Q  U  S  O  T
E  C  C  U  P  J  N  J  I  Q  Y  P  W  E
A  R  H  E  D  T  F  B  F  S  E  T  O  P  A
S  L  E  E  V  E  F  G  S  N  G  X  N  F  M
E  X  H  N  Z  J  L  P  D  G  R  H  D  Z  R
D  F  N  E  U  J  J  I  C  H  O  C  K  E  Y
N  Z  E  B  L  F  K  P  G  R  A  M  K  B  F
C  R  Y  J  T  G  W  Z  L  H  V  B  P  R  R
B  E  I  X  Y  R  E  C  E  N  T  P  V  A  W
E  F  B  R  E  A  T  H  E  Z  X  C  Y  Y  P
```

BREATHE	BREEZE	CREASE
DELIGHT	DONKEY	EAGER
HOCKEY	KIDNEY	LEASE
PLEAD	QUEEN	RECENT
RESPOND	SCREECH	SLEEVE
SQUEAK	STEAM	ZEBRA

count aloud: count up and down by 20s between 0 and 200. Count up and down by 200s between 0 and 2000.

mental math:

- 400+50+300+40
- 320+300
- 320+320
- 60+200+20+400
- $40+$250

Numbers that are added are called "addends" The answer to an addition problem is the sum. We can add numbers in any order.

Find the sum of 7,4,3, and 6?

To solve this, look for the ones that add up to 10. 7 and 3=10 and 6 and 4=10. Your answer 20.

Your turn—do as above:

8+6+2_____   4+7+3+6_____   8+7+2+3_____

7+3+4_____   5+5+3_____   6+2+8+4_____

When adding larger numbers, remember to line them up in a column for easier addition. Start on the right and move to the left. If you have to carry over, do so.

$$
\begin{array}{r} 436 \\ +123 \\ \hline \end{array}
\qquad
\begin{array}{r} 650 \\ +\ 79 \\ \hline \end{array}
\qquad
\begin{array}{r} 752 \\ +183 \\ \hline \end{array}
$$

Compare 5+5+5_____4+5+6 (<>=)

Common and proper nouns

Give me an example of the following:

common nouns

Person	Place	Thing
girl	store	dog
boy	restaront	cat
kid	town	slide
grandma	country	car
grandpa	vilige	swing

Proper nouns

Person	Place	thing
Toni Soto	Walmart	Yellow slide
Stacey lin	Kroger	Mustang
Grandma Sara	BigBoy	Golden richrever
Mia Soto	MCDonalds	Gray cat
Mike Soto	Michigan	purple swing

Your other task for the day is to read. You can look online at www.plainandnotsoplain.com for book recommendations that we enjoyed reading or do an online search to find something that you are interested in. You should read for a minimum of one hour per day.

Write down the title of the book you are reading and how long you read for today.

Diary of a wimpy Kid

2 chapters

write sentences for your words

count aloud: count up and down by 20s between 0 and 200. Count up and down by 200s between 0 and 2000.

mental math:

- $25+$25
- $300+$400
- 30+450
- $750+$250
- $50+$350
- 360 seconds +360 seconds

Place value

hundred thousands	ten thousands	thousands	hundreds	tens	ones

You place a comma counting over every 3 places to separate the numbers. This also helps to make it easier to read. When reading a large number—within the commas read it as a 3 digit number. For example 321,233 Read the first set of numbers as three hundred twenty-one. Then determine which place value you are in, this one is thousands. So three hundred twenty-one thousands, two hundred thirty- three. We don't say the word "and". Just say in between the commas and then which value they are worth.

Your turn:

Use words to name 53270

Use digits to write "one hundred fifty thousand, two hundred thirty- four

Use digits to write sixty-three thousand, one hundred seventeen

Use digits to write two hundred six thousand, seven hundred one


```
  463          311          876
 +321          +87         +239
```

Proper nouns.

Copy the following sentences and write them correctly. Use a capital letter for the beginning of the sentence, capitalize the proper nouns and use correct punctuation.

1. our friend, brooklyn, works at the zoo
2. wow, that is the prettiest swan we have ever seen in lake lure
3. do you like the town of zirconia
4. how old is your sister lauren
5. my birthday is in februrary not in march
6. meet us at the new york zoo on tuesday
7. will you meet us in paris for thanksgiving
8. we will all join up at christmas to give presents to each other
9. how many sisters does sarah have
10. the summer months, june, july, and august are always a busy time for sam

1 Our friend, Brooklyn, works at the zoo.

2 Wow, that is the prettiest swan we have ever seen in Lake Lure.

3 Do you like the town of Zirconia.

4 How old is your sister Lauren?

5 My Birthday is in February not in march.

6 Meet us at the New york zoo on Tuesday.

7 Will you meet us in Paris for Thanksgiving.

8 We will all join up at Christmas to give presents to each other.

9 How many sisters does Sarah have.

10 The summer months, June, July, and August are always a busy time for sam.

Your other task for the day is to read. You can look online at www.plainandnotsoplain.com for book recommendations that we enjoyed reading or do an online search to find something that you are interested in. You should read for a minimum of one hour per day.

Write down the title of the book you are reading and how long you read for today.

DiARY of a wimpy Kid

1 chapter

Quiz

Addition and subtraction are inverse operations. This means that one operation undoes the other. If we add 3 and 5, we get 8. If we subtract 3 from 8 we get 5. For every addition fact, we can form a subtraction fact. For example:

2+3=5   5-3=2   3+2=5   5-2=3

These are called fact families

Write two addition facts and two subtraction facts for each fact family:

7,8,15

5,7,12

Which digit is in the thousands place in 4654

What is sixty-four plus two hundred six

Use word to name the number four hundred plus four tens plus four ones

Use digits to write eight hundred two

When seven is subtracted from fifteen what is the difference

Add to find the sum:

36+403+97   572+386+38

Half of the 18 students were girls. How many girls were there

Choose a proper noun of your own to complete the sentence.

1. I live in the state of _Ohio_.
2. We have a park called _Delco_.
3. A lake by us is called _lake eary_.
4. My state capital is _Columbus_.
5. We hike up the mountain called _Mount evrest_.
6. The nearest big town is called _Cinsinaty_.
7. My road is called _Tabor Ave_.
8. My church is called _Our laddy of the emaculet cuseption_.
9. Our pastor is named _Father Joshof_.
10. My mom's name is _Stacie_.

Fill in the following with common nouns not proper.

1. My favorite foods to eat are _Junk food_, _ice cream_, and _Chips_.
2. My favorite animal is _Dog_.
3. My favorite outside activity is _Swim_.
4. The animal I least like is _Cat_.
5. My least favorite food is _Vegtibles_.
6. A sport played outdoors is _Soccer_.
7. A sport played indoors is _basket ball_.
8. _fish_ you will find in a body of water.
9. _Clowds_ you will find up in the air.
10. _people_ you will find on the land.

Use a crayon or colored pencil and highlight all the proper nouns one color and all the common nouns another color. Notice that none of them are capitalized☺

river	mississippi river	georgia	state
oak	tree	lauren	girl
town	zirconia	doll	sarah
teacher	mr. maryon	country	ireland
mt. mitchell	restaurant	jesus	person

Your other task for the day is to read. You can look online at www.plainandnotsoplain.com for book recommendations that we enjoyed reading or do an online search to find something that you are interested in. You should read for a minimum of one hour per day.

Write down the title of the book you are reading and how long you read for today.

Diary of a wimpy Kid

1 chapter

week 3 spelling words

arrive

childhood

chime

climate

delight

digest

fighting

grind

ideal

prize

sight

silence

spying

style

thigh

timing

title

violin

count aloud: count up and down by 50s between 0 and 500. Count up and down by 500s between 0 and 5000.

mental math:

- $250+$250
- $75+$125
- 60 degrees+20 degrees
- 600-200
- 6000-2000
- 860+70

Subtraction. We line up the numbers in column form and we start on the right and move to the left. Remember you cannot take away if the number on top is smaller. You will have to borrow from the neighbor. We borrow (10) because between each place value is times ten.

```
  346          319          600
 -264          -73         -123
```

What digit in 596, shows the number of tens

One hundred is equal to how many tens

Write five hundred forty is greater than five hundred fourteen

remember to rewrite these in column form to make them easier:

$346-$178=   415-378=   429+85+671=

Regular plural nouns

A plural noun names more than one person, place, or thing. Most nouns are made plural by adding an "s" to the end of the word.

Tables   cups   baseballs

Make the following plural by adding an s.

Crayon becomes _Crayons_

Phone becomes _Phones_

Hair becomes _Hairs_

Pen becomes _Pens_

Some nouns need an "es" added to the end of the word to make them plural. Nouns ending in the letters "s, x, or z or in a ch or sh sound need es".

Bosses   taxes   benches   dishes

Loss becomes _Losses_

Fox becomes _Foxes_

Box becomes _Boxes_

Lunch becomes _Lunches_

Wish becomes _Wishes_

Make the following plural:

Car _Cars_   couch _Couches_

Bench _Benches_   Doll _Dolls_

Wish _Wishes_   watch _watches_

Girl _Girls_   kiss _Kisses_

Chair _Chairs_   box _boxes_

Your other task for the day is to read. You can look online at www.plainandnotsoplain.com for book recommendations that we enjoyed reading or do an online search to find something that you are interested in. You should read for a minimum of one hour per day.

Write down the title of the book you are reading and how long you read for today.

DIARY of a wimpy kid

1 chapter

Begin memorizing these common prepositions. It is one of those things like math facts that if you know them, it will make your future in grammar so much easier. This week take the first column and memorize.

about	before	down	like	past	until
above	behind	during	near	since	up
across	below	except	of	through	upon
after	beneath	for	off	to	with
against	beside	from	on	toward	within
along	between	in	onto	under	without
around	beyond	inside	outside	underneath	
at	but	into	over		
	by				
	concerning				

```
S  R  L  S  P  Y  I  N  G  M  C  H  I  M  E
E  Y  N  S  T  Y  L  E  T  A  T  Q  V  A  X
Q  R  I  Y  T  I  T  L  E  D  H  Z  P  L  M
X  S  D  I  K  R  P  B  C  R  I  V  P  E  H
M  I  E  R  U  R  D  T  H  R  G  K  R  V  Q
U  L  A  B  Y  J  J  F  I  G  H  T  I  N  G
A  E  L  R  K  J  T  A  L  M  J  Q  Z  S  T
L  N  Z  B  R  K  N  M  D  T  I  L  E  H  J
E  C  X  R  S  I  S  V  H  H  I  N  G  N  C
G  E  M  N  L  T  V  B  O  K  Z  I  G  U  L
R  K  O  O  S  Y  J  E  O  G  L  P  Y  G  I
I  J  I  E  S  C  H  V  D  E  M  D  R  Q  M
N  V  G  S  I  G  H  T  D  U  O  X  W  E  A
D  I  P  V  W  C  A  X  Z  X  P  X  C  L  T
D  I  U  K  F  X  S  B  V  G  E  M  O  R  E
```

ARRIVE	CHILDHOOD	CHIME
CLIMATE	DELIGHT	DIGEST
FIGHTING	GRIND	IDEAL
PRIZE	SIGHT	SILENCE
SPYING	STYLE	THIGH
TIMING	TITLE	VIOLIN

count aloud: count up and down by 25s between 0 and 200

mental math:

- $5000+$4500
- 6000-4000
- 500yards-400yards
- 125 feet+125 feet
- 6+6-2+5
- 640+260

In the number sentence, there is a missing addend. The letter w is used to represent the missing addend

$$8+w=15$$

A number sentence with an equal sign is often called an equation. Since eight plus seven equals 15, we know that the missing addend is 7. Notice we did that by subtracting.

Your turn: Find the missing addend

$24 +m=37$ subtract to find the missing addend

Find the missing addend

$15+20+6+w=55$

$35+m=67$ m=_____

$n+27=40$ n=_____

Use the digits 4,5,6 and write a three digit odd number greater than 500

What is five hundred ten minus fifty one

More on plural

If a word ends in the letter "y" then the y is changed to an "i" before adding the es.

Countries	**cities**	**flies**

Strawberry becomes _Strawberries_

However, words that end in "y" with a vowel before the y only add the s.

Boys	**keys**	**donkeys**

Toy becomes _Toys_

Change the following into plural nouns:

Activity _Activitys_   essay _essays_

Enemy _Enemies_   valley _Valleys_

Display _Displayes_   party _Parties_

Fly _Flys_   trolley _trolleys_

In some cases, the noun has to change its spelling before making the plural form. If a noun ends in f or fe, and the f sound can still be heard in the plural form, just add s. However if the final sound of the plural form is v, then change the f to ve and add the s.

Roofs (f sound)	**gulfs (f sound)**
Calves (v sound)	**loaves (v sound)**

Change the following into plural nouns:

Calf _Calves_   knife _Knifes_

Wolf _Wolves_   cliff _Cliffs_

Circle the correct spelling of the plural nouns in the following sentences.

1. I have made many new (friendes/**friends**) this year at school.

2. Two little (**foxes**/foxs) ran through the (woodes/**woods**) today.

3. The (**leaves**/leafs) are falling here and turning beautiful colors.

4. One leaf is the color of the (cherrys/**cherries**) on our tree at home.

5. In church, I am going to be in the (playes/**plays**) that they put on.

6. When I get home I am going to have to wash the dinner (**dishes**/dishs.)

Your other task for the day is to read. You can look online at www.plainandnotsoplain.com for book recommendations that we enjoyed reading or do an online search to find something that you are interested in. You should read for a minimum of one hour per day.

Write down the title of the book you are reading and how long you read for today.

DiARY of A Wimpy Kid
_____

1 chapter
_____

write sentences for your words

REVIEW

What is five hundred minus forty two

What digit in 325,875 shows the number of hundreds

We can count to 30 by 3s or by 10s. We do not count to 30 when counting by

a. 2s   b.4s   c.5s   d.6s

Think of one odd number and one even number and add them. Is the sum odd or even

Compare 100-10_____100-20

rewrite the following in column form:

$363-$179= $570-$91=

367+56+654=   32+248+165

12+4=80 r=_____

Give an example for each of the following rules below:

Rule: Nouns ending in the letters s, x, or z or in a ch or sh sound need es.

| Couches | bushes | battleaxes |
| buses | bratzes | |

Rule: Words that end in y with a vowel before the y add s.

| sta | | |

Rule: If a word ends in the letter y, then the y is changed to an i before adding the es.

| Stories | Panties | yesterdaies |

Rule: If a noun ends in f or fe, and the f sound can still be heard in the plural form add s.

| Knifes | stuffs | kliffs |

Make a list of ten of your favorite things. Then on the lines next to them, write them in plural form.

Singular	Plural
1 dogs	boxer
2 buttanfly	Monark Butterfly
3 ice cream	cookie douch ice cream
4 chips	Hotche touse
5 cake	Chocalite cake
6 Melk	Chocalite melk
7 phone	I-phone 6
8 tablet	Kindle
9 pants	Swetpants
10 shirt	tangtop

V
O
W
E
L

A
e
i
o
u
And
y

Your other task for the day is to read. You can look online at www.plainandnotsoplain.com for book recommendations that we enjoyed reading or do an online search to find something that you are interested in. You should read for a minimum of one hour per day.

Write down the title of the book you are reading and how long you read for today.

DiARy of A Wimpy Kid

1 chapter

Quiz

REVIEW

3,6,9,12,_____,_____,_____

6,12,18,24,_____,_____,_____

How many $100 bills are needed to make $1000

Is half of 37,295 a whole number? Why or why not

Jadyn, Brooklyn, and Autumn collect trading cards. Together they have a total of 63 cards. If Jadyn has 27 cards and Brooklyn has 15 cards, how many cards does Autumn have?

Stephen is 5 years old

Jentzen is 11 years old

Evan is 6 years older than Stephen

How old is Evan?

Some words are irregular nouns and they change completely.

Example:

Man===men

Woman===women

Child===children

Foot===feet

Tooth===teeth

Goose===geese

Mouse===mice

Person===people

Some words do not change at all:

Cod===cod

Wheat==wheat

Rye==rye

The best way to learn these plural forms is by reading, writing, and practicing. Most you can tell are wrong by how they sound. Find the following irregular plurals in the word search puzzle. The words can be forward, backward, horizontal, or diagonal.

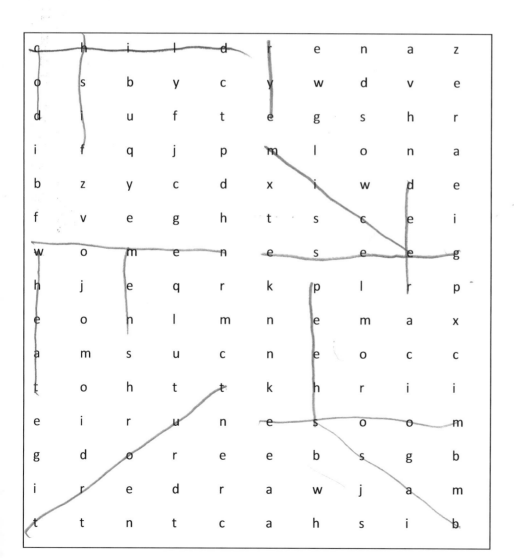

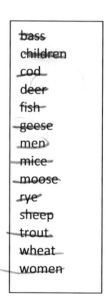

bass

children

cod

deer

fish

geese

men

mice

moose

rye

sheep

trout

wheat

women

Your other task for the day is to read. You can look online at www.plainandnotsoplain.com for book recommendations that we enjoyed reading or do an online search to find something that you are interested in. You should read for a minimum of one hour per day.

Write down the title of the book you are reading and how long you read for today.

DeAR Dumb DIARY.

20min

week 4 spelling words

arrow

buffalo

burro

chose

chrome

cloak

compose

cove

foam

gopher

gown

knowing

loan

loaves

roast

rows

soak

solo

count aloud: count up and down by 25s between 0 and 200. Count up and down by 250s between 0 and 2000.

mental math:

- $6000+$3200
- $5000+$3000
- 375+125
- 350 seconds +300 seconds
- 540-140
- 7+6+3+4

Story problems

The troop hiked 8 miles in the morning and 9 miles in the afternoon. Altogether, how many miles did the troop hike? When you see the word altogether, in all, how many, the sum of...those are all clues to add +

8 miles +9 miles =17 miles

After Mike paid Sarah $120 for rent, Sarah had $645. How much money did Sarah have before Mike paid Sarah for rent?

We know that she had 645 dollars, if we take away or subtract the 120 dollars we will find out what she had before. Take away, how many more, difference those are all subtraction clues.

Your turn:

Tammy wants to buy a camera. She has $24. The camera costs $41. How much more does she need?

The Maryons traveled 397 miles one day and 406 miles the next day. Altogether how many miles did they travel?

Marks team scored 63 points and won the game. If the team scored 29 points in the second half, how many points did the team score in the first half?

Review

Change the underlined singular noun to a plural noun. Write the new sentence.

1. Many tourists came to the <u>island</u>.
2. People love the quiet <u>beach</u> and warm days.
3. They swim and collect shells with their <u>child</u>.
4. Islanders love welcoming new <u>person</u> to their home.
5. Do you know about the local <u>goose</u> that swim with you?
6. Our drinks are served in <u>glass</u> that are topped with umbrellas.
7. The only bad thing are the many <u>mouse</u> that live here.
8. My two front <u>tooth</u> fell out last week.

1 Many tourists came to Hawihhi.

2 People love the quiet Sandy beach and warm days.

3 They sim and collect shells with their children.

4 Islanders love welcoming new people to their home.

5 Do you know about the local geese that swim with you.

6 Our drincks are servedinglass thar topped with umbrellas

7 The only bad thing arethe many mice that live here.

8 My two front teeth fellout last week.

Write the plural forms of each noun

Chief	Festival	Sweater	Essay
Cook			
Address	Potato	Laser	Scent
Addres			
Loaf	Thief	Charter	Quality
Slice			
Forty	Torch	Pattern	success
40			
Occasion	Man	Goose	wheat

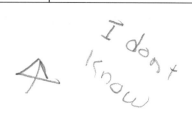

51

Your other task for the day is to read. You can look online at www.plainandnotsoplain.com for book recommendations that we enjoyed reading or do an online search to find something that you are interested in. You should read for a minimum of one hour per day.

Write down the title of the book you are reading and how long you read for today.

Dear Dumb DIARY.

20 min

Begin memorizing these common prepositions. It is one of those things like math facts that if you know them, it will make your future in grammar so much easier. This week take the first column and memorize.

about	before	down	like	past	until
above	behind	during	near	since	up
across	below	except	of	through	upon
after	beneath	for	off	to	with
against	beside	from	on	toward	within
along	between	in	onto	under	without
around	beyond	inside	outside	underneath	
at	but	into	over		
	by				
	concerning				

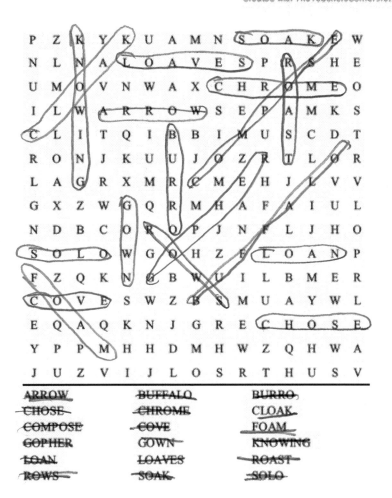

P Z K Y K U A M N S O A K E W
N L N A L O A V E S P R S H E
U M O V N W A X C H R O M E O
I L W A R R O W S E P A M K S
C L I T Q I B B I M U S C D T
R O N J K U U J O Z R T L O R
L A G R X M R C M E H J L V V
G X Z W G Q R M H A F A I U L
N D B C O R O P J N F L J H O
S O L O W G O H Z F L O A N P
F Z Q K N G B W I L B M E R
C O V E S W Z B S M U A Y W L
E Q A Q K N J G R E C H O S E
Y P P M H H D M H W Z Q H W A
J U Z V I J L O S R T H U S V

ARROW	BUFFALO	BURRO
CHOSE	CHROME	CLOAK
COMPOSE	COVE	FOAM
GOPHER	GOWN	KNOWING
LOAN	LOAVES	ROAST
ROWS	SOAK	SOLO

53

In mathematics we study numbers. We also study shapes such as circles, squares, and triangles. the study of shapes is called geometry. The simplest figures in geometry are the point and the line. A line does not end. Part of a line is called a line segment or segment. A line segment has two endpoints. Sometimes dots are drawn at each end of a line segment to represent the dots. The last visible point on each end of the line segment is considered to be an endpoint. A ray begins at a point and continues without end.

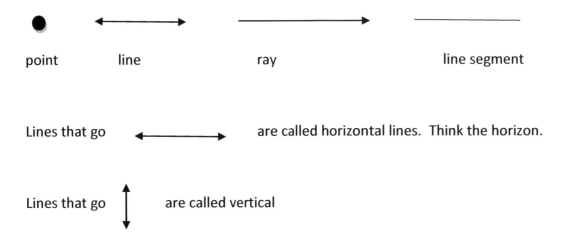

point   line   ray   line segment

Lines that go ⟷ are called horizontal lines. Think the horizon.

Lines that go ↕ are called vertical

Two lines that will never touch are called parallel lines. Two lines that will intersect at one point are called intersecting lines.

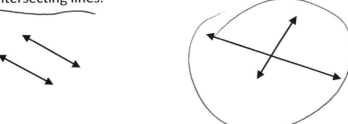

Practice:

862-79= 783

$$\begin{array}{r} 2 \\ \cancel{8}\cancel{6}2 \\ -\ \ 79 \\ \hline 783 \end{array}$$

508-39= 469

$$\begin{array}{r} 4\ \ \ \\ \cancel{5}\cancel{0}8 \\ -\ \ 39 \\ \hline 469 \end{array}$$

654-232=

765+45+53= 863

$$\begin{array}{r} 765 \\ +\ 45 \\ \hline 810 \\ +\ 53 \\ \hline 863 \end{array}$$

765+641+102= 1,508

$$\begin{array}{r} 765 \\ +641 \\ \hline 1406 \\ +102 \\ \hline 1,508 \end{array}$$

80+98+432= 602

$$\begin{array}{r} 80 \\ +90 \\ \hline 120 \\ +432 \\ \hline 602 \end{array}$$

54

Homophones

Homophones are words that sound alike but have different spellings and meanings.

Write the correct homophone in the blank.

1. I had to have the _____ of the shoe repaired. (soul, sole)
2. After he was sick for days, his face was _Pail_____. (pail/pale)
3. Luckily the accident caused me _no___ _pane_(know/no) (pane/pain)
4. After running out of _flour____, the baker had to stop. (flour/flower)
5. We have ___read_____many books off our shelves. (red/read)
6. Jadyn sat on the bottom _stairs___without being noticed. (stares/stairs)
7. A fierce storm __blew_____through my town. (blew/blue)
8. She purchased a beautiful new dress _for____ the wedding. (fore/for)
9. Walking down the _isle_____to get married can by scary. (I'll/aisle/isle)
10. Cats have been __banned_____from the park. (band/banned)
11. I'd rather receive my _mail____electronically than on paper. (mail/male)
12. To plant tomatoes you have to _____seeds. (so/sew/sow)
13. Sadie sat and scratched the place where the _flee__bit her. (flea/flee)
14. The police can _sees_____your property if needed. (sees/seas/seize)
15. It was interesting to ___hear_____ her sing. (here/hear)
16. We chose to visit Lansing, the _Capital___ of Michigan. (capital/capitol)
17. We drove __to_____the city in __two_____days. (to/too/two)
18. My sisters couldn't hide __their_____sadness. (their/there)
19. We appreciated the _Peace_when the children went to bed. (piece/peace)
20. We walked up and down the _rows_____of corn plants. (rows/rose)
21. Many elderly people share __tales___of their childhood. (tales/tails)
22. We found that __it's_____ an exciting place to be. (its /it's)
23. We wondered if the _weather_____was going to change or not.
(weather/whether)
24. Carrots are _root_____vegetables. (route/root)
25. I wore a __hole__in one of my shoes from _so___much walking.
(whole/hole) (so/sew)

Your other task for the day is to read. You can look online at www.plainandnotsoplain.com for book recommendations that we enjoyed reading or do an online search to find something that you are interested in. You should read for a minimum of one hour per day.

Write down the title of the book you are reading and how long you read for today.

Dear Dumb DIARY

20 min

write sentences for your words

Draw me a line segment

Draw me a line

Draw me a ray

Draw me two parallel lines

Draw me two intersecting lines

Draw me a vertical line

Draw me a horizontal line

What comes next 5,10,15,_20_ , _25_ , _30_

38+427=_465_

$$\begin{array}{r} 4\,2\,7 \\ +\ \ 3\,8 \\ \hline 4\,6\,5 \end{array}$$

$580-$94=_346_

$$\begin{array}{r} 5\,8\,0 \\ -\ \ 9\,4 \\ \hline 3\,4\,6 \end{array}$$

Write two addition and two subtraction facts for the fact family 4,6,10

4+6=10
6+4=10
10-6=4
10-4=6

More homophone work

Read each sentence. If you find a misused homophone, rewrite the sentence correctly. If there is no error write: The sentence is correct as is.

1. I went to bed so late that I had trouble falling asleep last knight.

   I went to bed so late that I had trouble falling asleep last night

2. Our fruit salad had apples, oranges, and pairs.

   Correct

3. Don't stare at me!

   Correct

4. There are too people behind me in line.

   There are two people behind me in line.

5. As we drove to the country, we saw a heard of cattle in the road.

   Correct

6. The building was made of concrete and steal.

   Correct.

7. I could not find anything I knead at the mall.

   I could not find anything I need at the mall.

8. The baby is always hungry an our after eating.

   The baby is always hungry an hour after eating.

9. As we walked threw the crowd, I lost my hat!

   Correct

10.

Your library books are dew today.

   Correct

Your other task for the day is to read. You can look online at www.plainandnotsoplain.com for book recommendations that we enjoyed reading or do an online search to find something that you are interested in. You should read for a minimum of one hour per day.

Write down the title of the book you are reading and how long you read for today.

Dear Dumb DiARy

2 chapters

Quiz

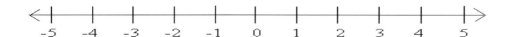

By carefully marking numbers on a line, we can a make a number line. A number line shows numbers at a certain distance from zero. Numbers to the left of zero are negative numbers. We read the minus sign by saying "negative three". The small marks above each number are called tick marks.

The numbers shown on the number line are called integers. Integers include all the counting numbers, the negatives of all the counting numbers, and the number zero.

This sequence counts down by ones. What are the next six numbers in the sequence 5,4,3,........the answer is: 2,1,0,-1,-2,-3

Your turn:

Draw a number line marked with the whole numbers from 0 to 5.

How many segments are there on a number line from 2 to 7?

Write the comparison using digits

Eighteen thousand is less than eighty thousand

The number 57 is between which pair of numbers:

40 and 50   50 and 60   60 and 70   70 and 80

During the first week of summer vacation, Evan earned $18 cutting grass and $12 babysitting. How much did he earn altogether?

Homonyms	Homophones	Homographs
Multiple meaning words	Words that sound alike	Same spelling, different pronunciation, different meanings
The spruce tree.... To spruce up....	Addition for math Edition of a book	Desert=abandon Desert=area of land
Suit yourself .... Wore a suit....	I want to go I like it too One plus one is two	Bass=fish Bass=instrument
Weigh on the scale... Scale the wall...	Capitol building State capital	Close==nearby Close==to shut
The price is fair... Go to the fair...	Pick a flower Bake with flour	Bow=to bend down Bow==ribbon

Homonyms practice

1. I _ate_ the entire pie. (ate/eight)
2. Can you _beat_ on the drum?) (beet/beat)
3. That shirt has a weird _scent_ .(scent/cent)
4. There is a _hole_ in the ground. (whole/hole)
5. Do not _waist_ the food. (waist/waste)
6. Stephen is my _son_ . (son/sun)
7. Have you _seen_ my hair? (seen/scene)
8. The suns _raise_ are bright. (raise/rays)
9. Please _Pause_ the movie. (paws/pause)
10. I do not _know_ the answer to that. (no/know)
11. Go grab my fishing _real_ (real/reel)
12. The bear has a big _Paw_ . (pa/paw)
13. I lost the _oar_ when I was kayaking. (or/ore/oar)
14. The _maid_ will clean the dishes. (made/maid)
15. Can you tie a _knot_ ? (not/knot)
16 I was so sick with the _flu_ yesterday. (flu/flew)
17. _I'll_ grab the drinks. (isle/I'll)
18. Can we _dye_ the shoes? (die/dye)
19. Let's go swim in the _creek_ . (creak/creek)
20. Put on the emergency _brake_ when parking. (brake/break)
21. The prisoner was in his _sell_ . (sell/cell)

Your other task for the day is to read. You can look online at www.plainandnotsoplain.com for book recommendations that we enjoyed reading or do an online search to find something that you are interested in. You should read for a minimum of one hour per day.

Write down the title of the book you are reading and how long you read for today.

_____

_____

week 5 spelling words

argue	argue
blue	blue
confuse	confuse
due	due
duke	duke
dune	dune
excuse	excuse
include	include
issue	issue
museum	museum
plume	plume
ruby	ruby
rude	rude
statue	statue
tissue	tissue
truth	truth
tube	tube
tulip	tulip

Tally marks are used to keep track of a count. Each tally mark counts as one. Here we show the tallies for the numbers one through six.

| | || | ||| | |||| | ⅢⅢ | ⅢⅢ |

| 1 | 2 | 3 | 4 | 5 | 6 |

Notice that the tally marks for five is a diagonal mark crossing four vertical marks.

Making tally marks just makes it easier to count.

Go through your home and use tally marks to count the following objects:

number of windows	
number of doors—include closets	
number of pets	
number of siblings	
number of overhead fans	
number of rugs	
number of chairs	

Add 324 plus 321equals   subtract 3532 minus 398

Subject Pronouns

A pronoun is a word that is used in place of a noun. Pronouns can make writing and speaking more interesting. Subject pronouns are pronouns that replace the subject of the sentence. **MEMORIZE THESE**

I   you   he   she   it   we   they

French fries are good for dinner. French fries taste good with ketchup.
French fries are good for dinner. They taste good with ketchup.

Fill in the blanks with pronouns that could replace the words.

Jadyn and Brooklyn=___*they*___

Lauren =___*She*___

bat=___*It*___

Evan=___*he*___

balls=___*it*___

Circle each pronoun.

1. *She* went to the park today.
2. *He* went to play baseball.
3. *They* are coming over tonight.
4. *It* is over there.

Write a pronoun that replaces the underlined word.

5. The ball smashed my window! *it*___
6. Greg and I are taking the books to the library. *we*___
7. Sara, enjoys coming over for coffee. *She*___
8. Church camp, begins in July and will be fun! *It*___

Fill in the blanks with a pronoun.

9. ___*we*___ are going on a trip.
10. ___*it*___ is blue and big.
11. ___*we*___ showed Stephen the verse about healings.
12. ___*I*___ am going to church today.

What does singular mean? *Singular means a word that dousen't change.*

What does plural mean?_____

Write S if the underlined pronoun is singular. Write P if it is plural.

1. We are going on a plane ride._____
2. I am going to music practice tonight._____
3. They are being goofy in class._____
4. He is feeling better._____

Your other task for the day is to read. You can look online at www.plainandnotsoplain.com for book recommendations that we enjoyed reading or do an online search to find something that you are interested in. You should read for a minimum of one hour per day.

Write down the title of the book you are reading and how long you read for today.

_____

_____

Begin memorizing these common prepositions. It is one of those things like math facts that if you know them, it will make your future in grammar so much easier. This week take the first column and memorize.

about	before	down	like	past	until
above	behind	during	near	since	up
across	below	except	of	through	upon
after	beneath	for	off	to	with
against	beside	from	on	toward	within
along	between	in	onto	under	without
around	beyond	inside	outside	underneath	
at	but	into	over		
	by				
	concerning				

```
B   B   U   U   E   X   J   H   P   C   B   W   R   D   K
K   Z   J   Y   N   X   A   D   V   B   O   U   D   U   G
J   T   C   O   N   F   U   S   E   R   K   C   J   K   S
P   L   U   M   E   J   A   D   R   O   Z   D   M   E   R
Y   D   R   C   T   E   U   A   E   K   D   U   R   W   N
D   W   Z   S   U   L   A   S   R   K   E   Q   A   W   M
Y   D   N   G   C   Z   U   D   R   S   G   T   K   S   U
Y   L   R   N   Y   C   V   T   U   L   I   P   T   T   M
C   A   I   W   X   U   H   M   B   N   V   W   Y   A   C
R   Q   Z   E   X   Y   O   E   Y   C   E   N   C   T   N
U   Y   T   U   B   E   H   I   O   P   A   M   R   U   A
D   O   I   P   P   T   I   S   S   U   E   C   A   E   N
E   Y   R   G   U   U   S   S   U   V   R   E   D   J   K
X   L   Y   R   I   B   L   U   E   O   U   L   N   N   Q
N   W   T   B   C   G   B   E   P   D   N   G   I   M   I
```

ARROW	ARGUE	BLUE
CONFUSE	DUE	DUKE
DUNE	EXCUSE	INCLUDE
ISSUE	MUSEUM	PLUME
RUBY	RUDE	STATUE
TISSUE	TRUTH	TUBE
TULIP		

count aloud: count by 25 cents from 25 cents to three dollars. Then from three dollars to 25 cents

mental math:

- 6500-500 $= 6000$
- 2000-100 $= 1900$
- 360-20 $= 340$
- 425-125 $= 300$
- 50+50-25 $= 125$
- 8+8-1+5-2 $= 18$

Multiplication

If there are 5 rows of desk with 6 desks in each row, how many desks are there in all? You can draw it out to help. $5 \times 6 = 30$

To solve you can count out each individual desk, but that would take some time. Or we can count by the number of desks in each row. 5,10,15,20,25,30. Or we can multiply 5 times 6. The x is called a times sign.

Multiplication helps to get your answer more quickly☺ If I have ten children and each child was going to get four pieces of candy, how many pieces do I need? I can count by tens four times. Or I can count by 4's ten times to get my answer.

Keep working on those multiplication facts to help you memorize them and speed up this process.

What multiplication problems is represented by the X's $6 \times 3 = 18$

XXXXXX

XXXXXX

XXXXXX

Subject Pronoun

Circle the underlined words with a pronoun that could replace it.

1. Collin is studying Albert Einstein.
   a. he *(circled)*
   b. you
   c. her
   d. it
2. Lauren thinks it is boring.
   a. he
   b. it
   c. they
   d. she *(circled)*
3. A school lesson can sometimes be long.
   a. him
   b. it *(circled)*
   c. they
   d. he
4. Jadyn and Ashlyn are coming to school today.
   a. they *(circled)*
   b. them
   c. us
   d. we
5. The ball hit Brooklyn.
   a. they
   b. it *(circled)*
   c. I
   d. he
6. Evan and I want to come along.
   a. We *(circled)*   b. me   c. they   d. us

Rewrite the following paragraph by replacing some of the subjects with subject pronouns.

Ice cream is my family's favorite treat. Ice cream is the best with chocolate syrup. My family really enjoys homemade ice cream too. Ice cream is so good on a hot summer day. My family will probably always like to eat ice cream.

It is my family's favorite treat. They really enjoy homemade ice cream too. It is so good on a hot summer day. They will probably always like ice cream

Handwritten margin: I you he She it we they

71

Your other task for the day is to read. You can look online at www.plainandnotsoplain.com for book recommendations that we enjoyed reading or do an online search to find something that you are interested in. You should read for a minimum of one hour per day.

Write down the title of the book you are reading and how long you read for today.

_____

_____

write sentences for your words

Adding and subtracting dollars and cents.
To add and subtract dollars and cents, we align the decimal points so that we add or subtract digits with the same place value. We write the decimal point in the answer.

```
   $ 3.45
   $ 6.23
+  $ 0.50
   $10.18
```

**Very important to line them up or you will get a wrong answer.

Your turn:

$4.50-$3.80=

$321.80+$1.08+$1= if you need to add some zeros as place holders do so

Add $5, $8.75,$10,$0.35

Kim brought a $5 bill to school to pay for lunch. What amount will she have left after paying for a lunch that costs $3.25?

$543.05-$3.89=

Object pronouns

Pronouns are wordS that are used in the place of a noun. An object pronoun replaces the noun that is the receiver of the action in the sentence. **MEMORIZE THESE**

Mrs. Maryon cooked dinner for Mr. Maryon.
Mrs. Maryon cooked dinner for him.

me   you   him   her   it   us   them

Rewrite the following sentences and replace the underlined object noun with object pronouns.

1. I needed an eraser. Sam gave his eraser to <u>I.</u>

   I need an eraser. Sam gave his eraser to me.

2. My sister and I are going to the park. Mom drove <u>my sister and I.</u>

   My sister and I are going to the park. Mom drove us.

3. Evan threw a ball to his brother, Stephen. Evan likes playing ball with <u>Stephen.</u>

   Evan likes playing ball with him.

4. Lauren cooked pasta for dinner. She cooked <u>pasta</u> with meatballs.

   She cooked it with meatballs.

Write 3 more sentences that use object pronouns. Underline them.

1. *My sister and I got knew pants. Dad drove My sister and I.*

2. *Stacey and me go to the same school. Stacey and me walk.*

3. *Grandma made piezza for dinner. Grandma made piezza with peparonies.*

Your other task for the day is to read. You can look online at www.plainandnotsoplain.com for book recommendations that we enjoyed reading or do an online search to find something that you are interested in. You should read for a minimum of one hour per day.

Write down the title of the book you are reading and how long you read for today.

_____

_____

Quiz

Write a multiplication problem for each of the following addition problems:

8+8+8+8   25+25+25

8x4   25x3

Find each sum or difference

$5.25+$8.92 $43.27-$3.99

5.25   43.27
8.92   - 3.99
─────   ──────
.33   39.28

Draw a number line marked with numbers from -3 to 3

-3 -2 -1 1+ 2+ 3+

Use tally marks to show the number 9

-9 -8 -7 -6 -5 -4 -3 -2 -1 1+ 2+ 3+ 4+ 5+ 6+ 7+ 8+ 9+

Lauren hiked 33 miles in one day. If she hiked 15 miles after noon, how many miles did she hike before noon?

33
-15
────
18

She hiked 18 miles before noon.

Write two addition facts and two subtraction facts for the fact family 5,4,9

5+4=9
4+5=9
9-4=5
9-5=4

Dad paddled the canoe down the river 25 miles each day for 4 days. How far did he go in 4 days?

< > =

7,14,21, 28 , 35 , 42   3+3+3+3 ___=___ 4+4+4
                               12 = 12

Pronouns agreement

A pronoun replaces a noun in a sentence. The noun that is replaces is called the antecedent. All pronouns have antecedents. Pronouns must agree in gender and number with their antecedents and what their antecedents refer to.

Michael must bring his own drink to the party.
He must bring his own drink to the party.(agrees in gender)
He must bring her own drink to the party. (does NOT agree in gender)

Tony must bring three balls to practice.
Tony must bring them to practice. (agrees in number)
Tony must bring it to the practice. (does NOT agree in number)

Circle the correct pronoun in parentheses. Remember they must agree in number and gender.
1. Collin did well on (her/his) book report.
2. Sara did not do well on (her/its) spelling test.
3. She missed four words. (he/they) were hard.
4. The show was funny, and (it/they) made them both laugh.
5. They ate a small pizza. (its/it) was delicious.
6. The ball smashed the window. (it/her) made a big hole.
7. Brooklyn helped Stephen with (his/her) shoes.
8. Mom and Dad are going to see the movie with the neighbors. They will have a good time with (them/they).
9. Sam and I are twins. (we/us are ten years old.)
10. (I/me) like to swim in the pool.

What are the subject pronouns?

_____,_____,_____,_____,_____,_____,_____

What are the object pronouns?

_____,_____,_____,_____,_____,_____,_____

What is a noun?_____

Make plural the following nouns:

Couch _____	bush_____	ox_____
Boss_____	Fly_____	strawberry_____
Man_____	mouse_____	foot_____
Deer_____	Goose_____	loaf_____

Your other task for the day is to read. You can look online at www.plainandnotsoplain.com for book recommendations that we enjoyed reading or do an online search to find something that you are interested in. You should read for a minimum of one hour per day.

Write down the title of the book you are reading and how long you read for today.

_____

_____

week 6 spelling words

barnyard

blastoff

brand-new

chairperson

cupboard

hide-and-seek

homesick

ice skate

peanut butter

polar bear

post office

seagulls

snowstorm

topsy-turvy

town crier

yardstick

zip code

count aloud: count by 25 cents from 25 cents to three dollars. Then by 50 cents to five dollars.

mental math:

- 3500+500
- 2500-500
- $7.50+$2.50
- 10+10-5+10-5
- How much money is 3 quarters
- One foot is 12 inches. Two feet is 24 inches. How many inches in 3 feet
- If a square is 5 inches on each side, what is distance around the square

Find the missing number of

f-15=24. We need to find the first number in the subtraction problem. When 15 is subtracted from f, the difference is 24. So f must be more than 24. We will do the opposite of subtraction which is addition to solve. If we add 24 plus 15, by reading it backwards we can get the answer of 39. Then we plug in the numbers to see if we are correct.

Your turn:

find the missing number of 45- s=21

Find the missing number of n-24=48

Find the missing number of 63-p=20

Draw a number line marked with integers from -5 to 5

Use words to name $4.48

Verbs

A verb is a word that tells that action or the state of being in a sentence.

The children **play** basketball. The word play is a verb. It tells what the children do.

Circle the verb.

1. Brooklyn (paints) a picture.
2. Evan (throws) a football to Collin.
3. We (play) at the park every Sunday.
4. We (eat) pizza at the table.
5. Everyone (cheers) for us at the competition.

Add a verb of your own to complete the sentences.

1. Sadie _Cheers_ across the lawn.
2. The cat _scratch_ my brother.
3. We _ate_ a cake.
4. Everyone _gave_ hugs to Daddy.
5. We all _give_ praises to God.

Verbs for present, past, and future.

When a verb tells about now it ends with –s.

    Today the girl <u>plays</u> with her cat.

When a verb tells about past, it ends with –ed.

    Yesterday she <u>played</u> with the cat.

When a verb tells of the future it has the word will in it.

    Tomorrow I <u>will play</u> with the cat.

Write which tense the verb is in. (present, past, or future.)

1. Greg will go fishing with Evan after work. _future_
2. Collin cleaned up the garage for his Dad. _Past_
3. Amy makes dinner in the kitchen. _Present_

Choose the correct form of the verb.

4. Evan (plays, (played)) video games last night.
5. Two girls (perform, (will perform)) in the talent show tomorrow.
6. Amy ((wants), wanted) to ride her bike now.
7. The friends (will visit, (visited)) us at the lake last night.
8. Yesterday, I ((mixed), will mix) the cake batter.
9. Now Autumn ((plays), played) with her friends.
10. Tomorrow Stephen ((will ride), rides) his bike.
11. Last night Evan ((played), plays) video games.
12. He ((will go), go) to the football game tomorrow.
13. Dad ((will give), gives) Evan his gift tomorrow.

Your other task for the day is to read. You can look online at www.plainandnotsoplain.com for book recommendations that we enjoyed reading or do an online search to find something that you are interested in. You should read for a minimum of one hour per day.

Write down the title of the book you are reading and how long you read for today.

_____

_____

Begin memorizing these common prepositions. It is one of those things like math facts that if you know them, it will make your future in grammar so much easier. This week take the first column and memorize.

about	before	down	like	past	until
above	behind	during	near	since	up
across	below	except	of	through	upon
after	beneath	for	off	to	with
against	beside	from	on	toward	within
along	between	in	onto	under	without
around	beyond	inside	outside	underneath	
at	but	into	over		
	by				
	concerning				

no word scramble☺

Use digits to write eight hundred eighteen thousand, eighty

818,080

Use tally marks to make the number 11

 IIII I

Jadyn is reading a 260 page book. She has read 85 pages. How many more pages does she have left to read?

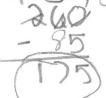
260
- 85
(175)

She has 175 pages left.

Tammy mixed 32 ounces of soda with 24 ounces of juice to make punch. How many ounces of punch did she make?

32
+24
56

She made 56 ounces of punch.

Write the equation: Fifty-six is less than sixty-five

56 < 65

Add $43.10 +$1.54

43.10
+ 1.54
44.64

600-m=364 m=236
5680
-364
236

$573+$96+$427=

573
+ 9 6
42 7
1,096

436+y=634 y=198
5684
-436
198

100-n=48 n=52

100
-48
52

6+48+9+w=100 w=32

100
- 63
37

Change the underlined verb to the tense in (). Write the word

1. Some cats <u>enjoyed</u> getting baths. (present)_____
2. Our family <u>will agree</u> with them. (present)_____
3. God's love never <u>failed.</u> (present)_____
4. I <u>copy</u> a paper about birds. (future)_____
5. I <u>baked</u> a cake tomorrow. (future)_____
6. They <u>find</u> a bunch of flowers. (future)_____
7. Sadie <u>will bark</u> loudly. (past)_____
8. Jadyn <u>frosts</u> the cake. (past)_____
9. Madelyn <u>plays</u> with dolls.(past)_____

Write the past tense of the following verbs:

Present	past
add	
ask	
call	
joke	
look	
report	
observe	
	cheered
	walked
	laughed
	whispered
	warned

Your other task for the day is to read. You can look online at www.plainandnotsoplain.com for book recommendations that we enjoyed reading or do an online search to find something that you are interested in. You should read for a minimum of one hour per day.

Write down the title of the book you are reading and how long you read for today.

_____

_____

write sentences for your words

Write two addition and two subtraction facts for the fact family 2,8,10

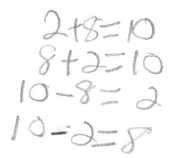

2+8=10
8+2=10
10−8= 2
10−2=8

Change this addition problem to a multiplication problem 10+10+10+10

10×4=40

In a class of 23 students, there are 12 girls. Do girls make up more than or less than half of the class. Explain

yes, Because it is more than the boys.

Draw a horizontal segment and a vertical ray

horizontal

Crystal has $7.00 in her wallet and $4.37 in a coin jar. How much does she have altogether?

$11.37

Ethan had a collection of rocks. He gave Collin 17 rocks. Ethan now has 56 rocks. Write a subtraction equation that can be used to find the number of rocks Ethan had before he gave some away. Then solve.

4 16
5 6
−1 7
39

90

Irregular verbs: past and present tense

Some verbs do not add –ed to show past action. They are called irregular verbs. Because irregular verbs do not follow a regular pattern, you must remember their spellings. Here are some:

Present	past	past with has, have, or had
Begin	began	(has,have,had)begun
Do	did	(has, have, had)done
Find	found	(has, have, had)found
Give	gave	(has, have, had)given
Go	went	(has, have,had)gone
Run	ran	(has,have,had)run
See	saw	(has, have,had)seen
Take	took	(has, have, had)taken
Think	thought (has, have, had)thought	
Wear	wore	(has, have, had)worn
Am	was	
Bring	brought	
Eat	ate	
Get	got	
Is	was	
Let	let	
Put	put	
Rise	rose	
Sleep	slept	

Choose the correct form of the irregular verb in () to complete each sentence.

1. My mother (*took*, taken) many pictures of us.
2. I have (saw, *seen*) photos of Dad as a little boy.
3. He (go, *went*) to swim lessons, just as I did.
4. I once (think, *thought*) he did not like swimming.
5. He (*wore*, worn) an orange swim suit.

Write each correct form of the verb on the line.

6. I have (begin) to keep a journal. _began_
7. I (take) the name from a book. _took_
8. I have (give) my cat a bone. _given_
9. It is about a cat who has (go) to Paris. _went_
10. She (do) everything I ask of her. _does_
11. The cat (run) away. _ran_
12. Have you (saw) my rock collection? _seen_
13. All the girls (wear) skirts yesterday at the dance. _wore_
14. He had (took) a cookie from the tray. _~~take~~ took_
15. Madelyn (get) a bike for her birthday. _got_

Your other task for the day is to read. You can look online at www.plainandnotsoplain.com for book recommendations that we enjoyed reading or do an online search to find something that you are interested in. You should read for a minimum of one hour per day.

Write down the title of the book you are reading and how long you read for today.

_____

_____

Quiz

count aloud: count up and down by 50s between 0 and 500

mental math:

- 50+50+50 = 150
- 500+500+500 1,500
- 24+26 50
- 240+260 500
- 480-200 280
- 10+6-1+5+10 30

6 X1	2 X6	5 X2	3 X8	4 X2	3 X6	1 X2	2 X2	1 X1	6 X4
6	12	10	24	8	18	2	4	1	24
3 X5	8 X2	4 X6	3 X4	1 X0	3 X7	4 X6	4 X8	3 X2	5 X4
15	16	24	12	0	21	24	32	6	20
8 X2	6 X0	1 X9	3 X4	9 X2	5 X5	1 X5	9 X9	1 X2	6 X2
16	0	9	12	18	25	5	90	2	12
3 X1	5 X6	3 X3	3 X0	4 X0	3 X6	4 X4	3 X8	5 x10	3 X10
3	30	9	30	0	18	16	24	50	30
5 X9	5 X4	1 X7	7 X2	6 X6	5 X2	4 X2	7 X6	8 X6	8 X8
45	20	7	14	36	10	8	42		
9 X6	5 X7	2 X4	5 X6	9 X2	0 X0	1 X4	1 X3	4 X7	9 X4
54	35	8	30	18	0	4	3	28	36
10 X2	5 X3	10 X6	5 X3	5 X8	5 X1	5 X0	4 X4	3 X2	3 X9
20	15	60	15	40	5	0	16	6	27

Circle the action verbs in each of the following sentences. Replace the verb with another action verb of your own.

1. The hungry teenagers gulped down the snacks. _____
2. The toddlers screamed with delight at the clown._____
3. Jadyn's necklace sparkled in the moonlight. _____
4. Brookyn spun around and around on the merry-go-round._____
5. The newspapers fluttered across the yard in the wind. _____

Choose the correct verb tense in ()

1. Her family (calls, calling) her Brookie.
2. Madelyn sometimes (acts, acting) very silly.
3. She (pretends, pretending) she is an animal.
4. Jentzen (runs, ran) around the house now.
5. My mother (taken, took) lots of photos of us.
6. I have (saw, seen) pictures of Dad as a little boy.
7. I once (think, thought) he hated swimming.
8. Then I (find, found) an old photo of him.
9. He(swim, swam) in the lake.
10. Brooklyn (laugh, laughs) when she hears a joke.

What are the subject pronouns?
I , you , he , She , it , we , they

What are the object pronouns?
me, you, him, her , it , us , them ,

What is a noun? purson, place, or thing

What is a verb? The action of being astate of a Sentincy

What is a pronoun? is something that changes a noun

95

Your other task for the day is to read. You can look online at www.plainandnotsoplain.com for book recommendations that we enjoyed reading or do an online search to find something that you are interested in. You should read for a minimum of one hour per day.

Write down the title of the book you are reading and how long you read for today.

_____

_____

week 7 spelling words

baseball	baseball
basketball	basketball
breakfast	breakfast
classroom	classroom
driftwood	driftwood
firefly	firefly
flagpole	flagpole
harmless	harmless
knickknack	Knickknack
lifetime	lifetime
motorcycle	motorcycle
paperback	paperback
playhouse	playhouse
railway	railway
switchboard	switchboard
taxicab	taxicab
textbook	textbook
tiptoe	tipto

Draw a number line with integers from -3 to 10

-3 -2 -1 0 1 2 3 4 5 6 7 8 9 10

Mike was the ninth person in line. How many people were in front of him

8

Use tally marks to show thirteen

$\cancel{||||}$ $\cancel{||||}$ |||

Write two addition and two subtraction facts for the fact family of 1,9,10

$1+9=10$
$9+1=10$
$10-9=1$
$10-1=9$

Tickets to an amusement park are on sale for $1.00 each. On the first day of sale, the park sold one hundred sixty-four tickets. After three days, the park sold 239 tickets. How many tickets did the park sell the second day?

239
-164
075

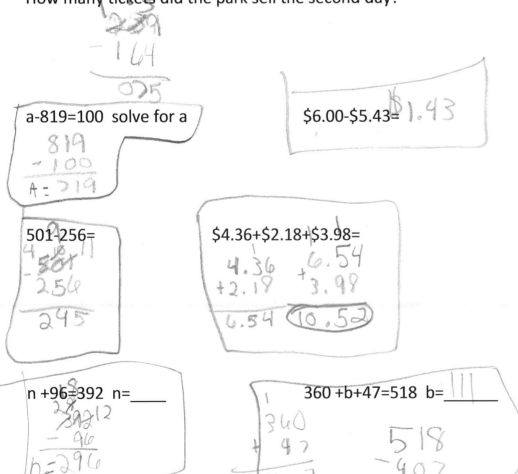

a-819=100 solve for a

819
-100
A = 719

$6.00-$5.43= $1.43

501-256=

501
-256
245

$4.36+$2.18+$3.98=

4.36   6.54
+2.18   +3.98
6.54   10.52

n +96=392 n=____

392
-96
n=296

360 +b+47=518 b=____

360
+ 47
407

518
-407
111

Synonym or Antonym

Draw a circle around each word that is a synonym of the first word. Draw a box around each word that is an antonym of the first word..

Accomplish	achieve	fail	Breathe	Sit
Answer	silence	reply	Work	Sleep
Artificial	Man made	genuine	Cook	clean
Bargain	Deal	Rip off	Remote	Scarce
Faithful	loyal	unreliable	Good	Hastily
Genuine	real	misleading	Clean	Dirty
Many	limited	Numerous	Painful	Tired
Labor	Child's play	work	Soothe	Unhappily
Reliable	problematic	Crazily	Dependable	Hush
Complete	unfinished	Answer	finish	Charge
Hazard	safeguard	Brittle	Alert	Danger
Hurry	procrastination	Choose	Pick	rush
Praise	compliment	Negative	Many	sad
Forfeit	Choose	Generous	Gain	Lose
Adjacent	Nearby	Clean	Remote	Sudden
Pompous	Festive	Noisy	Proud	Modest
Exquisite	Careful	Beyond	Hideous	Delightful
Impeccable	Perfect	Scarce	Painful	Flawed
Hairy	Furry	Attract	Annoy	Smoothe
Despondently	Elegantly	Crazily	Unhappily	Happily
Interrogate	Cross-examine	Dislike	Hush	Persecute
elude	Scold	Avoid	Frighten	Confront
Collect	Accumulate	scatter	Bright	dark

Analogy
Circle the correct analogy

Harm is to destroy as like is to	love	dislike
Cure is to heal as buy is to	store	purchase
Declare is to say as ask is to	question	answer
Pick is to choose as attempt is to	try	win
Card is to deck as flower is to	bouquet	petal
Tiredness is to sleep as curiosity is to	exploration	rest
High is to low as near is to	around	far
Germ is to disease as bomb is to	loud	explosion
Front is to back as grumpy is to	frown	happy
Soap is to clean as towel is to	wet	wipe

Your other task for the day is to read. You can look online at www.plainandnotsoplain.com for book recommendations that we enjoyed reading or do an online search to find something that you are interested in. You should read for a minimum of one hour per day.

Write down the title of the book you are reading and how long you read for today.

_____

_____

Begin memorizing these common prepositions. It is one of those things like math facts that if you know them, it will make your future in grammar so much easier. This week take the first column and memorize.

about	before	down	like	past	until
above	behind	during	near	since	up
across	below	except	of	through	upon
after	beneath	for	off	to	with
against	beside	from	on	toward	within
along	between	in	onto	under	without
around	beyond	inside	outside	underneath	
at	but	into	over		
	by				
	concerning				

```
A   B   L   I   F   E   T   I   M   E   Y   M   M   L   U
G   A   C   P   F   Z   F   R   V   M   F   O   L   U   X
K   S   Q   S   W   I   T   C   H   B   O   A   R   D   O
N   K   H   M   I   D   G   N   S   R   B   S   K   D   R
P   E   F   O   M   G   E   T   S   E   S   O   Y   O   G
B   T   T   Q   R   C   S   S   E   O   K   P   P   D
R   B   A   O   K   I   A   A   L   B   C   Y   L   A   D
E   A   F   R   O   L   B   M   T   A   E   Y   A   P   R
A   L   I   C   C   F   R   X   N   L   N   B   Y   E   I
K   L   R   Y   H   A   E   K   O   Q   A   Y   H   R   F
F   Q   E   C   H   T   K   P   R   C   E   J   O   B   T
A   L   F   L   Y   C   G   Z   I   V   R   S   U   A   W
S   E   L   E   I   A   T   X   C   T   I   C   S   C   O
T   H   Y   N   L   V   A   D   M   I   I   T   E   K   O
Z   N   K   F   R   T   R   A   I   L   W   A   Y   U   D
```

BASEBALL	BASKETBALL	BREAKFAST
CLASSROOM	DRIFTWOOD	FIREFLY
FLAGPOLE	HARMLESS	KNICKKNACK
LIFETIME	MOTORCYCLE	PAPERBACK
PLAYHOUSE	RAILWAY	SWITCHBOARD
TAXICAB	TEXTBOOK	

6 X1	2 X6	5 X2	3 X8	4 X2	3 X6	1 X2	2 X2	1 X1	6 X4
3 X5	8 X2	4 X6	3 X4	1 X0	3 X7	4 X6	4 X8	3 X2	5 X4
8 X2	6 X0	1 X9	3 X4	9 X2	5 X5	1 X5	9 X9	1 X2	6 X2
3 X1	5 X6	3 X3	3 X0	4 X0	3 X6	4 X4	3 X8	5 x10	3 X10
5 X9	5 X4	1 X7	7 X2	6 X6	5 X2	4 X2	7 X6	8 X6	8 X8
9 X6	5 X7	2 X4	5 X6	9 X2	0 X0	1 X4	1 X3	4 X7	9 X4
10 X2	5 X3	10 X6	5 X3	5 X8	5 X1	5 X0	4 X4	3 X2	3 X9
3 x3	9 x9	7 x7	5 x5	3 x7	6 x8	2 x2	10 x6	12 x12	6 x4
6 x6	4 x4	2 x2	10 x10	5 x7	0 x6	7 x4	3 x7	8 x8	6 x7

Linking verbs do not show action. They link or join a subject to a word in the predicate.

**Let's memorize the linking verbs

Is   are   am   was   were   be   being   been

Action verb: Sarah <u>runs</u> in the race.
Linking verb: Sarah <u>is</u> the fastest runner.

Underline the verbs in each sentence. They may be action or linking.

1. I read a story last night.
2. My story was about a warm, summer day.
3. It describes how we play in the lake.
4. I read it to my Mother.
5. Sarah was in the story.
6. Collin is a tall boy.

Add a verb of your own to complete the sentences. Write them. Then write action or linking to tell which verb you used.

7. The boys_____a snowman today._____
8. Sarah_____a carrot for the nose._____
9. Winter_____my favorite season._____
10. Sam_____one of my favorite friends._____
11. My friends_____sad about the cat._____

Circle the linking verb and underline the noun that it is linked to the subject.

1. The book is good.
2. We are ten miles away from home.
3. I am tired.
4. There were many bees in the hive.
5. He was going to the park.

Fill in the blanks with a linking verb.

1. I have_____to that park.
2. What _____the name of your sister?
3. I am _____good.
4. The puppies_____so cute.
5. We_____all going to play ball.
6. The girl_____loud.
7. I _____sad.

Your other task for the day is to read. You can look online at www.plainandnotsoplain.com for book recommendations that we enjoyed reading or do an online search to find something that you are interested in. You should read for a minimum of one hour per day.

Write down the title of the book you are reading and how long you read for today.

_____

_____

write sentences for your words

5+5+5_____3x5 is it < > =?

Use digits and symbols to write twelve equals ten plus two

What term is missing

....., 32, 40,48,_____,64,......

Use digits to write eight hundred eighty dollars and eight cents

Compare 346,129_____346,132

A dozen is 12. How many is half dozen?

Write a multiplication problem that shows how to find the total number of Os

000000

000000

000000

000000

Which number is greater -3 or 1

There are 3 feet in one yard. How many feet are in ten yards

Helping verbs

Helping verbs are the linking verbs plus more.

Is	are	am	was	were	be	being	been	has	had	have	do	does	did
	may	might	must	can	could		should		would				

Memorize this list too. Helping verbs help to form some of the tenses of main verbs. They express time and mood.

If you see an "ing" verb that is a clue that there is a helping verb in the sentence.

She was running for miles and miles.

Sometimes, more than one helping verb is used in a sentence. This is called a verb phrase.

She had been sleeping for a long time.

Circle the letter of the sentence that contains a helping verb. Remember helping verbs help to set the time and mood of sentences.

a) We are going to the movies.
b) We went to the movies.
c) They ran to the movies.

a) Sam helped me with my studies.
b) Sam will help me with my studies.
c) Sam helps me with my studies every day.

a) I should think so!
b) I think so.
c) I think you are correct.

Fill in the blanks with helping verbs.

1. We _____ _____ planning our vacation for many months.
2. I _____ looking forward to seeing you.
3. We _____traveling by car.
4. It _____fun choosing where we are going.
5. I_____like to go see you swim.

Your other task for the day is to read. You can look online at www.plainandnotsoplain.com for book recommendations that we enjoyed reading or do an online search to find something that you are interested in. You should read for a minimum of one hour per day.

Write down the title of the book you are reading and how long you read for today.

_____

_____

Quiz

6 X1	2 X6	5 X2	3 X8	4 X2	3 X6	1 X2	2 X2	1 X1	6 X4
3 X5	8 X2	4 X6	3 X4	1 X0	3 X7	4 X6	4 X8	3 X2	5 X4
8 X2	6 X0	1 X9	3 X4	9 X2	5 X5	1 X5	9 X9	1 X2	6 X2
3 X1	5 X6	3 X3	3 X0	4 X0	3 X6	4 X4	3 X8	5 x10	3 X10
5 X9	5 X4	1 X7	7 X2	6 X6	5 X2	4 X2	7 X6	8 X6	8 X8
9 X6	5 X7	2 X4	5 X6	9 X2	0 X0	1 X4	1 X3	4 X7	9 X4
10 X2	5 X3	10 X6	5 X3	5 X8	5 X1	5 X0	4 X4	3 X2	3 X9
3 x3	9 x9	7 x7	5 x5	3 x7	6 x8	2 x2	10 x6	12 x12	6 x4
6 x6	4 x4	2 x2	10 x10	5 x7	0 x6	7 x4	3 x7	8 x8	6 x7

Subject verb agreement

Subjects and verbs have to agree in a sentence. The best way to do this, is by how they make sense.

Choose which verb makes sense.

1. Jadyn (designing, designed) quilts to sell.
2. She (finished, finishes) two quilts last month.
3. Lauren (patch, patched) together some pieces.
4. She is (sewed, sewing) the pieces now.
5. I (help, helped) her with the pieces yesterday.
6. We (cooked, will cook) the dinner last night.
7. Greg (works, worked) last evening outdoors.
8. Amy (plans, planned) dinner already.
9. Evan (flew, fly) in an airplane last year.
10. Collin (talks, talked) on the phone last week.

Which word best fits in the sentence.

11. The little cat_____bravely.

    acted   are acted   were acting   are acting

12. A mouse_____around the room.

    were walking   was walking   is walked   were walked

Give me an example of a singular noun?_____

Give me an example of a plural noun?_____

Give me an example of a proper noun?_____

Give me an example of a common noun?_____

Your other task for the day is to read. You can look online at www.plainandnotsoplain.com for book recommendations that we enjoyed reading or do an online search to find something that you are interested in. You should read for a minimum of one hour per day.

Write down the title of the book you are reading and how long you read for today.

_____

_____

week 8 spelling words

aren't

can't

couldn't

didn't

hasn't

he's

I'd

isn't

let's

shouldn't

they're

they've

wasn't

weren't

we've

wouldn't

you'd

you're

Jadyn had $28. After she spent $12, how much money did she have?

After losing 234 pounds, Jumbo the elephant still weighed 4,368 pounds. How much did Jumbo weight before he lost the weight?

The price went up from $26 to $32. By how many dollars did the price increase?

use tally marks to show the number 15

Use words to name $206.50

For the fact family 7,8,15 write two addition and two subtraction facts

Brooklyn had $24. She spent $8. How much money did Brooklyn have left

b-256=67 what is b

Adjectives

Adjectives are words used to describe a noun or pronoun. Using colorful, lively, descriptive adjectives makes writing and speaking more interesting.

Most adjectives are common adjectives and are not capitalized. They can be before or after the noun they describe.

It was a breezy day.   The day was breezy.

Proper adjectives are formed from proper nouns and are always capitalized.

The chef likes baking Italian bread.

Write a list of 5 adjectives that describe your favorite animal.

Animal:_____

1. _____
2. _____
3. _____
4. _____
5. _____

Circle all the adjectives in the sentences below.

1. Mom made a tasty treat for us to eat.
2. Evan was a hungry boy.
3. Amy was a pretty, tall woman.
4. Greg was a short, handsome man.
5. The Sahara Desert is in the North African desert region.
6. The Arabian camel has one hump, while the Bactrian camel has two humps.
7. I like to eat Chinese food for my birthday dinner.

    Fill in the blanks with adjectives common or proper

1. Come look at this_____butterfly. (common)
2. My _____truck is broken. (proper)
3. I am eating this _____apple. (proper)
4. Collin has _____hair. (common)
5. We filled the bags with _____candy. (common)
6. Will you sew_____dresses? (common)
7. We will need_____pails for each child. (common)
8. Three_____bugs are on the floor. (common)
9. Watch out for that_____ball! (common)
10. Did you see the _____ woman? (proper)

Your other task for the day is to read. You can look online at www.plainandnotsoplain.com for book recommendations that we enjoyed reading or do an online search to find something that you are interested in. You should read for a minimum of one hour per day.

Write down the title of the book you are reading and how long you read for today.

_____

_____

Begin memorizing these common prepositions. It is one of those things like math facts that if you know them, it will make your future in grammar so much easier. This week take the first column and memorize.

about	before	down	like	past	until
above	behind	during	near	since	up
across	below	except	of	through	upon
after	beneath	for	off	to	with
against	beside	from	on	toward	within
along	between	in	onto	under	without
around	beyond	inside	outside	underneath	
at	but	into	over		
	by				
	concerning				

no crossword puzzle☺

6 X1	2 X6	5 X2	3 X8	4 X2	3 X6	1 X2	2 X2	1 X1	6 X4
3 X5	8 X2	4 X6	3 X4	1 X0	3 X7	4 X6	4 X8	3 X2	5 X4
8 X2	6 X0	1 X9	3 X4	9 X2	5 X5	1 X5	9 X9	1 X2	6 X2
3 X1	5 X6	3 X3	3 X0	4 X0	3 X6	4 X4	3 X8	5 x10	3 X10
5 X9	5 X4	1 X7	7 X2	6 X6	5 X2	4 X2	7 X6	8 X6	8 X8
9 X6	5 X7	2 X4	5 X6	9 X2	0 X0	1 X4	1 X3	4 X7	9 X4
10 X2	5 X3	10 X6	5 X3	5 X8	5 X1	5 X0	4 X4	3 X2	3 X9
3 x3	9 x9	7 x7	5 x5	3 x7	6 x8	2 x2	10 x6	12 x12	6 x4
6 x6	4 x4	2 x2	10 x10	5 x7	0 x6	7 x4	3 x7	8 x8	6 x7

Review: Fill in the blanks

Present	past	future
1. Amy <u>works.</u>	Amy <u>worked.</u>	Amy <u>will work.</u>
2. Lauren <u>sings.</u>	Lauren_____	Lauren _____ .
3. He <u>plays.</u>	He_____ .	He_____ .
4. Today I <u>come.</u>	Yesterday I_____ .	Tomorrow I_____ .

Write the correct form of the underlined verb.

5. Soon, we will all <u>praised </u>the Lord. _____
6. God's word <u>are</u> holy._____
7. The boy is<u> jumps</u> for joy._____
8. After Pastor finished, Sarah <u>walk </u>to her car._____
9. Evan <u>listen</u> to the message from the pastor._____

Choose the correct form of the verb to complete each sentence

10. Do you (like, liking) butterflies?
11. Greg always (laughs, laugh) at her jokes.
12. Her family (calls, calling) her the "jokester."
13. Stephen (crawl, crawls) on the floor.
14. The little child(acted, are acting) bravely.
15. A cat (is purred, was purring) in my lap.

Remember the irregular verbs?

Present	past	past with has, have, or had
Begin	began	(has,have,had)begun
Do	did	(has, have, had)done
Find	found	(has, have, had)found
Give	gave	(has, have, had)given
Go	went	(has, have,had)gone
Run	ran	(has,have,had)run
See	saw	(has, have,had)seen
Take	took	(has, have, had)taken
Think	thought	(has, have, had)thought
Wear	wore	(has, have, had)worn

Choose the correct form of the irregular verb in () to complete each sentence.

1. My mother (took, taken) many pictures of us.
2. I have (saw, seen)photos of Dad as a little boy.
3. He (go, went) to swim lessons, just as I did.
4. I once (think, thought) he did not like swimming.
5. He (wore, worn) an orange swim suit.
6. I have (begin, began) to keep a journal.
7. I (take, took) the name from a book.
8. I have (given, give) my cat a bone.
9. It is about a cat who has (go, gone) to Paris.
10. She (do, did) everything I ask of her.
11. The cat (run, ran) away.
12. Have you (saw, seen) my rock collection?
13. All the girls (wear, wore) skirts yesterday at the dance.
14. He had (took, taken) a cookie from the tray.

Your other task for the day is to read. You can look online at www.plainandnotsoplain.com for book recommendations that we enjoyed reading or do an online search to find something that you are interested in. You should read for a minimum of one hour per day.

Write down the title of the book you are reading and how long you read for today.

_____

_____

write sentences for your words

900-c=90 c=_____   g+843=1000 g=_____

Draw a horizontal segment

Draw two intersecting lines

Use digits and a comparison symbol to write: Eight hundred forty is greater than eight hundred fourteen

What number is missing

....24,30,36,_____48,54

4x3_____2x6 compare

The letter y stands for what in 36 +y=63

How many cents is half a dollar?

Greg had $32. He spent $15. How much does he have left?

Review

List me 5 adjectives that describe the following:

Cats	Snow	Sunshine
Mountains	Water	people
Ice cream	Chocolate	Spinach
Gum	Children	chickens

Your other task for the day is to read. You can look online at www.plainandnotsoplain.com for book recommendations that we enjoyed reading or do an online search to find something that you are interested in. You should read for a minimum of one hour per day.

Write down the title of the book you are reading and how long you read for today.

_____

_____

Quiz

6 ×1	2 ×6	5 ×2	3 ×8	4 ×2	3 ×6	1 ×2	2 ×2	1 ×1	6 ×4
3 ×5	8 ×2	4 ×6	3 ×4	1 ×0	3 ×7	4 ×6	4 ×8	3 ×2	5 ×4
8 ×2	6 ×0	1 ×9	3 ×4	9 ×2	5 ×5	1 ×5	9 ×9	1 ×2	6 ×2
3 ×1	5 ×6	3 ×3	3 ×0	4 ×0	3 ×6	4 ×4	3 ×8	5 ×10	3 ×10
5 ×9	5 ×4	1 ×7	7 ×2	6 ×6	5 ×2	4 ×2	7 ×6	8 ×6	8 ×8
9 ×6	5 ×7	2 ×4	5 ×6	9 ×2	0 ×0	1 ×4	1 ×3	4 ×7	9 ×4
10 ×2	5 ×3	10 ×6	5 ×3	5 ×8	5 ×1	5 ×0	4 ×4	3 ×2	3 ×9
3 ×3	9 ×9	7 ×7	5 ×5	3 ×7	6 ×8	2 ×2	10 ×6	12 ×12	6 ×4
6 ×6	4 ×4	2 ×2	10 ×10	5 ×7	0 ×6	7 ×4	3 ×7	8 ×8	6 ×7

Adverbs

We have learned about adjectives, they describe nouns. Now we are going to learn about adverbs, they describe verbs.

An adverb answers the question: how, when, where

We all listened **carefully**.   How did we listen? Carefully

Greg is coming **now.** When is Greg coming? Now

Look, over **there.** Where do we look? There

They often end in "ly"

Write the adverb that tells more about each underlined verb.
1. We <u>eat</u> quickly at snack time._____
2. We <u>will sing</u> later._____
3. They <u>race</u> around._____
4. Lauren <u>looked</u> carefully for her shoe._____
5. She <u>finds</u> her shoe there._____

Choose an adverb in () to complete each sentence.

6. My whole family gets ready (late, up).
7. We are going to the park at school (today, loudly).
8. I will read my bible (loudly, up) to the class.
9. Everyone will listen to me (down, quietly).
10. We will have treats (up, later)

Circle each adverb. Write if it tells **when, where**, or **how.**
11. I am going to leave early._____
12. I will make food quickly._____
13. Then my sister and I will go to the park._____
14. We see ducks over there in the pond._____
15. When I looked quietly, I saw a fish._____
16. Sarah quickly finished her work so she could get to dinner._____
17. Fruit often makes a great dessert._____
18. He accidentally hit the car._____
19. The snow fell gracefully on the ground._____
20. She rudely interrupted him._____

Your other task for the day is to read. You can look online at www.plainandnotsoplain.com for book recommendations that we enjoyed reading or do an online search to find something that you are interested in. You should read for a minimum of one hour per day.

Write down the title of the book you are reading and how long you read for today.

_____

_____

week 9 spelling words

additive

badge

chapter

daffodil

dragon

friction

gathering

kangaroo

magazine

pasture

patches

rapid

sassafras

standard

tacks

thankful

transplant

traveler

A ticket to a basketball game costs $24. How much would 3 tickets cost?

To solve, we could add 24 three different times or we could do a multiplication problem

24

x3
___

72

Remember how we have to carry the one from the 4x3?

Your turn:

Six different times next month, a salesperson must make a 325 mile round trip. How many total miles will the salesperson travel next month

327
X 3
_____

7654
x 2
_____

5432
x   5
_____

Good, Bad: Well, Badly

Good and bad are adjectives that modify nouns or pronouns. Well and badly are adverbs that modify verbs.
A guitar is a good instrument to invest in for boys.
Buying a drum set is a bad choice.
It's hard to play the drums well when you have a headache.
I played badly because my finger was sprained.

1. Laura used to play the flute _____(bad, badly) when she first started.

2. I felt Sam's choice to learn how to play the drums was a _____-(good/well) one.

3. Bob sang very _____(good/well) at the birthday party.

4. Steven made a _____(bad/badly) choice when he quit exercising.

5. Cindy made a _____(good/well) decision when she brought the books home to do extra studying.

6. Mr. Maryon said that I display a _____(good/well) attitude toward the little children.

7. Leaving an expensive tablet out where it can get damaged is a _____(bad/badly) thing to do

8. Lauren performed the dance solo _____(good/well) because she practiced everyday.

Compounds

There are 3 types of compound words. Closed compound—two separate words joined together that create a new meaning and written as one word.
Open compound—two separate words create a new meaning but the two words are not joined together.
Hyphenated compound—two or more words written separately but connected by a hyphen create a new meaning.
Add a word from the word box to form a new compound word.

1. cup_____
2. snow_____
3. home_____
4. barn_____
5. chair_____
6. yard_____
7. sea_____
8. hide-_____
9. brand-_____

10. polar_____
11. ice_____
12. peanut_____
13. blast_____
14. post_____
15. topsy-_____
16. town_____
17. zip_____
18. jack-_____

barnyard	blastoff
brand-new	chairperson
cupboard	hide-and-seek
homesick	ice skate
jack-o'-lantern	peanut butter
polar bear	seagull
snowstorm	topsy-turvy
town crier	yardstick
zip code	post office

131

Your other task for the day is to read. You can look online at www.plainandnotsoplain.com for book recommendations that we enjoyed reading or do an online search to find something that you are interested in. You should read for a minimum of one hour per day.

Write down the title of the book you are reading and how long you read for today.

_____

_____

```
G  C  A  K  D  R  A  G  O  N  W  W  C  L  M
A  D  A  F  F  O  D  I  L  V  Q  X  B  F  J
T  H  H  D  T  R  A  V  E  L  E  R  A  M  L
H  P  A  T  C  H  E  S  U  I  O  M  D  T  S
E  B  W  I  E  V  G  F  C  K  C  E  G  A  T
R  Y  T  Y  B  K  K  F  D  S  H  D  E  C  A
I  W  Y  R  P  N  A  X  W  A  A  S  F  K  N
N  M  K  F  A  X  K  N  H  S  P  L  R  S  D
G  A  G  H  S  N  C  Y  G  S  T  I  A  S  A
L  G  T  L  T  S  S  Q  Z  A  E  P  C  K  R
S  A  Y  R  U  R  G  P  J  F  R  C  T  W  D
V  Z  Q  S  R  K  T  G  L  R  U  O  I  T  Q
U  I  E  F  E  Q  H  G  Y  A  G  Z  O  N  T
U  N  S  R  A  P  I  D  V  S  N  B  N  Y  Z
B  E  A  D  D  I  T  I  V  E  P  T  F  Q  T
```

ADDITIVE	BADGE	CHAPTER
DAFFODIL	DRAGON	FRACTION
GATHERING	KANGAROO	MAGAZINE
PASTURE	PATCHES	RAPID
SASSAFRAS	STANDARD	TACKS
THANKFUL	TRANSPLANT	TRAVELER

6 ×1	2 ×6	5 ×2	3 ×8	4 ×2	3 ×6	1 ×2	2 ×2	1 ×1	6 ×4
3 ×5	8 ×2	4 ×6	3 ×4	1 ×0	3 ×7	4 ×6	4 ×8	3 ×2	5 ×4
8 ×2	6 ×0	1 ×9	3 ×4	9 ×2	5 ×5	1 ×5	9 ×9	1 ×2	6 ×2
3 ×1	5 ×6	3 ×3	3 ×0	4 ×0	3 ×6	4 ×4	3 ×8	5 ×10	3 ×10
5 ×9	5 ×4	1 ×7	7 ×2	6 ×6	5 ×2	4 ×2	7 ×6	8 ×6	8 ×8
9 ×6	5 ×7	2 ×4	5 ×6	9 ×2	0 ×0	1 ×4	1 ×3	4 ×7	9 ×4
10 ×2	5 ×3	10 ×6	5 ×3	5 ×8	5 ×1	5 ×0	4 ×4	3 ×2	3 ×9
3 ×3	9 ×9	7 ×7	5 ×5	3 ×7	6 ×8	2 ×2	10 ×6	12 ×12	6 ×4
6 ×6	4 ×4	2 ×2	10 ×10	5 ×7	0 ×6	7 ×4	3 ×7	8 ×8	6 ×7

Compound words and ABC order
Here is a list of more compound words. Put the following columns in ABC order. Rewrite them.

newscast   _____
weekend   _____
everybody   _____
up-to-date   _____
grandparent   _____
first aid   _____

wildlife   _____
homemade   _____
baby-sit   _____
brother-in-law   _____
three-dimensional   _____
starry-eyed   _____
self-defense   _____

teammate   _____
classmate   _____
part-time   _____
tongue-tied   _____
self-confidence   _____
weather-proofed   _____

water-repellant   _____
autograph   _____
forehead   _____
quick-witted   _____
daytime   _____
thoroughbred   _____

Your other task for the day is to read. You can look online at www.plainandnotsoplain.com for book recommendations that we enjoyed reading or do an online search to find something that you are interested in. You should read for a minimum of one hour per day.

Write down the title of the book you are reading and how long you read for today.

_____

_____

write sentences for your words

Draw a vertical line segment

Sam read 3 books. Each book had 120 pages. How many pages did he read. First answer once by adding and again by multiplying

The spider spun its web for 6 hours the first night and for some more hours the second night. If the spider spent a total of 14 hours spinning its web those two nights, how many hours did the spider spin the second night?

rewrite your problems vertically for easier solving

24x3=_____ $35 x4_____   56 x 6=_____

c+147=316 what is c_____   604-w=406 what is w_____

3 +n+15+9=60 what is n_____

Conjunctions

A conjunction joins words or groups of words together. There are three kinds of conjunctions:

Coordinating conjunction connect words, phrases or clauses using: and, but, or, nor, for, yet.

The rain is cold and wet.

Correlative conjunctions connects with pairs and are used together: both/and, not only/but also, either/or, neither/nor, whether/or

Both Sarah and Timmy went to the play. (sarah and timmy are a pair)

And	both/and	neither/nor	as long as
But	either/or	after	since

1. Mary wanted to have ice cream for a snack _____ Linda wanted popsicles.

2. _____ green _____ black were used in the mural.

3. Sarah wanted to go biking today_____ the big rainstorm.

4. Danielle didn't go biking_____ it was storming.

5. _____ Greg_____ Amy passed their First Aid class.

6. Collin wanted to stay inside and play Xbox _____ it was still storming.

7. _____ take out the trash_____ walk the cat.

8. We were going to see a movie,_____ we went out to eat, instead.

Circle the conjunctions in the following sentences.

1. I have fished in the Colorado River many times, but I never catch any fish.

2. The postman told me last winter that my poor luck was caused neither by my lack of skill nor by my choice of the wrong bait.

3. I saved my money and bought both the reel and the lure, for I was determined to make a big catch.

4. December was very cold, but I decided to try my luck at Lake Summit; I caught nothing.

5. Whether I go early in the morning or late in the afternoon, the fish either aren't hungry or won't eat.

6. Both his father and he played football in high school and in college.

7. Either you must wash the dishes, or you will have to clean the bathroom.

8. We waited for a long time, for the bus was late.

9. I like to play baseball and tennis.

10. Would you like to eat tacos or nachos?

Your other task for the day is to read. You can look online at www.plainandnotsoplain.com for book recommendations that we enjoyed reading or do an online search to find something that you are interested in. You should read for a minimum of one hour per day.

Write down the title of the book you are reading and how long you read for today.

_____

_____

Quiz

6 X1	2 X6	5 X2	3 X8	4 X2	3 X6	1 X2	2 X2	1 X1	6 X4
3 X5	8 X2	4 X6	3 X4	1 X0	3 X7	4 X6	4 X8	3 X2	5 X4
8 X2	6 X0	1 X9	3 X4	9 X2	5 X5	1 X5	9 X9	1 X2	6 X2
3 X1	5 X6	3 X3	3 X0	4 X0	3 X6	4 X4	3 X8	5 x10	3 X10
5 X9	5 X4	1 X7	7 X2	6 X6	5 X2	4 X2	7 X6	8 X6	8 X8
9 X6	5 X7	2 X4	5 X6	9 X2	0 X0	1 X4	1 X3	4 X7	9 X4
10 X2	5 X3	10 X6	5 X3	5 X8	5 X1	5 X0	4 X4	3 X2	3 X9
3 x3	9 x9	7 x7	5 x5	3 x7	6 x8	2 x2	10 x6	12 x12	6 x4
6 x6	4 x4	2 x2	10 x10	5 x7	0 x6	7 x4	3 x7	8 x8	6 x7

Conjunctions

Combine the following sentences to form one sentence with a connector word. (and, but, or, for, nor))

1. Kathy likes to ride horses. Lauren likes to brush them.

   _____

   _____

2. Can we go to the park? Can we go to the beach?

   _____

   _____

3. I was scared when I went to the ocean. I swam anyways.

   _____

   _____

4. Jadyn is nine years old. Jadyn likes to ride horses.

   _____

   _____

5. Karen is short. Karen is taller than her brothers.

   _____

   _____

Add a conjunction to each phrase that describes the planet Saturn.

6. Beautiful_____majestic
7. Far away,_____gigantic
8. Larger than Earth,_____lighter in comparison
9. Shorter days than Earth_____faster rotation
10. Atmosphere of mostly hydrogen_____helium
11. Beautiful rings_____not the only planet with them

Fill in the following clues with a closed compound word

Hoop, whistle, and you play =b_____

Pay a fare, has a driver= t_____

Sometimes called a lightning bug=f_____

Game played with bat and ball= b_____

You hang a red and white striped with stars on it=f_____

From moment born till death= l_____

A softcover book=p_____

Your other task for the day is to read. You can look online at www.plainandnotsoplain.com for book recommendations that we enjoyed reading or do an online search to find something that you are interested in. You should read for a minimum of one hour per day.

Write down the title of the book you are reading and how long you read for today.

_____

_____

week 10 spelling list

ancestor

attempt

central

definition

enforce

festival

generally

genuine

legend

medicine

necessary

pedal

reference

residence

section

sentence

temperature

tennis

compare 12 x1_____24x0

Five hundred four thousand is less than five hundred fourteen thousand, write with digits and a comparison symbol

What number is missing

...21,28,35,_____,49,56

What digit in 375 is in the hundreds place

What number is ten more than these tally marks

|||| |||| |||

Multiply vertically 321 x5=   432x 4=

Articles

The adjectives *a, an, the are* called articles. Articles go before nouns and sometimes other adjectives. Use "the" to name a specific noun.

The boys like to play. ---talking of specific boys

A and an do not name specific. Put "a" before a consonant and "an" before a vowel.

I am going to eat an apple. I am going to eat a pear.

Fill in the following with a, an, or the

1. I have _____bad headache.
2. Today's class was cancelled because_____teacher is sick.
3. My Dad works hard. He's _____engineer
4. Collin came home with a huge box. He bought_____new paddle.
5. How long does it take to get there? It takes about _____hour.
6. I want to change the channel. Okay, _____remote control is over there.
7. Why can't Tina come? She doesn't have _____passport.
8. Where does Barb live? In _____apartment on 5th avenue.
9. Oh, no where is it? Don't worry, _____key is in my pocket.
10. I don't understand what this word means. You need to buy_____dictionary.

Review

Name the part of speech that is underlined. Nouns, verbs, adjectives, adverbs, conjunction, pronoun
1. *Mary* likes *fish.*_____
2. You and I must change this. _____
3. What a hot day! They were very angry._____
4. They played and sang. _____
5. We soon quit. I am very sad. _____
6. Ed or Joe lost. _____
7. Give an example of singular common noun?_____
8. Give an example of proper noun?_____
9. Give an example of plural common noun?_____
11. Name the subject pronouns (7) _____

_____
12. Name the object pronouns (7) _____

_____

Your other task for the day is to read. You can look online at www.plainandnotsoplain.com for book recommendations that we enjoyed reading or do an online search to find something that you are interested in. You should read for a minimum of one hour per day.

Write down the title of the book you are reading and how long you read for today.

_____

_____

```
X  F  P  C  P  Y  X  F  B  L  K  Z  R  V  S
A  R  I  S  K  B  Z  W  A  K  J  J  E  G  E
N  R  E  M  E  X  P  R  M  V  V  R  F  E  C
C  E  W  E  G  N  T  R  O  A  U  D  E  N  T
E  S  T  D  N  N  T  N  E  T  R  E  R  U  I
S  I  E  I  E  A  D  E  A  I  G  F  E  I  O
T  D  N  C  Y  Q  P  R  N  X  E  I  N  N  N
O  E  N  I  I  L  E  L  S  C  N  N  C  E  J
R  N  I  N  G  P  E  W  F  Z  E  I  E  Q  X
N  C  S  E  M  A  D  N  E  D  R  T  M  Y  T
X  E  F  E  S  T  I  V  A  L  A  I  V  G  L
F  A  T  T  E  M  P  T  R  M  L  O  B  A  U
V  G  E  L  E  G  E  N  D  D  L  N  D  Q  P
N  E  C  E  S  S  A  R  Y  C  Y  E  A  S  A
P  A  K  Q  D  W  X  S  Y  B  P  I  B  F  A
```

ANCESTOR	ATTEMPT	CENTRAL
DEFINITION	FESTIVAL	GENERALLY
GENUINE	LEGEND	MEDICINE
NECESSARY	PEDAL	REFERENCE
RESIDENCE	SECTION	SENTENCE
TEMPERATURE	TENNIS	

6 X1	2 X6	5 X2	3 X8	4 X2	3 X6	1 X2	2 X2	1 X1	6 X4
3 X5	8 X2	4 X6	3 X4	1 X0	3 X7	4 X6	4 X8	3 X2	5 X4
8 X2	6 X0	1 X9	3 X4	9 X2	5 X5	1 X5	9 X9	1 X2	6 X2
3 X1	5 X6	3 X3	3 X0	4 X0	3 X6	4 X4	3 X8	5 x10	3 X10
5 X9	5 X4	1 X7	7 X2	6 X6	5 X2	4 X2	7 X6	8 X6	8 X8
9 X6	5 X7	2 X4	5 X6	9 X2	0 X0	1 X4	1 X3	4 X7	9 X4
10 X2	5 X3	10 X6	5 X3	5 X8	5 X1	5 X0	4 X4	3 X2	3 X9
3 x3	9 x9	7 x7	5 x5	3 x7	6 x8	2 x2	10 x6	12 x12	6 x4
6 x6	4 x4	2 x2	10 x10	5 x7	0 x6	7 x4	3 x7	8 x8	6 x7

Interjection

An interjection is an exclamatory word that expresses emotion. When the feeling is especially strong, the interjection is followed by an exclamation mark. The word that follows begins with a capital letter. When the feeling is less strong, the interjection is followed by a comma.

Ugh! The milk taste sour.

Yippee! We won!

Wow! It worked.

Oh, all right.

Common interjections	
Ah	Hurray
Aha	Oh
Alas	Ouch
Aw	Uh
Cheers	Uh-huh
Eh	Uh-uh
Hey	Well
Hi	Wow
Huh	Yeah

Write a sentence with the following interjections: (If you don't know the meaning look it up.)

1. alas

_____

_____

2. Ouch

_____

_____

3. Ugh

_____

_____

4. Huh

_____

_____

5. Yeah

_____

_____

6. Wow

_____

_____

7. Aw

_____

_____

8. Well

_____

_____

9. Hey

_____

_____

Your other task for the day is to read. You can look online at www.plainandnotsoplain.com for book recommendations that we enjoyed reading or do an online search to find something that you are interested in. You should read for a minimum of one hour per day.

Write down the title of the book you are reading and how long you read for today.

_____

_____

write sentences for your words

count aloud: count up and down by 5s between 1 and 51. Count up and down by 200s between 0 and 2000.

Mental math:

- 3 x30 plus 3x2
- 4 x20 plus 4x3
- 6 x$700
- one meter is 1000 millimeters. How many millimeters is 1 meter minus 100 millimeters
- 6 x4+1+10-5+3

Multiplying three numbers.

When faced with multiplying three numbers, we first multiply two of the factors together. Then we multiply the product we get by the third factor.

9x6x5 nine times six is 54 and then 54 times 5 equals270

Your turn:

Find the product of 5x3x2

Find the product of 2 x3x2

Find the missing factor w x3=18

There are 12 inches in a foot and 3 feet in a yard. How many inches long is a wall that is 5 yards long?

Interjections

Add commas and exclamation points where they are needed in the following sentences.

1. Yes we will finish the history project soon.
2. Wow I forgot that it must be done by Friday.
3. Jeff bring the microscope to the science lab quickly
4. Yikes That was a scary experiment that you did Mark.
5. Cool I would love to use the other lab.
6. Yes I'll try to set up the project in that room Susan.
7. Well that solved my problem.
8. Hey Mike Let's meet at the park.
9. Hurry It is going to rain.
10. Ugh That soup tastes horrible.

Review Verb Tenses

Fill in the blanks with the correct form of the verb.

I can't believe I (get)_____ that apartment. I (submit) _____my application last week, but I didn't think I had a chance of actually getting git. When I (show) _____up to take a look around, there were at least twenty other people who (arrive)_____ before me. Most of them already (fill)_____out their application and were already leaving. The landlord said I could still apply, so I did.

I (try)_____to fill out the form, but I couldn't answer half of the questions. They (want)_____me to include references, but I didn't want to list my previous landlord because I (have)_____some problems with him in the past and I knew he wouldn't recommend me. I (end) _____up listing my father as a reference.

It was total luck that he (decide)_____to give me the apartment. It turns out that the landlord and my father (go)_____to high school together. He decided that I could have the apartment before he (look)_____at my credit report. I really lucked out!

Your other task for the day is to read. You can look online at www.plainandnotsoplain.com for book recommendations that we enjoyed reading or do an online search to find something that you are interested in. You should read for a minimum of one hour per day.

Write down the title of the book you are reading and how long you read for today.

_____

_____

Quiz

Find the missing letter: 5m=30 (when two variables are together that means to multiply) so what times 5 is 30?

3b =21 what is b

Draw a horizontal line and a vertical line. Then write the words above the lines

In one class there are 33 students. Fourteen of the students are boys. How many are girls?

6x4x5=   5x6x8

$407x8= $7.32x6=*don't forget decimal

n-354=46 n=_____

Think of one digit odd number and a one digit even number. Multiply them. Is the product even or odd? how do you know?

6x4=8x?

Prepositions

Remember all of these? See if you can fill in the blanks of the missing ones.

about	before	down	like	_____	until
above	_____	_____	near	_____	_____
_____	below	except	_____	through	_____
after	beneath	____	____	___	____
_____	_____	_____	_____	_____	____
along	between	in	onto	under	without
		inside	outside	underneath	
_____	_____				
at	but	into	over		
	by				
	concerning				

A prepositional phrase is a group of words that begins with a preposition and ends with the object of the preposition.

Water makes up about 65 percent **of the human body.**

Circle the prepositional phrases:

1. The muscles in the human body number 600.
2. All adults should brush their 32 teeth with great care.
3. Our skin might burn in the hot sun.
4. Every person on earth is warm-blooded.
5. The man went through the hospital doors.
6. The temperature inside the body is about 98.6 degrees.
7. The dentist looked inside my mouth.
8. An adult skeleton consists of about 200 bones.
9. People who live in high altitudes may have more blood flowing in their veins.
10. Our skin helps protect our inner tissues from the outside world.
11. The horse jumped over the high fence.
12. The paper fell underneath the small bookcase.
13. I walked around the yard.
14. The book for him is new.
15. I ran after the cat, through the wooden door, and into the house.

Give me 5 words that describe your day today: (adjectives)

1. _____
2. _____
3. _____
4. _____
5. _____

Your other task for the day is to read. You can look online at www.plainandnotsoplain.com for book recommendations that we enjoyed reading or do an online search to find something that you are interested in. You should read for a minimum of one hour per day.

Write down the title of the book you are reading and how long you read for today.

_____

_____

week 11 spelling list

activities

citizen

difference

difficulties

exit

fiction

hippopotamus

individual

instrument

interesting

kitchen

listening

miniature

miserable

officer

principal

prisoner

shipment

6 X1	2 X6	5 X2	3 X8	4 X2	3 X6	1 X2	2 X2	1 X1	6 X4
3 X5	8 X2	4 X6	3 X4	1 X0	3 X7	4 X6	4 X8	3 X2	5 X4
8 X2	6 X0	1 X9	3 X4	9 X2	5 X5	1 X5	9 X9	1 X2	6 X2
3 X1	5 X6	3 X3	3 X0	4 X0	3 X6	4 X4	3 X8	5 x10	3 X10
5 X9	5 X4	1 X7	7 X2	6 X6	5 X2	4 X2	7 X6	8 X6	8 X8
9 X6	5 X7	2 X4	5 X6	9 X2	0 X0	1 X4	1 X3	4 X7	9 X4
10 X2	5 X3	10 X6	5 X3	5 X8	5 X1	5 X0	4 X4	3 X2	3 X9
3 x3	9 x9	7 x7	5 x5	3 x7	6 x8	2 x2	10 x6	12 x12	6 x4
6 x6	4 x4	2 x2	10 x10	5 x7	0 x6	7 x4	3 x7	8 x8	6 x7

Review of Verbs.

Underline the complete verbs in the following sentences. Be sure to include any helping verbs.

1. He stepped onto the plane.
2. Black soot and brilliant diamonds are both carbon.
3. Diamonds are crystals of carbon.
4. It must be heated very hot at the same time.
5. Miners usually find diamonds deep in the ground.
6. For centuries, most diamond mines were in India.
7. Now the biggest diamond mines are found in Africa.
8. One day in 1866, some children saw a pretty pebble in the river near Hopetown, South Africa.
9. It looked like frosted glass.
10. The children brought it home with them.
11. One day a neighbor offered money for it.
12. The children gave it to him for nothing.
13. The children did not know the value of the stone.
14. It was a diamond.
15. Word about this discovery spread very quickly.
16. Other people hunted for diamonds nearby.
17. Many of them were disappointed.
18. However, some people found diamonds in the area.
19. They were blessed with good fortune.
20. Diamonds were discovered in other parts of Africa as well.

Give me 5 words that describe how you feel about the mountains:

1. _____
2. _____
3. _____
4. _____
5. _____

Put parenthesis around the prepositional phrases

1. The cat hid under the steps.
2. The teacher asked my name and took me to a large room.
3. Service will begin when the Pastor comes into the sanctuary.
4. We learn the Bible for our teaching.
5. She laughed at the boy when he told a funny joke.

Your other task for the day is to read. You can look online at www.plainandnotsoplain.com for book recommendations that we enjoyed reading or do an online search to find something that you are interested in. You should read for a minimum of one hour per day.

Write down the title of the book you are reading and how long you read for today.

_____

_____

```
I  I  O  G  X  M  T  H  A  C  G  R  T  F  O
N  W  X  D  I  F  F  I  C  U  L  T  I  E  S
S  S  X  I  W  F  L  K  T  Y  U  D  O  H  T
T  D  M  N  H  Y  I  I  I  W  D  B  L  I  O
R  I  I  D  P  M  S  T  V  Z  K  R  E  P  F
U  F  S  I  R  I  T  C  I  O  W  C  P  P  F
M  F  E  V  I  N  E  H  T  S  F  U  L  O  I
E  E  R  I  S  I  N  E  I  E  A  A  X  P  C
N  R  A  D  O  A  I  N  E  X  P  F  N  O  E
T  E  B  U  N  T  N  Z  S  I  M  W  K  T  R
Q  N  L  A  E  U  G  U  C  T  Y  Y  G  A  G
U  C  E  L  R  R  H  N  X  T  B  B  U  M  X
C  E  Y  R  Y  E  I  B  I  U  G  C  S  U  I
U  I  N  T  E  R  E  S  T  I  N  G  I  S  C
D  E  H  Q  P  C  I  T  I  Z  E  N  Q  S  X
```

ACTIVITIES	CITIZEN	DIFFERENCE
DIFFICULTIES	EXIT	HIPPOPOTAMUS
INDIVIDUAL	INSTRUMENT	INTERESTING
KITCHEN	LISTENING	MINIATURE
MISERABLE	OFFICER	PRINCIPAL
PRISONER		

Use digits and symbols to write this comparision:

Eight times eight is greater than nine times seven

What are the next three integers in this counting sequence: 8,6,4,2,....

Jim and his friends each purchased a bookcase. The friends bookcase is half the height of Jims. If the friends bookcase is 3 feet tall, how tall is Jims?

Madelyn bought four folders for $0.37 each. Altogether how much money did the four folders cost?

mental math:

- 2x5x6
- 4x60 plus 4x5
- 9x9-1+10

The $45 dress was marked down to $29. By how many dollars had the dress been marked down?

3 x $4.83= $706x4=

Put () around the following prepositional phrases in each sentence below.

1. Micah left his shoes (at our house).
2. Paul left them (beneath the towels).
3. Mary looked closely (under the stairs) but couldn't find it.
4. Sam sent Danny a message to look (under the magazines).
5. Let's go play (in the woods).

Join the following 2 simple sentences to make a compound sentence.
Rewrite the new sentence with conjunction. You cannot use the same conjunction more than once.

a) Lauren likes her hair purple. Lauren likes her hair short.

   _____

   _____

b) Dad says she can dye her hair. Dad says he does not want her to shave it.

   _____

   _____

c) Would you like to come over? Would you like to go out to eat?

   _____

   _____

Present	Past	Past with has/had/have
speak	spoke	spoken
know		
make		
write		
sit		
say		
take		
think		
do		
see		
give		
come		
go		
buy		
forget		
tell		

Your other task for the day is to read. You can look online at www.plainandnotsoplain.com for book recommendations that we enjoyed reading or do an online search to find something that you are interested in. You should read for a minimum of one hour per day.

Write down the title of the book you are reading and how long you read for today.

_____

_____

write sentences for your words

Division

Searching for a missing factor is called division. It is the opposite of multiplication. The product is shown inside a symbol called a division box ‾‾‾| The two factors are outside the box are called factors.

$3\overline{)12}$ to solve this problem, we need to know what number times 3 equals 12. Since 3 x4=12, we know the missing factor is 4. We write our answer this way:

$$3\overline{)12} = 4$$

Your turn:

$$4\overline{)20} \qquad 5\overline{)25}$$

It can also be written like this $20 \div 4 =$ _____

An art teacher plans to distribute 80 sheets of paper equally to each of the ten students. How many sheets of paper should each student receive?

Multiplication and division are inverse operations. One undoes the other. If we start with 5 and multiply by 6 we get a product of 30. If we then divide 30 by 6 we get 5.

Write two multiplication facts and two division facts for the fact family 2,3,6

Adverbs review

Which of the following is the adverb:

1. Joshua accidentally deleted three hours of homework with one click.
   a) Deleted
   b) Homework
   c) Accidentally
   d) With

2. Mary worked briefly on her report.
   a) Report
   b) Briefly
   c) Worked
   d) her

3. We went to the beach yesterday.
   a) Yesterday
   b) Went
   c) Beach
   d) we

4. The kayak was speeding wildly through the rapids.
   a) Through
   b) Kayak
   c) Was
   d) Wildly

5. My brother always picks on me.
   a) Brother
   b) Picks
   c) Always
   d) On

6. The children worked enthusiastically on their first art project.
   a) Enthusiastically
   b) Children
   c) First
   d) Project

7. The horse was galloping fast, and Jadyn was frightened.
   a) Horse
   b) Frightened
   c) Fast
   d) Galloping

8. Kathy often practices her beam routine at gymnastics.
   a) Often
   b) Routine
   c) Gymnastics
   d) Practices

Your other task for the day is to read. You can look online at www.plainandnotsoplain.com for book recommendations that we enjoyed reading or do an online search to find something that you are interested in. You should read for a minimum of one hour per day.

Write down the title of the book you are reading and how long you read for today.

_____

_____

Quiz

Solve

24÷3=_____   81÷9=_____   40÷5=_____

4÷4=_____   10÷5=_____   16÷8=_____

24÷6=_____   8÷4=_____   8÷8=_____

6÷1=_____   20÷2=_____   30÷5=_____

356+ t+67=500 what is t_____

Find the missing factor is 6x6=4n

Use digits and symbols to write this comparions:

Nine times five is less than seven times seven

Jentzen cut a 15 inch long piece of wood in half. How long was each piece

Mental math:

- 4x5x6
- 5x8x3
- 7x7+1+25+25
- I have 4 quarters, 3 dimes, and 8 pennies. How much do I have?

Word Search Worksheets

noun	common	proper	verb	plural
singular	irregular	pronoun	present	past
future	action	helping	linking	adjectives
adverbs	conjunction	interjection	preposition	articles

•

```
p  r  e  p  o  s  i  t  i  o  n  j  n  z  j  d
a  s  q  g  f  q  x  j  i  h  p  b  k  s  t  v
n  e  n  b  j  z  d  f  x  f  z  r  m  e  p  j
s  l  p  j  v  m  w  u  j  w  w  e  i  v  a  n
b  c  c  n  j  p  a  t  p  z  p  v  r  i  n  h
r  i  h  r  a  x  t  u  l  m  r  d  r  t  u  e
e  t  u  s  c  p  q  r  c  r  e  t  e  c  o  l
v  r  t  u  l  t  z  e  e  r  s  l  g  e  n  p
d  a  a  u  b  o  a  p  a  d  e  v  u  j  o  i
a  h  r  a  u  w  o  l  a  z  n  n  l  d  r  n
v  a  h  c  f  r  u  p  u  c  t  y  a  a  p  g
l  d  y  d  p  g  l  r  a  n  t  z  r  f  b  s
g  n  i  k  n  i  l  o  o  s  d  i  w  y  m  u
p  n  o  i  t  c  n  u  j  n  o  c  o  t  q  y
z  w  s  r  l  b  n  o  m  m  o  c  z  n  m  t
i  n  t  e  r  j  e  c  t  i  o  n  m  s  a  q
```

Your other task for the day is to read. You can look online at www.plainandnotsoplain.com for book recommendations that we enjoyed reading or do an online search to find something that you are interested in. You should read for a minimum of one hour per day.

Write down the title of the book you are reading and how long you read for today.

_____

_____

week 12 spelling list

blocked

bother

column

common

dodge

gossip

honor

model

monster

octopus

oxen

problem

product

promise

robberies

soccer

toboggan

wobble

6 X1	2 X6	5 X2	3 X8	4 X2	3 X6	1 X2	2 X2	1 X1	6 X4
3 X5	8 X2	4 X6	3 X4	1 X0	3 X7	4 X6	4 X8	3 X2	5 X4
8 X2	6 X0	1 X9	3 X4	9 X2	5 X5	1 X5	9 X9	1 X2	6 X2
3 X1	5 X6	3 X3	3 X0	4 X0	3 X6	4 X4	3 X8	5 x10	3 X10
5 X9	5 X4	1 X7	7 X2	6 X6	5 X2	4 X2	7 X6	8 X6	8 X8
9 X6	5 X7	2 X4	5 X6	9 X2	0 X0	1 X4	1 X3	4 X7	9 X4
10 X2	5 X3	10 X6	5 X3	5 X8	5 X1	5 X0	4 X4	3 X2	3 X9
3 x3	9 x9	7 x7	5 x5	3 x7	6 x8	2 x2	10 x6	12 x12	6 x4
6 x6	4 x4	2 x2	10 x10	5 x7	0 x6	7 x4	3 x7	8 x8	6 x7

Simile

A simile is a comparison between two things using the word "like" or the word "as."
Example: It is as hot as the sun in here!
      My brother eats like a pig.
Instead of saying that one things "is" the other, a simile says that one thing is like another.

Each sentence contains a simile. What two things are being compared? Write the two things on the lines.

1. When Lauren dances, she floats across the stage like a feather.

_____   _____

2. Joey runs like the wind.

_____   _____

3. Their baby is as sweet as sugar.

_____   _____

4. The joke was so funny that I laughed like a hyena.

_____   _____

5. Your room is as messy as a pig sty.

_____   _____

Explain what each simile means in the following.

6. After playing all afternoon with Tina, baby Michael slept as soundly as a bear hibernating for the winter.

_____

_____

7. My brother is as cool as a cucumber.

_____

_____

8. It is raining like cats and dogs.

_____

_____

9. Even though she was being laughed at, Kara stood with her head up, as proud and immovable as a mountain.

_____

_____

Your other task for the day is to read. You can look online at www.plainandnotsoplain.com for book recommendations that we enjoyed reading or do an online search to find something that you are interested in. You should read for a minimum of one hour per day.

Write down the title of the book you are reading and how long you read for today.

_____

_____

```
S  F  M  E  F  G  W  K  D  F  P  W  D  P  Z
C  O  M  J  J  V  C  T  M  K  Y  E  U  R  I
D  O  C  O  D  O  K  B  B  O  K  K  K  O  H
R  R  M  C  N  X  X  O  C  D  E  V  B  O
I  X  L  M  E  S  V  E  O  T  P  E  E  L  N
A  L  W  F  O  R  T  L  N  O  H  L  L  E  O
C  I  H  W  A  N  B  E  I  P  F  E  Z  M  R
M  P  C  O  M  P  S  A  R  U  E  K  R  E  R
U  R  O  B  B  E  R  I  E  S  L  T  N  W  I
G  O  L  B  T  O  B  O  G  G  A  N  P  A  T
O  M  U  L  D  K  P  L  E  X  G  N  M  W  K
S  I  M  E  W  D  R  I  H  L  A  A  J  B  H
S  S  N  L  X  F  Z  Y  X  O  P  F  I  I  C
I  E  R  U  O  I  F  F  D  D  O  D  G  E  R
P  L  H  P  R  O  D  U  C  T  V  K  A  Y  S
```

BLOCKED	BOTHER	COLUMN
COMMON	DODGE	GOSSIP
HONOR	MODEL	MONSTER
OCTOPUS	OXEN	PROBLEM
PRODUCT	PROMISE	ROBBERIES
SOCCER	TOBOGGAN	WOBBLE

There are some different ways to show division: Here are three ways. These all mean the same thing…… twelve divided by 3

$$3\overline{)12} \qquad\qquad 12\div3 \qquad\qquad \frac{12}{3}$$

In 12÷3=4, the numbers are called the dividend (12) the divisor (3) and the quotient (4)

Write this division problem in two other forms:

24÷6

Show 10 divided by 2 in three forms

Show 21 divided by 3 equals 7 in three forms

Solve 60÷10=_____   42÷6=_____   12÷4=_____

Draw a horizontal line marked with even integers from -6 to 6

More examples of similes

As big as an elephant.
As black as coal.
As cheap as dirt.

Can you write 1-2 sentences using the word "as" for a simile?

1._____

_____

2_____

_____

Here are some using like:

Like a rose
Like stars
Like a baby

Can you write 1-2 sentences using the word "like' for a simile?

1._____

_____

2._____

_____

Put the following words in ABC order

Nouns   _____
Verbs   _____
Adverbs   _____
Adjectives   _____
Conjunctions _____
Interjections _____
Prepositions _____
Pronouns   _____
Articles   _____

Give me three common nouns:

1. _____
2. _____
3. _____

Give me three proper nouns:

1. _____
2. _____
3. _____

Your other task for the day is to read. You can look online at www.plainandnotsoplain.com for book recommendations that we enjoyed reading or do an online search to find something that you are interested in. You should read for a minimum of one hour per day.

Write down the title of the book you are reading and how long you read for today.

_____

_____

write sentences for your words

6 X1	2 X6	5 X2	3 X8	4 X2	3 X6	1 X2	2 X2	1 X1	6 X4
3 X5	8 X2	4 X6	3 X4	1 X0	3 X7	4 X6	4 X8	3 X2	5 X4
8 X2	6 X0	1 X9	3 X4	9 X2	5 X5	1 X5	9 X9	1 X2	6 X2
3 X1	5 X6	3 X3	3 X0	4 X0	3 X6	4 X4	3 X8	5 x10	3 X10
5 X9	5 X4	1 X7	7 X2	6 X6	5 X2	4 X2	7 X6	8 X6	8 X8
9 X6	5 X7	2 X4	5 X6	9 X2	0 X0	1 X4	1 X3	4 X7	9 X4
10 X2	5 X3	10 X6	5 X3	5 X8	5 X1	5 X0	4 X4	3 X2	3 X9
3 x3	9 x9	7 x7	5 x5	3 x7	6 x8	2 x2	10 x6	12 x12	6 x4
6 x6	4 x4	2 x2	10 x10	5 x7	0 x6	7 x4	3 x7	8 x8	6 x7

Metaphors

Metaphor compares two things that are not alike by saying that one thing is the other.
Example: My brother is a pirate because he is takes my things without asking.
They can be used to paint clearer pictures of what the author is trying to say.
Example: If you say your brother is a pirate, you know he is stealing things.

Practice:

1. Lisa is harmless as a dove when playing tricks on people.

_____

_____

2. My bag was a bag of bricks weighing me down on the way to school.

_____

_____

3. You are my sunshine, you make me happy when skies are gray.

_____

_____

4. The race was a piece of cake because I had trained hard.

_____

_____

Write a metaphor of your own:

_____

_____

Write a simile, remember to use like or as:

_____

_____

Write the linking verbs:

_____,_____,_____,_____,_____,_____,_____,_____,_____

List the prepositions:

about	before	down	like	____	until
____	____	except	____	through	____
after	beneath	____	____	___	____
____	____	____	____	____	____
along	between	in	onto	under	without
			outside	underneath	
____	____	____	____		
at	____	into	____		
	____				
	concerning				

Your other task for the day is to read. You can look online at www.plainandnotsoplain.com for book recommendations that we enjoyed reading or do an online search to find something that you are interested in. You should read for a minimum of one hour per day.

Write down the title of the book you are reading and how long you read for today.

_____

_____

Quiz

Write two multiplication facts and two division facts for the fact family 4,6,24

$24 \div 6 = 4$ $6 \times 4 = 24$
$24 \div 4 = 6$ $4 \times 6 = 24$

Use tally marks to show 17

Autumn reads 40 pages in one day. How many does she read in 4 days

$$\begin{array}{r} 40 \\ \times\ 4 \\ \hline 160 \end{array}$$

She reads __160__ pages in four days.

There are 806 men and women at church. If 432 of them are women, how many are men?

$$\begin{array}{r} 806 \\ -432 \\ \hline 374 \end{array}$$

There is 374 men at church.

What is the sum of five hundred twenty-six and six hundred eight-four

526   684

$$\begin{array}{r} 526 \\ +684 \\ \hline 1,210 \end{array}$$

24÷6=__4__   15÷3=__5__   10÷2=__5__

8m=24 what is m__meater__   90÷10=_____

Review---circle the letter of the best answer

1. Which sentence contains a common noun?
   a) I visited Table Rock State Park.
   b) I liked seeing the geese.
   c) I heard that you went to Caesars Head.

2. Which sentence contains a proper noun?
   a) I like to study history.
   b) Science is one of my favorite subjects.
   c) The U.S. Capitol is in Washington D.C.

3. Which sentence contains a regular plural noun?
   a) I liked seeing the moose on our trip.
   b) The geese were in the pond and then they flew away.
   c) The cats liked playing together.

4. Which sentence contains an irregular plural noun?
   a) The ducks loved playing in the water.
   b) Hamsters make great pets.
   c) The mice scurried under the oven.

5. Which sentence contains a subject pronoun?
   a) Marie went on a school field trip.
   b) She went on a school field trip.
   c) Mike went on a school field trip.

6. Which sentence contains an object pronoun?
   a) The school choir picked me.
   b) The school choir picked Ann to sing.
   c) They picked the best singer to perform.

7. Which sentence has an incorrect use of pronoun agreement?
   a) The sisters left him sweaters in the van.
   b) Cathy picked up her videos at the library.
   c) Mickey forgot his books at the library.

8. Which sentence contains an adjective?
   a) It is time for food.
   b) Hurry, or you will be late!
   c) Look at this colorful cup I bought.

9. Which sentence contains an adverb?
   a) Will you clean the bathroom sometime?
   b) I like your hair.
   c) Yikes! He is fast.

10. Do you remember the 3 articles? They go before a noun when you are talking about specific and non specific? _____, _____, _____

Your other task for the day is to read. You can look online at www.plainandnotsoplain.com for book recommendations that we enjoyed reading or do an online search to find something that you are interested in. You should read for a minimum of one hour per day.

Write down the title of the book you are reading and how long you read for today.

_____

_____

week 13 spelling words

bucket

button

crunchy

dusk

guppies

judges

lucky

public

refund

ruffle

skunk

spun

struck

subject

thunder

trust

ugly

umbrella

$23.18 x 6= $34.09x2=

5x6x7_____7x6x5 <>=

Eighty minutes of music can be placed on a CD. How many HOURS of music can be placed on three compact disc

$40.00-$24.68= $2-14¢= write it out vertically

4318 +m=4328 m=_____   Add the following: $23.07, $4.09, $60.75

In this equation, which is the divisior

27÷3=9

Write with digits and symbols

Ten times two is greater than ten plus two

Write the part of speech above the words in bold. Write ADJ for adjectives, ADV for adverbs, CONJ for conjunctions, INT for interjections, PREP for prepositions, and ART for articles.

Hurray! Happy Birthday!

Birthdays were **first** celebrated **in ancient** Rome. **The** Romans celebrated **the** birthdays **of** their **favorite** gods **and important** people, like **the** emperor. **In** Britain, they celebrate **the Queen's** birthday. **In the** United States, **the** birthdays **of** presents **and important** leaders, like Martin Luther King, are celebrated. **In** Japan, Korea, **and** China, the **sixtieth** birthday marks **a** transition **from an active** life **to** one **of** contemplation. **Many Eastern** cultures don't even recognize **the actual** date **of** birth. When **the first** moon **of the new** year arrives, everyone is **one** year older.

Your other task for the day is to read. You can look online at www.plainandnotsoplain.com for book recommendations that we enjoyed reading or do an online search to find something that you are interested in. You should read for a minimum of one hour per day.

Write down the title of the book you are reading and how long you read for today.

_____

_____

```
M  I  J  U  D  G  E  S  S  Y  T  L  C  I  K
S  Q  W  L  W  X  C  S  T  P  R  X  A  N  F
D  B  S  P  U  N  I  R  R  R  E  F  U  N  D
S  P  U  R  C  N  F  S  U  N  W  K  L  G  B
U  M  B  R  E  L  L  A  C  N  S  L  U  W  B
B  H  G  V  G  K  G  B  K  E  C  X  C  J  U
J  E  X  C  V  O  T  G  E  P  R  H  K  N  T
E  V  F  V  I  W  U  O  U  M  C  D  Y  H  T
C  X  P  K  X  B  Q  G  X  P  L  P  T  J  O
T  B  J  U  R  E  L  K  L  K  P  S  S  D  N
M  U  U  D  B  U  K  H  E  Y  U  I  D  V  G
N  C  Q  Y  D  L  F  L  O  R  K  B  E  T  K
A  K  B  H  X  N  I  F  T  Z  U  M  G  S  S
G  E  X  C  M  D  U  C  L  D  I  L  U  C  H
Q  T  X  S  T  H  U  N  D  E  R  D  L  X  O
```

BUCKET	BUTTON	CRUNCHY
DUSK	GUPPIES	JUDGES
LUCKY	PUBLIC	REFUND
RUFFLE	SKUNK	SPUN
STRUCK	SUBJECT	THUNDER
TRUST	UGLY	UMBRELLA

6 X1	2 X6	5 X2	3 X8	4 X2	3 X6	1 X2	2 X2	1 X1	6 X4
3 X5	8 X2	4 X6	3 X4	1 X0	3 X7	4 X6	4 X8	3 X2	5 X4
8 X2	6 X0	1 X9	3 X4	9 X2	5 X5	1 X5	9 X9	1 X2	6 X2
3 X1	5 X6	3 X3	3 X0	4 X0	3 X6	4 X4	3 X8	5 x10	3 X10
5 X9	5 X4	1 X7	7 X2	6 X6	5 X2	4 X2	7 X6	8 X6	8 X8
9 X6	5 X7	2 X4	5 X6	9 X2	0 X0	1 X4	1 X3	4 X7	9 X4
10 X2	5 X3	10 X6	5 X3	5 X8	5 X1	5 X0	4 X4	3 X2	3 X9
3 x3	9 x9	7 x7	5 x5	3 x7	6 x8	2 x2	10 x6	12 x12	6 x4
6 x6	4 x4	2 x2	10 x10	5 x7	0 x6	7 x4	3 x7	8 x8	6 x7

Write me 5 verbs describing you :

    1. _____

    2. _____

    3. _____

    4. _____

    5. _____

Write me 5 adjectives describing you:

    1. _____

    2. _____

    3. _____

    4. _____

    5. _____

Write me 5 prepositions that you would use describing how you would get out of bed in the morning:

    1. _____

    2. _____

    3. _____

    4. _____

    5. _____

Write me 5 common nouns of things you would like this year for Christmas;

    1. _____

    2. _____

    3. _____

    4. _____

    5. _____

Write me 2 proper nouns of something you want for Christmas;

    1. _____

    2. _____

Write me 5 proper nouns of who you would like to have visit at Christmas:

    1. _____

    2. _____

    3. _____

    4. _____

    5. _____

Your other task for the day is to read. You can look online at www.plainandnotsoplain.com for book recommendations that we enjoyed reading or do an online search to find something that you are interested in. You should read for a minimum of one hour per day.

Write down the title of the book you are reading and how long you read for today.

_____

_____

write sentences for your words

Fractions

A fraction describes part of a whole. The "whole" may be a single thing such as a whole pie or a whole inch or the whole thing might be a group such as a whole class of students or a whole bag of cookies.

We use two numbers to write a fraction. The bottom number is called the denominator, shows the number of equal parts in the whole. The top number is called the numerator, it shows how many of the equal parts are counted.

3 numerator
4 denominator

This is how we read these common fractions:

½ = one half
¼ = one fourth
¾ = three fourths or three quarters
1/10= one tenth

How many cents is one fourth of a dollar?

The word fourth means that the whole dollar (100 cents) is divided into four equal parts.

100÷4=25

In each fourth there are 25 cents

One fourth of a dollar is 25 cents

Three fourths ¾ of a dollar is 75 cents

One tenth of the 30 students ate pizza for lunch. How much students ate pizza?

One tenth means one of ten equal parts. We can find one tenth of 30 by dividing 30 by 10

30÷10=3

One tenth of the 30 is 3, so 3 students ate pizza

Types of sentences

A declarative sentence is a sentence that tells something. Begin a statement with a capital letter and end with a period (.) *think "I do declare.." old fashioned speaking.

An interrogative sentence is a sentence that ask something. Begin an interrogative sentence with a capital letter. End with a question mark (?).

Rewrite the following sentences correctly. Use a period at the end of a statement and a question mark at the end of a question. Remember to capitalize the first word.

1. what is the cat eating
   _____

2. the cat is looking for the mouse
   _____

3. i think the cat is cute
   _____

4. do you like cats
   _____

5. are you looking for the cat
   _____

6. my bike is very fast
   _____

7. where is your bike
   _____

8. can you and I go ride bikes
   _____

9. will you play with me
   _____

10. my bike is cool
    _____

Place a check mark in front of each Declarative statement.

_____1. Do you want to come to the park?
_____2. I can't wait to go play at the park.
_____3. Is the bird making noise?
_____4. The bird is making noise.
_____5. I am going to clean my room.
_____6. My room is clean today.
_____7. You should go tighten the bolts on your bed.
_____8. Lauren you are the best.
_____9. Are you going to clean your room?

Your other task for the day is to read. You can look online at www.plainandnotsoplain.com for book recommendations that we enjoyed reading or do an online search to find something that you are interested in. You should read for a minimum of one hour per day.

Write down the title of the book you are reading and how long you read for today.

_____

_____

Quiz

From yesterday:

Your turn

There were twelve pumpkins in a patch. One fourth of them were too small. How many were too small?

$$\frac{12}{1} \times \frac{1}{4} = \frac{12}{4} = 3 \text{ were to small}$$

Out of those 12 pumpkins, one tenth were too large. How many were too large?

$$\frac{12}{1} \times \frac{1}{10} = \frac{12}{10} = 1\frac{2}{10}$$

Those 12 pumpkins, half of them were just the right size. How many pumpkins is that?

$$\frac{12}{1} \times \frac{1}{2} = \frac{12}{2} = 6$$

Two half circles can be put together to form a whole circle. The equation below states that two halves equal a whole:

½ + ½ =1

Draw me a vertical line

Draw a set of parallel line segments

Draw a ray

206

Complete the following sentences by adding the correct punctuation.
1. Sadie walked briskly five times up the mountain.
2. Did you see the famous monument on your vacation ?
3. The spider spun a beautiful web.
4. I like the rhythm of that song ,
5. January in Vermont is freezing cold,
6. Is it cold in North Carolina in March ?
7. Little children like to mimic animal sounds.
8. Does your sister like to imitate you ?
9. The role of the mother is to nurture the children .
10. If you neglect your room, it will become messy.
11. Did you ignore the rules that I gave to you ?
12. The sun inevitably will rise in the morning.
13. What is the legal voting age in the United States ?
14. Kevin is very mature for his age.
15. Why do you yell ?

Write me 2 declarative sentences:
1. _I shall go away._
2. _I shall go to the movies._

Write me 2 interrogative sentences
1. _Can I hav a slice of cake._
2. _Am I done._

Identify what type of sentence this is:
The Hawaiian islands are really mountaintops. _declarative_
Were those mountains once active volcanoes? _Interrogative_
Are you coming to the parade with us today? _Interrogative_
I wish you would not complain about work. _declarative_
Will you come over to my home? _Interrogative_
Jadyn eats a balanced diet each day. _declarative_
The dry, cold air irritates sensitive skin. _declarative_
I have immense respect for your parents. _declarative_
Would you like to see my pet? _Interrogative._

Your other task for the day is to read. You can look online at www.plainandnotsoplain.com for book recommendations that we enjoyed reading or do an online search to find something that you are interested in. You should read for a minimum of one hour per day.

Write down the title of the book you are reading and how long you read for today.

_____

_____

week 14 spelling list

afford

carton

curtain

departing

directions

emergency

forlorn

further

girth

harbor

observe

origin

perfume

refer

starch

sturdy

temper

thirst

Problem	Answer	Problem	Answer	Problem	Answer	Problem	Answer	Problem	Answer
6 ×1	6	2 ×6	12	5 ×2	10	3 ×8	24	4 ×2	8
3 ×6	18	1 ×2	2	2 ×2	4	1 ×1	1	6 ×4	24
3 ×5	15	8 ×2	16	4 ×6	24	3 ×4	12	1 ×0	0
3 ×7	21	4 ×6	24	4 ×8	32	3 ×2	6	5 ×4	20
8 ×2	16	6 ×0	0	1 ×9	9	3 ×4	12	9 ×2	18
5 ×5	25	1 ×5	5	9 ×9	81	1 ×2	2	6 ×2	12
3 ×1	3	5 ×6	30	3 ×3	9	3 ×0	0	4 ×0	0
3 ×6	18	4 ×4	16	3 ×8	24	5 ×10	50	3 ×10	30
5 ×9	45	5 ×4	20	1 ×7	7	7 ×2	14	6 ×6	36
5 ×2	10	4 ×2	8	7 ×6	42	8 ×6	48	8 ×8	64
9 ×6	54	5 ×7	35	2 ×4	8	5 ×6	30	9 ×2	18
0 ×0	0	1 ×4	4	1 ×3	3	4 ×7	28	9 ×4	36
10 ×2	20	5 ×3	15	10 ×6	60	5 ×3	15	5 ×8	40
5 ×1	5	5 ×0	0	4 ×4	16	3 ×2	6	3 ×9	27
3 ×3	9	9 ×9	81	7 ×7	49	5 ×5	25	3 ×7	21
6 ×8	48	2 ×2	4	10 ×6	60	12 ×12	144	6 ×4	24
6 ×6	36	4 ×4	16	2 ×2	4	10 ×10	100	5 ×7	35
0 ×6	0	7 ×4	28	3 ×7	21	8 ×8	64	6 ×7	42

3-15-20

imperative sentence is a sentence that gives a command or makes a request. They end with a period (.).
**think of something being imperative—important and needs to be done now.

Get the door, please.

An exclamatory sentence shows strong feeling. It ends with an exclamation point (!). **You are exclaiming something with excitement.

What a great God we serve!

Rewrite the following sentences correctly. Remember to begin with a capital letter and end with a proper punctuation.

1. pick up your shoes please.

_____

2. hurry, or you will miss the bus .

_____

3. go feed the cat now .

_____

4. come here Alyssa .

_____

5. watch out for the ball

_____

6. please cut the grass tomorrow .

_____

7. wow, that ice cream was big !

_____

8. this car is fast !

_____

Your other task for the day is to read. You can look online at www.plainandnotsoplain.com for book recommendations that we enjoyed reading or do an online search to find something that you are interested in. You should read for a minimum of one hour per day.

Write down the title of the book you are reading and how long you read for today.

_____

_____

```
S  R  K  A  G  J  D  B  M  G  H  D  F  S  E
T  N  W  A  F  I  I  E  N  G  R  E  M  T  M
U  M  O  B  S  E  R  V  E  M  E  P  Y  A  E
R  M  X  K  N  E  T  T  H  L  A  J  R  R  R
D  O  H  O  S  Y  C  G  H  F  A  R  F  C  G
Y  K  X  Z  E  C  T  G  D  Z  T  T  O  H  E
F  C  U  R  T  A  I  N  H  J  H  I  R  L  N
U  P  C  V  P  Z  O  R  I  G  I  N  L  C  C
R  C  A  H  E  S  N  B  A  S  R  G  O  R  Y
T  V  R  E  A  V  S  H  L  S  S  Y  R  N  M
H  H  T  R  K  R  R  G  Q  I  T  U  N  P  J
E  M  O  E  M  T  B  X  T  F  I  Q  W  F  W
R  F  N  F  J  U  D  O  F  T  E  M  P  E  R
T  B  F  E  R  Y  P  E  R  F  U  M  E  Y  Q
Q  U  J  R  V  S  C  V  K  A  F  F  O  R  D
```

AFFORD	CARTON	CURTAIN
DEPARTING	DIRECTIONS	EMERGENCY
FORLORN	FURTHER	GIRTH
HARBOR	OBSERVE	ORIGIN
PERFUME	REFER	STARCH
STURDY	TEMPER	THIRST

Perimeter

When you measure the length of the sides of an object and then add them all up you get the perimeter.

= 12 inches

	4inches	
2 inches		

We know that a rectangle's sides are congruent or the same so both sides would be 4 and the other side would be 2

4 + 4 +2+2=12 inches

What is the perimeter of your book to the nearest inch?_____

What is the perimeter of this piece of paper in inches?_____

What is the perimeter of the door frame in feet?_____

Greater than or less than

42 x 3_____56   5x5_____25

$\frac{4/2}{\times 3}$
126

5432   3255   5432
+432   +4325   -678
5864   7,580   4,754

327   7654   5432
X 3   x 2   x 5
981   14,708   27,160

214

Add correct punctuation to the following sentences:

1. Watch out for the ice.
2. Where are we going for dinner?
3. You're it!
4. What time is it?
5. Oranges are my favorite citrus fruit.
6. Brrrr!
7. Stop!
8. Will you come over today?
9. Please give me the paper.
10. Stop being such a complainer.
11. What will we do today?
12. Will you come over?
13. Heads up.

Put a check if the sentence is imperative.

_____1. Vote for Sarah for class president.
__✓__2. Please pick up that piece of trash.
_____3. Drink all of your milk up.
__✓__4. Carry your brother for me.
_____5. Let's go to the park.

Write me 2 imperative sentences.

1. _____I need you to go home now._____

2. _____

Write me 2 exclamatory sentences.

1. _____Vote for me because I can help,_____

2. _____

Look up on thesaurus.com other words that are synonyms of the words below: (3each)

Carry=_To take from one plase to another_

Drink=_To swollow a liquid._

Drive=_To controle an atalmoble._

Look=_To aim an eye to see._

Pick=_____

Shoot=_____

3-23-

215

Your other task for the day is to read. You can look online at www.plainandnotsoplain.com for book recommendations that we enjoyed reading or do an online search to find something that you are interested in. You should read for a minimum of one hour per day.

Write down the title of the book you are reading and how long you read for today.

_____

_____

write sentences for your words

Shapes

A rectangle has how many sides?_____
Draw me one

A square has how many sides?_____
Draw me one

A circle has how many sides?_____
Draw me one

When two triangles are the same size and shape, we say they are congruent. Which two
are congruent

Here are some more geometrical shapes

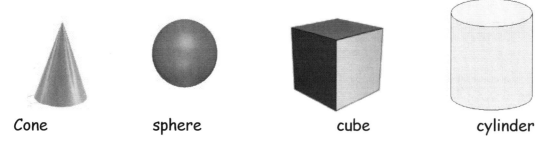

Cone   sphere   cube   cylinder

List some things that are this shape
Cone_____
Sphere_____
Cube_____
Cylinder_____

REVIEW

Add the correct ending punctuation.

Write E for exclamatory sentence or C for an imperative sentence.

1. _____Remember the safety rules
2. _____Always wear a helmet when riding your bike
3. _____Watch out, for the car
4. _____Stay on the right side of the road
5. _____Use your hand signals when making a turn
6. _____Beware of strangers
7. _____How fit you will be
8. _____Please be careful when riding your bike
9. _____Ride with your sister always
10._____Wow, my bike is fast

Add the correct ending punctuation. Interrogative end with a (?) and declarative end with a (.).

11._____Do you know how to swim
12._____We like to go to the beach
13._____The water is cool
14._____Did you bring sunscreen
15._____This is going to be fun
16._____Does your brother like to swim
17._____Do you want to eat here
18._____Did you want to stay all day
19._____Let's get in over there
20. _____The lake here is beautiful.

What are the 4 types of sentence:

_____   _____

_____   _____

Your other task for the day is to read. You can look online at www.plainandnotsoplain.com for book recommendations that we enjoyed reading or do an online search to find something that you are interested in. You should read for a minimum of one hour per day.

Write down the title of the book you are reading and how long you read for today.

_____

_____

Quiz

Calendar

How many months are there in one year?_____

What number month is your birthday?_____

How many days of the week are there?_____

Write the days of the
week?_____,_____,

_____,_____

_____,_____

_____,_____

Name me a month that spring occurs?_____

Name me a month that winter occurs?_____

Name me a month when summer occurs?_____

Name me a month when falls occurs?_____

What day was it yesterday?_____

What day is it tomorrow?_____

What day do we goto church on?_____

What day does the weekend begin on?_____

When is your birthday?_____

What is todays date—the month, day, and year?_____

What year is it?_____

What year were you born in?_____

Copy the 4 types of sentences and spell them 6 times each.

1. _____
2. _____
3. _____
4. _____
5. _____
6. _____

1. _____
2. _____
3. _____
4. _____
5. _____
6. _____

1. _____
2. _____
3. _____
4. _____
5. _____
6. _____

1. _____
2. _____
3. _____
4. _____
5. _____
6. _____

What punctuation ends an interrogative sentence:_____

What punctuation ends an exclamatory sentence:_____

What punctuation ends a declarative sentence:_____

What punctuation ends a imperative sentence: _____

Your other task for the day is to read. You can look online at www.plainandnotsoplain.com for book recommendations that we enjoyed reading or do an online search to find something that you are interested in. You should read for a minimum of one hour per day.

Write down the title of the book you are reading and how long you read for today.

_____

_____

week 15 spelling words

although

another

athlete

birth

channel

chauffeur

chiffon

chocolate

choir

chrome

exchange

radish

sheriff

shovel

Thursday

whether

whiskers

whisper

Write the following times on the clock:

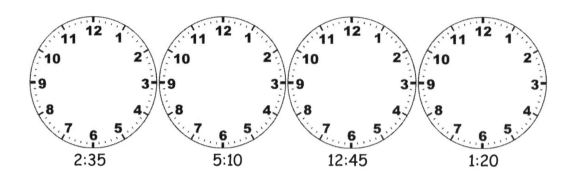

2:35   5:10   12:45   1:20

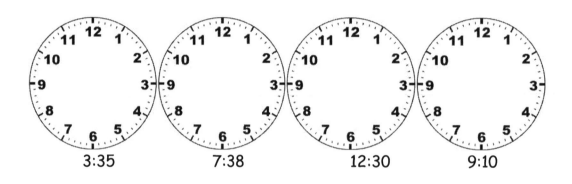

3:35   7:38   12:30   9:10

Write the following times

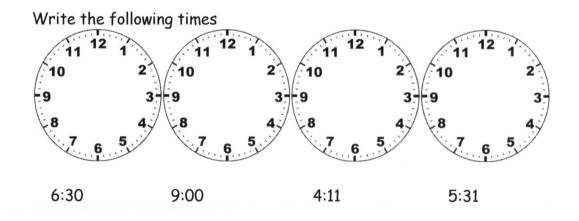

6:30   9:00   4:11   5:31

Simple sentences

Simple sentences are sentences with one independent clause. Independent clauses present a complete thought and can stand alone as a sentence. Simple sentences do not have any dependent clauses. Dependent clauses do not present a complete thought and cannot stand alone as sentences.

A sentence fragment is a group of words that is missing either a subject or predicate. It does not express a complete thought.

Mark which of the following express a complete thought and can stand alone as a simple sentence.

1. _____Cats can.
2. _____Let's go to the park to play.
3. _____We like.
4. _____Do you like to play?
5. _____Pigs pink.

The subject of a sentence tells who or what does something.
Mark dropped the box. Mark is the subject of this sentence.
The ball rolled away. The ball is the subject of this sentence.

Circle the subject.

1. Sarah ate the green apples.
2. Evan loves chocolate ice cream.
3. Mom made me my new dress.
4. They are going to the park.
5. We ate the bag of chips.
6. Elsa liked eating cookies and drinking milk.
7. Jadyn liked eating peanut butter and jelly sandwiches.
8. Autumn and Brooklyn like eating peanut butter and honey sandwiches.
9. He is going to the park.
10. We are going to play.

Choose a subject for the following sentences.

11._____loves to work on cars.
12._____climbs up the tree.
13._____rolls into the street.
14._____runs across the field.
15._____always feeds the cat.

Your other task for the day is to read. You can look online at www.plainandnotsoplain.com for book recommendations that we enjoyed reading or do an online search to find something that you are interested in. You should read for a minimum of one hour per day.

Write down the title of the book you are reading and how long you read for today.

_____

_____

```
Q  W  P  Q  T  K  T  A  H  B  H  P  M  G  L
K  C  C  H  U  J  I  H  T  G  I  C  A  A  H
C  C  Z  H  Q  W  R  J  U  H  T  R  E  X  P
C  Y  O  D  I  E  H  O  H  R  L  C  T  C  G
I  H  K  E  H  F  H  I  U  O  S  E  L  H  Y
W  O  O  T  X  T  F  E  S  L  L  D  T  F  C
B  H  O  I  L  C  F  O  E  K  N  H  A  E  H
K  N  I  A  R  F  H  N  N  J  E  I  M  Y  O
A  M  K  S  U  M  N  A  A  R  T  R  F  P  C
G  O  J  A  P  A  K  I  N  B  U  I  S  D  O
G  N  H  M  H  E  V  F  Y  G  Y  M  O  F  L
M  C  I  C  Z  L  R  W  I  G  E  Y  X  A  A
V  S  H  E  R  I  F  F  I  C  F  U  P  O  T
R  E  N  W  N  Z  G  L  Y  C  H  R  O  M  E
S  H  O  V  E  L  W  H  E  T  H  E  R  A  A
```

ALTHOUGH	ANOTHER	ATHLETE
BIRTH	CHANNEL	CHAUFFEUR
CHIFFON	CHOCOLATE	CHOIR
CHROME	EXCHANGE	SHERIFF
SHOVEL	THURSDAY	WHETHER
WHISKERS	WHISPER	

You have been practicing writing numbers. When you write the numbers such as "21" it is written with a hyphen twenty-one. 45 is written forty-five

Write the following numbers in words:

14_____27_____

59_____ 76_____

100_____45_____

Write the words for the following

1st_____

2nd_____

3rd_____

4th_____

5th_____

6th_____

7th_____

8th_____

9th_____

10th_____

The predicate tells what the subject of a sentence does or is.
Sarah <u>joined the class choir.</u>
The ball <u>is red and green.</u>

Underline the predicate.

1. Stephen gets the big shovel.
2. She digs in the sand.
3. Jentzen throws dirt at me.
4. Jentzen and Stephen enjoy playing in the sand box.
5. They wait to eat lunch.
6. Stephen liked baking cookies and eating chocolate.
7. Brooklyn and Sarah like eating jam and bread.
8. We love steak and fries.
9. Tammy and Elizabeth ate tortillas and salsa.
10. Tammy likes to drink coffee.

Add a predicate to the following phrases.

11. The rain_____.
12. The sun_____.
13. We_____.
14. Lauren and Jadyn_____.
15. They_____.
16. Mom and Dad_____.
17. The bike_____.
18. My pen_____.
19. The paper_____.
20. Butterflies and bumblebees_____.

Make your own sentences by adding the word into it. Make sure the verb form is correct.

1. play (yesterday)

_____

_____

2. swim (tomorrow)

_____

_____

Your other task for the day is to read. You can look online at www.plainandnotsoplain.com for book recommendations that we enjoyed reading or do an online search to find something that you are interested in. You should read for a minimum of one hour per day.

Write down the title of the book you are reading and how long you read for today.

_____

_____

write sentences for your words

Practicing division facts. Remember division is opposite of multiplication

24÷3=_____   81÷9=_____   40÷5=_____

4÷4=_____   90÷9=_____   56÷8=_____

24÷6=_____   27÷3=_____   8÷8=_____

6÷1=_____   20÷2=_____   63÷9=_____

56÷7=_____   6÷3=_____   45÷5=_____

6÷3=_____   6÷6=_____   10÷5=_____

18÷3=_____   4÷1=_____   15÷5=_____

30÷3=_____   24÷4=_____   42÷6=_____

28÷7=_____   50÷5=_____   8÷2=_____

35÷7=_____   72÷8=_____   16÷2=_____

28÷7=_____   36÷6=_____   64÷8=_____

21÷3=_____   27÷9=_____   40÷5=_____

81÷9=_____   42÷7=_____   9÷3=_____

4÷2=_____   10÷1=_____   44÷11=_____

16÷4=_____   5÷5=_____   36÷9=_____

18÷3=_____   18÷9=_____   30÷5=_____

Compound sentences

Compound sentences are sentences with two or more simple sentences joined by a coordinating conjunction, punctuation, or both. As in simple sentences, there are no dependent clauses in compound sentences.

Combine each pair of simple sentences into a compound sentence.

1. Stephen likes broccoli. Jentzen likes carrots.

_____

_____

2. Jadyn likes crocheting. Brooklyn likes sewing.

_____

_____

3. Lauren hates cats. Brooklyn loves cats.

_____

_____

4. I will go to the park. I might go to the zoo.

_____

_____

5. I will wear the blue skirt. I might wear my brown skirt.

_____

_____

6. I like coffee. I do not like tea.

_____

_____

Your other task for the day is to read. You can look online at www.plainandnotsoplain.com for book recommendations that we enjoyed reading or do an online search to find something that you are interested in. You should read for a minimum of one hour per day.

Write down the title of the book you are reading and how long you read for today.

_____

_____

Quiz

```
$ 32.76          $  271.12          $ 32.89          $ 21.00
+$  8.00         +$ 110.43          -$ 11.75         -$ 15.00
```

Solve:

$4.03 + $2.99+ 54¢=_____

$87.86-$12.96=_____

Write the following:

Two thousand, four hundred fifty-two:_____

One thousand, five hundred sixty-one:_____

Nine thousand, two hundred forty-three:_____

5000+500+50+5=_____

3000+200+9=_____

500,000+40,000+3,000+200+90+8=_____

400,000+20,000+1,000+900+20+6=_____

Complex sentences

Complex sentences have one independent clause and two or more dependent clauses. The independent and dependent clauses are connected with a subordinate conjunction or a relative pronoun. Remember dependent clauses do not present a complete thought and cannot stand alone as sentences. The dependent clause can by anywhere in the sentence.

Common subordinate conjunctions include: after, although, as, because, before, if, since, when, where, while, until, and unless.

Ex: Since he got a math tutor, his math grades have improved.

The independent and dependent clauses can also be connected with relative pronouns like who, whose, which, and that.

Ex: Mr. Smith, who is a math teacher, tutors Stephen.

By combining simple sentences into complex sentences adds variety and clarity to writing.

Circle the letter that best answers each question:

1. Which of the following sentences contain two simple, individual sentences?
   a) He is wearing his baseball uniform. He is holding his baseball bat.
   b) He is wearing his baseball uniform and holding his baseball bat.
   c) He is wearing his baseball uniform, although the game was cancelled.

2. Which of the following sentences contain a compound sentence?
   a) She is eating a salad. She is drinking lemonade.
   b) She is eating a salad, and she is drinking lemonade.
   c) She is drinking lemonade, since she is thirsty.

3. Which of the following sentences contain a complex sentence?
   a) Mary went jogging. Rose went jogging.
   b) Mary and Rose went jogging.
   c) Before breakfast, Mary and Rose went jogging.

4. Which of the following sentences contain a complex sentence?
   a) Mike was learning about moose at school. Mike was learning about elk at school.
   b) Mike and Sam were learning about woodland animals at school.
   c) Mike, who loved animals, was learning about moose and elk at school.

Write 2 sentences about your birthday . Make them complete and not fragments. They must express a complete thought.

1_____

_____

2_____

_____

Your other task for the day is to read. You can look online at www.plainandnotsoplain.com for book recommendations that we enjoyed reading or do an online search to find something that you are interested in. You should read for a minimum of one hour per day.

Write down the title of the book you are reading and how long you read for today.

_____

_____

week 16 spelling list

blind

blue

climb

close

frog

fruit

plate

plump

sleep

slow

small

smell

speak

spin

swarm

sweep

track

trap

Write < > =

762_____543   22,987_____23,789   756____765

987,789____987,879   23,876____22,000   890____980

766____766   4329_____3297   555_____5555

432,287+432=_____

5432x8=_____

Write ten sentences about your family. Follow which kind to write based on the clues below:

1.declarative_____

_____

2..interogative _____

_____

3. imperative _____

_____

4.exclamatory _____

_____

5. compound subjects _____

_____

6. compound predicate _____

_____

7. compound adjectives _____

_____

8.compound verbs _____

_____

9. 2 adjectives_____

_____

10. 2 verbs_____

_____

Your other task for the day is to read. You can look online at www.plainandnotsoplain.com for book recommendations that we enjoyed reading or do an online search to find something that you are interested in. You should read for a minimum of one hour per day.

Write down the title of the book you are reading and how long you read for today.

_____

_____

```
C   Y   D   F   M   O   S   L   A   R   S   C   Q   C   Z
J   E   S   S   D   J   W   C   L   I   M   B   T   H   V
Y   A   T   N   K   P   A   B   C   L   F   K   R   K   K
Q   A   I   C   P   R   R   O   O   L   K   V   A   Y   T
G   L   A   Y   C   Q   M   L   B   L   U   E   P   N   H
B   R   H   R   K   K   P   L   U   M   P   Y   S   X   O
T   Q   N   K   O   R   C   L   O   S   E   B   T   P   N
C   E   N   V   Z   P   P   L   A   T   E   O   E   L
I   O   E   Z   Z   E   I   U   Z   M   G   D   S   L   Y
Z   C   D   S   E   W   S   W   R   O   S   Z   E   Z   B
P   Z   M   L   C   F   W   C   R   I   S   M   A   L   L
G   O   S   O   F   R   E   F   E   L   S   X   N   X   B
Z   Z   N   W   B   U   E   Y   D   R   W   I   M   V   Y
D   T   G   R   X   I   P   F   V   Q   P   O   X   E   Z
Y   H   Y   Y   S   T   P   O   L   S   O   C   B   N   B
```

BLIND	BLUE	CLIMB
CLOSE	FROG	FRUIT
PLATE	PLUMP	SLEEP
SLOW	SMALL	SMELL
SPEAK	SPIN	SWARM
SWEEP	TRACK	TRAP

Write the correct letter in the box next to the figure.

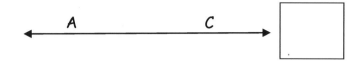

A. Line AC

B. Line LM

C. Line segment LM

D. Line segment WZ

E. Parallel lines

F. Perpendicular lines

G. Point D

H. Point Z

I. Ray DE

J. Ray Wt

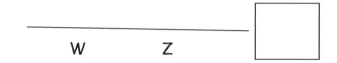

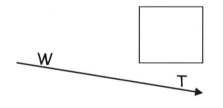

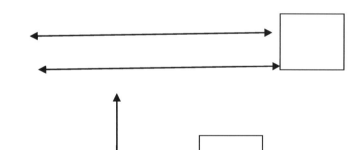

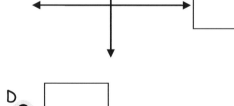

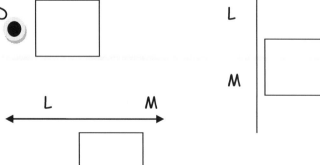

Fact and Opinion

A fact is something that is proven to be true. An opinion is what someone believes. People hold differing opinion, some of which are unfair or untrue.

Label each as a Fact (F) or opinion (O)

1. _____Girls are odd because they like to play with dolls.

2. _____Sarah has blonde hair and a flat nose.

3._____Timothy was saving all the water for himself.

4._____Chris is strange because he doesn't know what rock music is.

5. ____Fish swim in the water.

6._____Cats have long tails.

7._____North Carolina is a mountainous state.

8. ____North Carolina is the prettiest state ever.

9.____We should always wash our hands.

10.____We should always walk if we can.

11. ____Walking is good for our hearts.

12._____Walking up a mountain is harder than walking in the woods.

13. ____Running is better than walking.

14. ____Tablets are cooler than laptops.

15. ____Everyone should have a cell phone.

Write a fact:

_____

Write an opinion:

_____

Your other task for the day is to read. You can look online at www.plainandnotsoplain.com for book recommendations that we enjoyed reading or do an online search to find something that you are interested in. You should read for a minimum of one hour per day.

Write down the title of the book you are reading and how long you read for today.

_____

_____

write sentences for your words

Draw a pentagon   Draw a hexagon

If there are 12 eggs in a dozen, how many eggs are in ½ dozen?_____

If there are 100 centimeters (cm) in one meter, how many cm are in ½ meter?_____

If there are 16 ounces in a pound, how many ounces are in ½ pound?_____

If there are 4 quarts in a gallon, how many quarts are in ½ gallon?_____

If there are 60 seconds in a minute, how many seconds are in ½ minute?_____

If there are 1,000 meters in a kilometer, how many meters are in ½ kilometer?_____

If there are 30 days in most months, how many days are in ½ month?_____

If there are 24 hours in a day, how many hours are in ½ day?_____

If there are 36 inches in one yard, how many inches are in ½ yard?_____

If there are 2,000 pounds in a ton, how many pounds are in ½ ton?_____

Draw an octagon

Writing a paragraph

A paragraph is made up of a group of sentences. A paragraph should have, and stick to, a single topic. Each sentence should focus on the topic with plenty of information and supporting details related to the topic.

Elements of a paragraph: There are 3 parts to a paragraph

1. Beginning: The topic sentence is the beginning of the paragraph. It tells what the paragraph is going to be about. It also expresses the feeling of the paragraph.

2. Middle: The middle is the main part of the paragraph. The sentences here give more information and supporting details about the topic sentence.

3. End: After all of the information and details are writing, the ending sentence concludes, or sums up, the paragraph's main idea.

Choose one of the following topic sentences and write a paragraph. Follow the rules above. 1-topic sentence, 2-3 middle, supporting sentences, and 1 ending sentence to sum it all up.

1. There are several reasons why I like Saturdays.
2. It is fun to take a walk in the snow.
3. Some movies are really funny.
4. Swimming in the lake is fun.

Your other task for the day is to read. You can look online at www.plainandnotsoplain.com for book recommendations that we enjoyed reading or do an online search to find something that you are interested in. You should read for a minimum of one hour per day.

Write down the title of the book you are reading and how long you read for today.

_____

_____

Quiz

Put commas in the correct places. Remember to start on the right.

4256727899   432215876   567854321

7654   4321   6543   8907   5655
-4321   -4211   -3897   -5678   -3478
‾‾‾‾‾   ‾‾‾‾‾   ‾‾‾‾‾   ‾‾‾‾‾   ‾‾‾‾‾

What is the VALUE of the underlined digit or how much is it worth?

432,8_7_6,543 _____   _3_21,765_____

Write the standard form of the expanded version:

400,000+20,000+4,000+900+80+8=_____

30,000,000+2,000,000+400,000+30,000+7,000+600+80+2

_____

70,000+400+6=_____

A narrative gives the details of an event or events in the form of a story.

The first sentence organizes the whole story (main idea—topic sentence.)
Time-order words like first, next, last, finally, then-- show the sequence of events.
An exclamatory sentence adds interest
Vivid details help readers picture the scene.
Have a strong ending to show some writing personality.

Remember the rules for writing a paragraph and write your own paragraph about the following: Choose one:

The time I found the cat in my bed.

Walking in the woods, I found a golden spoon.

When I woke up I found a large box wrapped in paper.

I found all my clothes missing from my drawers.

_____
_____
_____
_____
_____
_____
_____
_____
_____
_____
_____
_____
_____
_____
_____
_____
_____
_____
_____
_____
_____
_____
_____

Your other task for the day is to read. You can look online at www.plainandnotsoplain.com for book recommendations that we enjoyed reading or do an online search to find something that you are interested in. You should read for a minimum of one hour per day.

Write down the title of the book you are reading and how long you read for today.

_____

_____

week 17 spelling list

cactus

celebrate

cement

certain

citizen

citrus

convoy

cumbersome

cyclone

dangerous

gallery

gesture

gopher

gurgle

gypsum

gypsy

region

Multiplication with zeros

Any time you have a number times a multiple of ten you just add extra zeros.

If you have 342 x 100= there are 2 zeros so your answer is 34,200

If you have 567 x 1000= there are 3 zeros so your answer is 567,000

Solve:

354x10=_____   4325x1000=_____

5423x100=_____   543x100=_____

53 x 10000=_____   3,231x 10000=_____

1. I bought a ball for $2.42, a bat for $1.75, and a mitt for $1.25 How much did I spend in all?

2. My plants grew 2 " last month, 3" this month, and I expect they will grow 1 $\frac{1}{2}$ more inches in the coming months. How tall will my plants be?

3. My girls weight 23 lbs, 46 lbs, 57 lbs, and 76 lbs. How many lbs all together do they weigh?

4. My boys have driven 3,243 miles this year. My girls have driven 1, 768 miles. How many more miles did the boys drive?

Proofreading a Paragraph
Go through the following paragraph and fix the errors. There will be the following:

Punctuation
Spelling
Capitalization
Verb usage
Sentence fragments

this past weekend, I hav the most relaxing time ever! hour family go to the osean. and rented a beach house All twelve of us stayed the entire weekend. We had fun swimming in the ocean relaxing in the sun and having campfires at night time since my family is very busy this past year, spending time together this weekend was a nice change. me looks forward to doing this again very soon

Rewrite in cursive:

_____

_____

_____

_____

_____

_____

_____

_____

_____

_____

_____

_____

_____

_____

_____

Your other task for the day is to read. You can look online at www.plainandnotsoplain.com for book recommendations that we enjoyed reading or do an online search to find something that you are interested in. You should read for a minimum of one hour per day.

Write down the title of the book you are reading and how long you read for today.

_____

_____

```
W  Y  G  Y  P  S  Y  O  Z  B  Q  C  D  E  M

D  A  N  G  E  R  O  U  S  B  J  V  T  N  C

G  G  F  U  E  U  C  D  C  I  H  A  X  M  E

X  U  U  L  R  B  J  Y  A  E  R  I  J  U  M

U  M  L  R  E  J  N  G  C  B  R  B  M  S  E

L  A  F  Z  G  F  W  Y  E  L  P  T  U  J  N

G  L  C  X  I  L  G  L  Y  S  O  R  A  D  T

G  D  O  U  O  F  E  L  I  N  T  N  J  I  E

O  G  N  K  N  C  I  D  C  I  M  U  E  M  N

P  Y  V  A  K  R  C  A  C  T  U  S  R  J  P

H  P  O  U  Z  B  C  W  C  I  T  I  Z  E  N

E  S  Y  K  X  P  K  K  P  N  J  D  B  B  Q

R  U  K  N  Q  L  O  I  Z  N  I  U  V  A  H

H  M  K  B  P  T  L  I  J  Z  W  L  W  N  B

J  I  A  C  Z  C  U  M  B  E  R  S  O  M  E
```

CACTUS	CELEBRATE	CEMENT
CERTAIN	CITIZEN	CITRUS
CONVOY	CUMBERSOME	CYCLONE
DANGEROUS	GALLERY	GESTURE
GOPHER	GURGLE	GYPSUM
GYPSY	REGION	

261

count aloud: count up and down by 25s between 0 and 200
mental math:
- 3 x40 plus 3x15
- 4 x50 plus 4x4
- The parking lot has 560 spots. Two hundred spots are empty. How many spots are filled?
- One minute is 60 seconds. How many seconds are in 3 minutes.

At Mountain View Academy, there are 4 classes of 5th graders with 30 students in each class. Altogether, how many students are in the 4 classes?

The coach separated 48 players into 6 teams with the same number of players on each team. How many players were on each team?

Jared raked leaves and filled 28 bags!! On each trip he could carry away 4 bags with leaves. How many trips did it take Jared to carry away all the bags?

On the shelf were 4 cartons of eggs. There were 12 eggs in each carton. How many eggs were in all four cartons?

Jadyn opened a bottle containing 32 ounces of milk and poured 8 ounces of milk into a bowl of cereal. How many ounces of milk remained in the bottle?

Same word different meanings

Each of the following words has more than one meaning. Give both meanings.

1. spring _____   _____

2. run   _____   _____

3. ruler _____   _____

4. deck _____   _____

5. suit _____   _____

6. cold _____   _____

7. tire _____   _____

8. rose _____   _____

9. play _____   _____

10. fly _____   _____

11. bowl _____   _____

12. seal _____   _____

13. fall _____   _____

14. face _____   _____

15. foot _____   _____

16. box _____   _____

Circle the resource book you would use to find:

 A recipe for baking cheesecake.

Encyclopedia   cookbook   The Life of a Beaver

Your other task for the day is to read. You can look online at
www.plainandnotsoplain.com for book recommendations that we
enjoyed reading or do an online search to find something that you
are interested in. You should read for a minimum of one hour per
day.

Write down the title of the book you are reading and how long you
read for today.

_____

_____

write sentences for your words

The set of drums costs eight hundred dollars. The band has earned four hundred eighty-seven dollars. How much more must the band earn in order to buy the drums?

Write two multiplication and two division facts for the fact family 3,4,12

$72 \div 8 =$ $6n = 42$ $36 \div 9 =$

$6n = 48$ $70/10$ $7\overline{)56}$

$367 \times 8 =$ rewrite vertical $\$5.04 \times 7 =$

$268 + m = 687$ $r - 4568 = 6318$

$5003 - w = 876$

If a dozen items are divided into two equal groups, how many will be in each group?

What are the net three terms in this counting sequence
….50,60,70,80,90,_____,_____,_____

Persuasion

A persuasion paragraph is one that persuades the reader to try something you are writing about. You want to convince them that what you are telling them about is a good thing. It may not be a good thing, but you are going to try and convince them that it is. Here is an example.

I went to the restaurant and tried frog legs. They were delicious. They are deep fried like a chicken nugget and taste like a chicken leg. I dipped mine in barbeque sauce and it was very good. I think everyone should try them.

Choose one of the following and persuade the reader to do it: Use rules for writing paragraphs.

Why girls should wear skirts.
Why cities should offer parks in the community.
Why everyone should have internet access.
Why everyone should participate in outdoor activities.

_____

_____

_____

_____

_____

_____

_____

_____

_____

_____

_____

_____

_____

_____

_____

_____

_____

_____

_____

_____

Your other task for the day is to read. You can look online at www.plainandnotsoplain.com for book recommendations that we enjoyed reading or do an online search to find something that you are interested in. You should read for a minimum of one hour per day.

Write down the title of the book you are reading and how long you read for today.

_____

_____

Quiz

Use words to show how this problem is read 10/2

The fraction ½ is equivalent to what decimal and what percent?
If you have ½ of the total whole thing, you have ½ of the 100% so you have 50%.
The decimal is if you have ½ of 1 whole. Half of one whole is 0.50 like half of 1.00 is .50 cents.

Multiply 3 numbers: do two numbers at a time, then the next one.

4 x 5 x 3= _____   10x2x5=_____

40x2x3=_____   3x3x3=_____

Remember tally marks? Make me tally marks for the following numbers:

6   8

12   21

Fill in the blanks:

1 gallon is_____quarts   1 yard is _____feet

1 foot is_____inches   1 mile is_____feet

1 quart is_____pints   1 pint is _____cups

Where would you look for the following:

1. A description of how mice make their homes.
Almanac   The Life of a Mouse   The Guinness Book of World Records

2. Another word for "rule":
Thesaurus   math textbook   world atlas

3. A map of Africa:
Thesaurus   world atlas   The Guniness Book of World Records

4. The difference between a muffler and a mantle:
Dictionary   science textbook   cookbook

5. Information about the author, CS Lewis:
Almanac   encyclopedia   Guidebook for Art Instruction

6. Which is the world's largest building:
The Guinness Book of World Records   dictionary   thesaurus

7. Why a beaver slaps its tail:
Dictionary   The Life of a Beaver   atlas

8. The pronunciation of "colonel"
Dictionary   almanac   The Hobbit

9. What camphor is used for
Dictionary   The Life of a Beaver   thesaurus

10. The average snowfall on December 25
Almanac   cookbook   spelling workbook

11. I am writing a paper and have too many usages of the word "place" what else could I use:

Dictionary   almanac   thesaurus

Your other task for the day is to read. You can look online at www.plainandnotsoplain.com for book recommendations that we enjoyed reading or do an online search to find something that you are interested in. You should read for a minimum of one hour per day.

Write down the title of the book you are reading and how long you read for today.

_____

_____

week 18 spelling list

affection

autograph

cough

enough

familiar

foreign

frequent

furniture

geography

laughter

muffler

paragraph

philosophy

physical

raffle

slough

tough

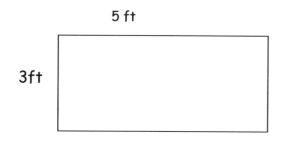

5 ft

3ft

What is the area:
What is the perimeter:

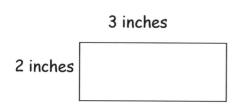

10 ft

2ft

What is the area:
What is the perimeter:

3 inches

2 inches

what is the area:
What is the perimeter:

We know that multiplication and division are the inverse of each other, right? We have done simple division for example 10÷2=5 and we know that 5x2=10 the opposite. Not all division problems will come out evenly. Let's say we divide 16÷5=?

5 | 16

To answer this question, we think, "what number of fives is close to but not more than 16?" We answer this with 3. We write 3 above the box and then multiply to show that 3 times 5 is 15.

$$\begin{array}{r} 3 \\ 5\overline{\smash{\big)}16} \\ \underline{-15} \\ 1 \end{array}$$

The amount leftover is called the remainder. Here the remainder is 1, which means one leftover. 16÷5=3 r1

YOUR TURN:

If you had 16 people waiting in line for a water ride and each boat holds 6 people. How many boats do you need to fit everyone? Set it up with division

Don't confuse verbs that have similar meanings

Lay means put or place
Lie means rest or recline

Set means put something somewhere
Sit means sit down

Let means allow
Leave means allow to remain

Teach means show how
Learn means find out

Lend means give to someone
Borrow means get from someone
Fill in with the correct verb:

1. Tell your cat to _____(lay, lie) down in front of the barn.
2. Please, _____(lay, lie) that saddle down in front of the stall.
3. _____(set, sit) on that bale of hay and rest your feet.
4. Will you _____(let, leave) me wear your boots tomorrow?
5. Don't _____(let, leave) these oats there.
6. I want to _____(teach, learn) how to trim my horse's tail.
7. We will certainly be happy to _____(teach, learn) you.
8. Please _____(set, sit) this cup of coffee on the table.

Circle the word that best describes the mood or tone of the person speaking.
1. When Tommy told her not to drink from the spring, Jesse questioned, "Why not? It's mine."

     Reluctant   worried   stubborn

2. When Sarah was calmed, everyone relaxed. Susan began to explain the family's story. "We are friends, we really are. But you got to help us."

  Persuasive   happy   helpless

3. Sam recalled a story of when his boys were little with a twinkle in his eye. "When they turned 18, they just up and left!"

  Stern   sad   stubborn

Your other task for the day is to read. You can look online at www.plainandnotsoplain.com for book recommendations that we enjoyed reading or do an online search to find something that you are interested in. You should read for a minimum of one hour per day.

Write down the title of the book you are reading and how long you read for today.

_____

_____

```
C  F  E  J  P  O  L  F  R  E  Q  U  E  N  T
G  O  N  N  H  D  A  C  O  U  G  H  W  D  J
E  R  O  S  Y  V  U  A  M  P  N  F  E  S  F
O  E  U  D  S  O  G  F  D  A  X  U  E  T  Y
G  I  G  E  I  X  H  F  C  R  O  R  D  U  P
R  G  H  D  C  Q  T  E  U  A  K  N  R  F  H
A  N  V  B  A  N  E  C  B  G  L  I  B  F  I
P  P  B  M  L  F  R  T  T  R  P  T  A  G  L
H  T  R  S  A  W  G  I  L  A  U  U  L  C  O
O  L  W  A  U  R  F  O  O  P  R  R  J  Z  S
L  S  W  P  U  X  S  N  I  H  E  E  B  E  O
A  U  T  O  G  R  A  P  H  K  E  D  O  N  P
F  A  M  I  L  I  A  R  V  S  L  O  U  G  H
X  M  U  F  F  L  E  R  A  F  F  L  E  S  Y
A  K  N  K  W  B  F  T  O  U  G  H  K  E  U
```

AFFECTION	AUTOGRAPH	COUGH
ENOUGH	FAMILIAR	FOREIGN
FREQUENT	FURNITURE	GEOGRAPH
LAUGHTER	MUFFLER	PARAGRAPH
PHILOSOPHY	PHYSICAL	RAFFLE
SLOUGH	STUFF	TOUGH

Divide. Write each answer with a remainder. rewrite them with the division bar signs

23÷5=   50÷6=

23÷4=   34÷9=

Which of these will have a remainder?

60÷10   44÷5   18÷2

Draw two horizontal lines, one above the other

At a dinner party, each guest is to receive a small bag of gifts. How many gifts should be placed in each bag if there are 8 guests and 32 gifts altogether?

Descriptive writing

You may be asked one day to describe something. When you are describing something use images and sense words to make your descriptive writing come alive.

Write a good main idea sentence or topic sentence. This tells what your paragraph will be about.

Develop and elaborate ideas. Use different sentences that tell about your main sentence. Try and "paint a picture' in the mind of your reader.

Choose one of the following and write a paragraph about it

Describe a favorite person
Describe your favorite place to visit
Describe your favorite outfit
Describe what it feels like to eat ice cream
Describe what it is like to cook a marshmallow.

_____

_____

_____

_____

_____

_____

_____

_____

_____

_____

_____

_____

_____

_____

_____

_____

_____

_____

Your other task for the day is to read. You can look online at www.plainandnotsoplain.com for book recommendations that we enjoyed reading or do an online search to find something that you are interested in. You should read for a minimum of one hour per day.

Write down the title of the book you are reading and how long you read for today.

_____

_____

write sentences for your words

Compare 46,208_____46,028

How many $\frac{1}{4}$ circles equal a half circle?

The fraction $\frac{1}{2}$ is equivalent to what decimal? _____what percent?____

Seventy-five chairs are to be placed in a large room and arranged in rows of ten. How many chairs will be in the last row?

Mr Bill has 10 quarters, if he gives each of his 3 grandchildren 3 quarters, how much money will he have left?

What comes next 50,40,40,20,10,_____,_____,____

Use words to show how this problem is read $4\overline{\smash{\big)}12}$

$36.15-$29.81=   3904x4=

Which reference book would you use for the following:

1. Which source would you use to learn how to make pancakes?

  Dictionary   atlas   cookbook

2. Which source might show where Triple Falls is?

 Dictionary   atlas   thesaurus

3. Which source would describe the peacock?

Book on insects   encyclopedia   newspaper

4. Which source would describe the sounds a cricket make?

Book on insects   thesaurus   atlas

5. Which source would give the meaning of "constable"

Newspaper   atlas   dictionary

6. Which source would describe the most recent world events?

Newspaper   encyclopedia   thesaurus

7. Which source would tell you how to divide "accommodations" into syllables?

Dictionary   book on insects   thesaurus

8. Which source could give a synonym for "pull"?

Thesaurus   cookbook   encyclopedia

9. Which source might best forecast tomorrow's weather?

Newspaper   atlas   encyclopedia

10. Which source would show you kitchen measurement equivalents?

Cookbook   dictionary   atlas

Your other task for the day is to read. You can look online at www.plainandnotsoplain.com for book recommendations that we enjoyed reading or do an online search to find something that you are interested in. You should read for a minimum of one hour per day.

Write down the title of the book you are reading and how long you read for today.

_____

_____

Quiz

The fraction ¼ is equivalent to 0.25 decimal and 25%. Think in terms of money quarters to remember this.

If you had ¾ how much percent would you have?_____ how much decimal?

Two digit multiplication---ask if you need to know how to do them. Think of the turtle heads...to help you stay in line.

(do 4x2, then 4x2. Then drop an egg (0) and do the 1x4 and 1x4

```
  44              72              22              11
 X12             x14             x14             x63
```

Fill in the chart:
There are _____hours in 1 day

There are _____minutes in 1 hour

There are _____seconds in 1 minutes

How many hours are in 6 days?_____

1 ft=_____in   1 lb=_____oz   1 pt=_____cups

1 yd=_____ft   1 mile=_____ft   1 gal=_____qt

The guide words in my dictionary are scream and scrubber. In the list below tell which words are found on the page (O), before the page (B), or after the page (A)

1. scribe _____

2. screw _____

3. scorn _____

4. screen _____

5. scurry _____

6. scout _____

7. seal _____

8. second _____

9. script _____

10. school _____

11. Scuff _____

12. Screech_____

13. Sea _____

14. Scrawl_____

15. Same _____

16. Scroll _____

17. Scrub _____

18. Sand _____

19. Serf _____

20. Selfish _____

Put the following in ABC order—label with #

_____Skirt
_____Pants
_____Socks
_____Slippers
_____Shoes
_____Nylons
_____Shirt
_____Tank top
_____boots
_____coat
_____vest

Your other task for the day is to read. You can look online at www.plainandnotsoplain.com for book recommendations that we enjoyed reading or do an online search to find something that you are interested in. You should read for a minimum of one hour per day.

Write down the title of the book you are reading and how long you read for today.

_____

_____

week 19 spelling words

ballet

castle

crumb

doubt

height

knack

knight

known

knuckle

listen

plumber

soften

thumb

weight

wreck

wren

wrench

wrestle

More practice—remember to do your turtle heads and if you have to carry some over, do so but don't forget to add. Ask your teacher if you need help.

32	32	65	88
X11	x21	x27	x22

Rewrite the following and solve:

55 x 22=_____   43 x 81=_____

87+ 26,654 + 3=_____

22 + _____=39

**remember 12 inches equals 1 foot and if you need to borrow in the subtraction do so. You borrow 7 days for a whole week

7ft. 3 in.	3 wks 2 days	89-27=x
+2 ft. 9in.	- 3 days.	X=_____

Analogies
Choose the words that best completes each analogy.

Ounce=weight   as degree=?
- a) Temperature
- b) Measure
- c) Pound
- d) Heavy

Robin=bird as collie=?
- a) dog
- b) Hunter
- c) Catch
- d) Bark

Turtle=reptile as cat=?
- a) Mammal
- b) Lizard
- c) Cat
- d) Poodle

Snake=slither as frog=?
- a) Croak
- b) Hop
- c) Pond
- d) Bite

Fish=aquarium, as bird=?
- a) Tree
- b) Cage
- c) Air
- d) Water

Radio=listen as television=?
- a) Watch
- b) Show
- c) Screen
- d) Broadcast

Your other task for the day is to read. You can look online at www.plainandnotsoplain.com for book recommendations that we enjoyed reading or do an online search to find something that you are interested in. You should read for a minimum of one hour per day.

Write down the title of the book you are reading and how long you read for today.

_____

_____

```
J  K  N  O  W  N  W  R  E  N  W  O  K  O  C
Y  E  P  K  S  O  F  T  E  N  R  C  J  S  H
O  C  L  N  L  D  Y  B  V  K  E  D  N  U  X
D  V  U  A  V  C  J  E  P  R  S  E  F  S  P
U  H  M  C  D  X  Z  Q  W  G  T  T  R  D  J
H  G  B  K  N  I  G  H  T  S  L  W  L  A  S
N  X  E  Z  N  G  B  V  I  E  E  P  C  V  O
A  H  R  V  S  M  G  L  R  D  O  U  B  T  Q
P  Y  K  N  U  C  K  L  E  V  Q  W  H  E  X
L  C  M  H  B  J  F  M  S  V  P  G  D  U  H
C  B  T  E  W  C  A  G  H  E  I  G  H  T  Q
R  X  W  R  E  N  C  H  F  E  R  U  T  H  W
B  H  K  D  S  U  O  S  W  C  A  S  T  L  E
F  C  B  A  L  L  E  T  F  F  T  L  Q  P  Q
L  L  Z  D  M  F  Z  Q  C  R  U  M  B  U  Z
```

BALLET	CASTLE	CRUMB
DOUBT	HEIGHT	KNACK
KNIGHT	KNOWN	KNUCKLE
LISTEN	PLUMBER	SOFTEN
THUMB	WEIGHT	WRECK
WREN	WRENCH	WRESTLE

Multiplying money
When you multiply dollars and cents, you do so the same way when you multiply other numbers. When you are finished, you count over how many decimal places over are in your problem and then move it over in your answer. This will be helpful for decimal multiplication later on this year☺

$5.75 $4.32 $2.67
X   43   x   9   x31
_____   _____   _____

Roman numerals from 10 to 100, counting by tens
X   XX   XXX   XL   L   LX   LXX   LXXX   XC   C

I is 1   V is 5   X is 10   C is 100   L is 50

Can you write the following numbers based on the chart:

17 _____35_____40_____70_____

Write words for the following:

1st_____6th_____

2nd_____ 7th _____

3rd_____ 8th_____

4th_____ 9th_____

5th_____ 10th_____

Word Search Worksheets

sentence	paragraph	simple	compound	dependent
independent	clause	complex	fragment	declarative
interrogative	exclamatory	imperative		

g)

```
m  e  u  i  z  s  p  o  e  g  n  r  e  c  e  q
s  v  t  x  c  h  l  m  f  j  o  s  q  o  v  d
u  i  p  n  p  r  e  n  n  e  u  i  b  s  i  e
u  t  u  l  e  l  f  v  y  a  t  m  x  s  t  x
w  a  j  x  y  d  c  u  l  u  k  p  e  c  a  c
t  g  j  p  d  p  n  c  z  e  q  e  l  t  r  l
n  o  l  y  y  n  e  e  r  l  y  r  p  n  a  a
e  r  z  d  a  f  c  p  p  g  t  a  m  e  l  m
m  r  i  n  m  w  n  a  g  e  k  t  o  d  c  a
g  e  u  u  u  w  e  r  b  d  d  i  c  n  e  t
a  t  x  o  t  w  t  a  z  b  x  v  t  e  d  o
r  n  x  p  r  i  n  g  e  h  x  e  l  p  u  r
f  i  i  m  s  x  e  r  d  y  d  p  n  e  w  y
w  l  b  o  z  l  s  a  k  b  m  l  w  d  c  c
l  e  a  c  s  k  r  p  x  i  b  d  y  n  o  q
p  z  n  i  p  x  v  h  s  l  o  j  a  i  z  e
```

What are the 4 types of sentences?

_____

_____

_____

_____

Your other task for the day is to read. You can look online at www.plainandnotsoplain.com for book recommendations that we enjoyed reading or do an online search to find something that you are interested in. You should read for a minimum of one hour per day.

Write down the title of the book you are reading and how long you read for today.

_____

_____

write sentences for your words

FRACTIONS

Fractions show a part of a whole. They are written like this

$\underline{3}$ numerator

5   denominator

You can make an equivalent fraction by dividing or multiplying both the numerator and denominator by the same number. Here is an example:

$\dfrac{1 \times 2}{4 \times 2} = \dfrac{2}{8}$ multiply both the numerator and denominator by 2

$\dfrac{9 \div 3}{12 \div 3} = \dfrac{3}{4}$ divide both the numerator and denominator by 3

This shows you that both of those numbers above are equal.

This is also helpful in learning how to simplify your fractions and reduce it down to lowest terms. It is much easier to say I have ¾ of a candy bar instead of 9/12.

A fraction is in the lowest terms when its numerator and denominator have no common factors greater than 1. Remember the trees? So to put a fraction to it's lowest terms, divide its numerator and denominator by common factors, until they have no common factor greater than 1.

Here is an example.

$\dfrac{5 \div 5}{10 \div 5} = \dfrac{1}{2}$ ***remember whatever you do to the numerator has to be done to the denominator

½ is the reduced to lowest terms. Reduce the following fractions to lowest terms:

$\dfrac{4}{16} =$ _____ $\dfrac{6}{24} =$ _____ $\dfrac{5}{30} =$ _____ $\dfrac{2}{10} =$ _____

Which of the following is the best answer:

1. Which of the following sentences makes the best topic sentence?
    a) Lauren was on a journey.
    b) Lauren started on her journey with only her pack on her back.
    c) Lauren had a backpack.
2. Which of the following topic sentences is the beginning of a descriptive paragraph?
    a) The day started out bright and sunny.
    b) School cafeterias should be open before and after school hours.
    c) Building a bookcase can be fast and easy.
3. Which of the following sentences is a sentence from the middle of a paragraph?
    a) A recycling program should be started in our school for three reasons.
    b) Recycling helps the environment.
    c) Recycling will benefit us all.
4. Which of the following sentences is from a narrative paragraph?
    a) The bears can weigh up to 800 pounds.
    b) Littering is unsanitary and inconsiderate.
    c) Pat journeyed many days and many nights.

Write a short descriptive paragraph describing something you ate recently.

_____

_____

_____

_____

_____

_____

_____

_____

_____

_____

_____

_____

_____

_____

_____

_____

_____

_____

Your other task for the day is to read. You can look online at www.plainandnotsoplain.com for book recommendations that we enjoyed reading or do an online search to find something that you are interested in. You should read for a minimum of one hour per day.

Write down the title of the book you are reading and how long you read for today.

_____

_____

Quiz

Which fraction is not equal to ½

9/18   10/25   25/50   50/100

It cost $3.48 to rent the movie. Sam gave the clerk $5.00. How much money should he get back?

A week is 7 days. How many days is 52 weeks?

½ of the contents of a 20-ounce bag of snack mix is granola. ¼ of the contents is coconut.
How many ounces of granola is in the bag?_____
How many ounces of coconut is in the bag?_____

40÷6=   20÷3=   60=nx10

$3.08   2514
x   7   x 3

Use words to show how this problem is read 7$\overline{)35}$

4x3x10   12x2x10

Write two multiplication facts and two division facts for the fact family 7,8,56

English sayings and phrases. Every culture has it's own phrases that can be difficult to understand if you are not from here. Do you know what these sayings really mean?

1. "I am going to catch forty winks."

_____

_____

2. " Wow! Do you have a chip on your shoulder?"

_____

_____

3. "We should count our blessings."

_____

_____

4. She worked up to the eleventh hour.

_____

_____

5. My husband lost his job, but every cloud has a silver lining.

_____

_____

6. Why are you wearing your birthday suit?

_____

_____

7. Good friends are few and far between.

_____

_____

8 The grass looks greener on the other side of the road.

_____

_____

9. I'm gonna kill two birds with one stone.

_____

_____

10. She likes to make a mountain out of a mole hill.

_____

_____

11. Don't sit on the fence, choose a side.

_____

_____

Your other task for the day is to read. You can look online at www.plainandnotsoplain.com for book recommendations that we enjoyed reading or do an online search to find something that you are interested in. You should read for a minimum of one hour per day.

Write down the title of the book you are reading and how long you read for today.

_____

_____

week 20 spelling list

accounts

adventures

arches

blouses

classes

compasses

couches

decisions

dresses

erasers

eyelashes

inches

indexes

larynxes

syllables

telescopes

toothbrushes

walruses

Improper fractions and mixed numbers

When the numerator of a fraction is equal to or greater than the denominator, the fraction is called an improper fraction. Here are some examples of improper fractions. $\underline{5}, \underline{7}, \underline{13}$. When

$$5 \quad 4 \quad 3$$

you have an improper fraction they should be written as whole numbers and one part that is a fraction. Instead of saying $\underline{7}$ you should say $1\frac{3}{4}$.

$$4$$

The bar in a fraction means the same thing as a division sign. When you see 7/4 it says 7 divided by 4. If you were to write that out as a division problem like this:

$$4\overline{)\,7}$$ Then solve.

When you have a remainder, instead of writing it as a remainder (3), you write it as the numerator and the divisor (4) becomes the denominator. Answer is $1\frac{3}{4}$

Let's practice changing these improper fractions to proper fractions with whole numbers. Do them as a division problem so you can get an answer. You will eventually do them in your head.

$\dfrac{14}{3}$ = _____ $\dfrac{4}{3}$ = _____ $\dfrac{11}{5}$ = _____

$\dfrac{7}{2}$ = _____ $\dfrac{3}{2}$ = _____ $\dfrac{16}{5}$ = _____

$\dfrac{4}{3}$ = _____ $\dfrac{8}{8}$ = _____ $\dfrac{32}{32}$ = _____

Identify the following sentences: There are 4 types remember them?
1. Walk up the steps and then turn right._____
2. Greg took a risk and accepted the new job. _____
3. How much money did you get?_____
4. Wow, we got home really fast!_____

Identify whether the following is a simple sentence, compound sentence, complex sentence, or a sentence fragment.
5. Greg and Amy wrapped and delivered all the presents.
_____

6. Between the lake,
_____

7. The mom challenged her children. The mom encouraged them.
_____

8. Grill the corn until it is slightly brown.
_____

9. The lake was blue. The lake was warm.
_____

10. During the night,
_____

Write me a sentence telling when you are going to the park.
_____
_____

Write me a sentence describing the drink.
_____
_____

Write me a sentence telling me about your family.
_____

Tell me how you will brush the cat.
_____
_____

Tell me where the frog was hidden.
_____
_____

Your other task for the day is to read. You can look online at www.plainandnotsoplain.com for book recommendations that we enjoyed reading or do an online search to find something that you are interested in. You should read for a minimum of one hour per day.

Write down the title of the book you are reading and how long you read for today.

_____

_____

```
N  I  H  K  C  F  X  O  S  H  G  M  X  O  O
R  N  T  X  O  A  M  P  I  M  B  A  T  C  R
O  C  E  G  M  D  K  M  W  E  W  D  O  L  F
L  H  L  F  P  E  M  O  A  R  E  V  O  A  M
A  E  E  B  A  C  X  I  L  A  Y  E  T  S  N
R  S  S  L  S  I  A  P  R  S  E  N  H  S  C
Y  X  C  O  S  S  C  S  U  E  L  T  B  E  O
N  I  O  U  E  I  C  Y  S  R  A  U  R  S  U
X  N  P  S  S  O  O  L  E  S  S  R  U  A  C
E  D  E  E  Q  N  U  L  S  O  H  E  S  R  H
S  E  S  S  W  S  N  A  H  F  E  S  H  C  E
V  X  H  Q  G  K  T  B  S  Y  S  V  E  H  S
U  E  O  M  M  M  S  L  H  X  J  Q  S  E  P
D  S  T  U  M  E  E  E  Q  Y  G  O  Z  S  P
Q  T  E  Z  D  R  E  S  S  E  S  L  P  P  L
```

ACCOUNTS	ADVENTURES	ARCHES
BLOUSES	CLASSES	COMPASSES
COUCHES	DECISIONS	DRESSES
ERASERS	EYELASHES	INCHES
INDEXES	LARYNXES	SYLLABLES
TELESCOPES	TOOTHBRUSHES	WALRUSES

309

Identify which of the following is an example of: mixed number, fraction, improper fraction, whole number

33_____   2 ½ _____

¾ _____ $\frac{49}{17}$ _____

4521-213=   732+389=

632x22=   128x89=

What is the tenth term in this counting sequence...
8,16,24,32

Capitalization

The names of cities, states, and countries are considered proper nouns and are all capitalized.
Write the following correctly:

sacramento   _____

tuxedo   _____

north carolina   _____

hendersonville   _____

africa   _____

north america   _____

alaska   _____

ohio   _____

japan   _____

detroit   _____

city   _____

israel   _____

Look up the following online with parents permission:

What is the most populated country in the world?

_____

The city in the United States that has the largest population is?

_____

What is the most populated state?

_____

What is the least populated state?

_____

What is the largest continent?

_____

What continent is its own country?

_____

Your other task for the day is to read. You can look online at
www.plainandnotsoplain.com for book recommendations that we
enjoyed reading or do an online search to find something that you
are interested in. You should read for a minimum of one hour per
day.

Write down the title of the book you are reading and how long you
read for today.

_____

_____

write sentences for your words

The operations of arithmetic are addition, subtraction, multiplication, and division. When there is more than one operation in a problem, parentheses can show you the order for which ones to do first. Parentheses separate a problem into parts. We do the parts in the parentheses first:

6 x (5+4)=   you first add the 5 +4 and get 9. Then multiply the 6x9

Remember do the parentheses first then go outside.

Your turn:
(4x2) -6   (6-4) x 2

(8x4)-2   (12-4) -1

How much is one half of a dollar plus one fourth of a dollar

How many horseshoes are needed to shoe 25 horses

Lauren removed some eggs from a carton of one dozen eggs. If nine eggs remained in the carton, how many eggs did she remove

Write two multiplication and two division facts for the fact family 3,5,15

rewrite these with the bar division to solve easier:

60÷7   50÷6   44÷11

Which digit is 256 shows the number of hundreds

Capitalize the months of the year and the days of the week.

Unscramble the following to get the days of the week

afdiyr   _____

s anudy   _____

yomadn   _____

ursya a td   _____

y d ustae   _____

y ruahtsd   _____

yeewdndas   _____

Unscramble the months of the year

raanuyj   _____

ch r m a   _____

eeebcdmr   _____

erootbc   _____

uabeyfrr   _____

y am   _____

rail p   _____

bovmneer   _____

eeesmtpbr   _____

t gauus   _____

unje   _____

uj y l   _____

How many days in the following:

January _____   February _____

March   _____   April   _____

May   _____   June   _____

July   _____   August   _____

September _____   October   _____

November _____   December _____

Your other task for the day is to read. You can look online at www.plainandnotsoplain.com for book recommendations that we enjoyed reading or do an online search to find something that you are interested in. You should read for a minimum of one hour per day.

Write down the title of the book you are reading and how long you read for today.

_____

_____

Quiz

count aloud: count up by 5s from 3 to 42 (3,8,etc)
mental math:
- 10 x 10 cm
- 10 x100 cm
- ½ of 12 inches
- ¼ of 12 inches
- What day of the week is 8 days after Sunday

The factors of a number are all the whole numbers that can divide it without leaving a remainder. For example, the factors of 6 are 1,2,3, and 6 because each of these numbers divides into 6 without leaving a remainder.

List the factors of 20

List the factors of 23

Which of these numbers is NOT a factor of 30?
2   3   4   5

At the tree farm, 9 rows of trees with 24 trees in each row were planted. How many trees were planted?

My haircut costs $6.75. I paid for it with a ten dollar bill.   What is my change?

Lauren bought four cartons of milk for $1.12 each. Altogether, how much did she spend?

Fill in the blanks.

1. The United States celebrates Independence Day on _____4th.
2. We celebrate _____in the month of December.
3. Fools come out to play on this _____day.
4. _____is the shortest month of the year.
5. Summer begins in the month of _____.
6. Farmers bring in their crops, including pumpkins in the month of _____.
7. Winter begins in _____.
8. Your birthday is in _____.
9. We celebrate what in November?_____
10. Which day of the week is the Lord's day?_____
11. Which day of the week do they consider hump day?_____
12. Which two days are the weekend?_____ _____
13. Which day do we begin school each week?_____
14. Which month is Valentines Day?_____
15. What do we celebrate at the beginning of the year?_____

Write the days of the week:
_____
_____
_____
_____
_____
_____
_____

Write the months of the year:
_____
_____
_____
_____
_____
_____
_____
_____
_____
_____
_____
_____

Your other task for the day is to read. You can look online at www.plainandnotsoplain.com for book recommendations that we enjoyed reading or do an online search to find something that you are interested in. You should read for a minimum of one hour per day.

Write down the title of the book you are reading and how long you read for today.

_____

_____

week 21 spelling words

anniversary

beauty

birthday

chimney

decoy

dictionary

highway

holiday

industry

monkey

mortuary

party

quantity

salary

strawberry

survey

turkey

valley

Factors

What are the factors of the following numbers:

4_____

8_____

9_____

15_____

12_____

6 x (7+8)   (6x7) +8

9n-54   55÷8

1234 x5= $5.67x3=   987x6=

Use words to name the number 894,201

What is the tenth term in the counting sequence
5,10,15,20…..

Think of a whole number, multiply it by 2. Is the answer odd or even?

The names of specific streets, places, and people are proper nouns and are capitalized.

Capitalize the names of specific streets. Ohio Avenue
Do not capitalize if you have just the word road or street in a sentence. Go across the street.
Capitalize the name of specific place. Caesars Head
Capitalize first and last name of people. Amy Maryon along with any titles. Dr. Aaron Clark
Do not capitalize nonspecific titles, streets, or places in a sentence. My best friend is running for president.

1. river   mississippi river
2. georgia   state
3. month   june
4. lauren   girl
5. town   zirconia
6. christmas   holiday
7. teacher   mr. maryon
8. country   ireland
9. mt. mitchell   hills
10.   jesus   person

Copy the following in columns and capitalize if needed:

_____

_____

_____

_____

_____

_____

_____

_____

_____

Write the name of a specific river_____
Write the name of specific person _____
Write the name of specific town _____
Write the name of specific month _____
Write the name of specific state _____
Write the name of specific day _____

Your other task for the day is to read. You can look online at www.plainandnotsoplain.com for book recommendations that we enjoyed reading or do an online search to find something that you are interested in. You should read for a minimum of one hour per day.

Write down the title of the book you are reading and how long you read for today.

_____

_____

```
M  A  D  Y  S  I  H  B  C  D  A  B  L  J  J
U  X  I  Z  A  N  U  I  L  G  S  F  V  R  E
S  X  C  M  N  D  F  R  G  B  T  K  A  R  M
A  T  T  Y  N  U  O  T  H  H  E  J  L  V  Z
L  Z  I  B  I  S  L  H  Q  S  W  A  L  O  G
A  Z  O  E  V  T  J  D  Q  T  J  A  E  I  G
R  T  N  A  E  R  O  A  U  J  H  W  Y  Y  H
Y  E  A  U  R  Y  L  Y  A  S  F  S  E  M  O
D  S  R  T  S  O  T  C  N  S  U  K  E  O  L
E  B  Y  Y  A  W  I  T  N  R  R  I  N  I  I
C  G  N  K  R  H  Z  Z  I  U  R  T  V  K  D
O  E  O  P  Y  P  A  R  T  Y  Q  N  J  E  A
Y  M  O  R  T  U  A  R  Y  G  E  G  Q  Y  Y
N  I  M  N  G  W  I  F  C  H  I  M  N  E  Y
L  E  X  G  S  T  R  A  W  B  E  R  R  Y  W
```

ANNIVERSARY	BEAUTY	BIRTHDAY
CHIMNEY	DECOY	DICTIONARY
HIGHWAY	HOLIDAY	INDUSTRY
MONKEY	MORTUARY	PARTY
QUANTITY	SALARY	STRAWBERRY
SURVEY	TURKEY	VALLEY

Count up from 5s from 4-54.

mental math:

- 10x34
- 32x100
- ½ of $8
- ¼ of $8
- ¾ of $8
- if the distance around a square is 8 cm what is the length of each side?

Long division---everyone's favorite. Let your teacher walk you through this one. Lets say that you have 234 students. The students will travel on 5 buses. Is it possible for each bus to carry the same number of students?

Write it out here and divide it through. We use the same method for the shorter division as the long, we just continue until we can't bring down any more.

Solve 5n=365. When two numbers are multiplied, 5 and n. The products is 365. We can find an unknown factor by dividing the product by the known factor.

$5\overline{)365}$

Your turn:

$2\overline{)432}$ $\qquad$ $5\overline{)325}$ $\qquad$ $7\overline{)497}$

Cause and effect

The cause is the reason for the action or why something happened. The effect is the result of the action what actually happened.

Underline the causes.

1. Because she knew her face so well, Sue didn't need a mirror.
2. Because the Stuarts had drunk water from the spring, they did not age.
3. Sarah went into town, because her two boys were returning home.
4. The Stuarts had taken the cat, because he trespassed on their property.
5. Because Sam and Lila brought no fish home, we had pancakes for dinner instead.

Circle the effects

6. The Mathers boys never lived in the same place for long because their employment always changed.
7. Because we did not have any flour, we had to have eggs for breakfast.
8. I put up the umbrella, so the children did not get sunburned.
9. I am tired, because I stayed up late last night.
10. I have a flat tire, because I ran over a nail.

Complete the following similes:

Sam was as artistic as:_____

Sadie's teeth were like_____

Mom's mind worked fast like _____

Madelyn was as sad as_____

Mrs. Paul was like _____

Analogies

Snow is to shovel as _____are to rake.

Boys are to men as girls are to _____

_____are to neck as belts are to waist.

Lives are to life as calves are to _____.

Mouse is to mice as goose is to _____.

Write the months of the year:

_____,_____

_____,_____

_____,_____

_____,_____

_____,_____

_____,_____

Your other task for the day is to read. You can look online at www.plainandnotsoplain.com for book recommendations that we enjoyed reading or do an online search to find something that you are interested in. You should read for a minimum of one hour per day.

Write down the title of the book you are reading and how long you read for today.

_____

_____

write sentences for your words

Practice more from yesterday, just keep going until you get it.

$3 \overline{)324}$ $3 \overline{)9,636}$ $8 \overline{)872}$

$2 \overline{)474}$ $5 \overline{)365}$ $7 \overline{)463}$

Words like mother, father, aunt, and uncle can be used as proper nouns or common nouns. When they are used as proper nouns, capitalize them.

Mother, where are my shoes?
My mother does not know where my shoes are.

Official names such as those of businesses and their products, are capitalized. Nonspecific names of products are not capitalized, even if they follow the business product name.

Papa's Pizza (name of business)
I like Papa's Pizza pizza (business name followed by a product name)

Circle the letter that matches the description.

1. The word mother not used to replace a name.
   a. Mother, please pass the bacon.
   b. My mother was the leader of the choir.
2. The word grandfather used as a name.
   a. Grandfather William was a police officer
   b. My grandfather is a good griller.
3. The word aunt not used to replace a name
   a. My aunt has the cutest cat.
   b. Aunt Sarah is a doctor.
4. Official business name followed by product name
   a. Oat Chewy granola bars
   b. Oat Chewy
5. Official business name without product name
   a. Yummy Pet pet food
   b. Yummy Pet

Titles of books, movies, plays, works of art are capitalized.

The first and last words of titles are always capitalized as well as every word in between except for the "smaller words" examples: a, an, the, in, of, at, and, but . These words should be capitalized if they are the first word in the title. Most titles are also underlined. Song titles and essay are in quotes.

book: <u>Catcher in the Rye</u>   play: <u>The Music Man</u>
movie: <u>Diary of a Wimpy Kid</u>   work of art: <u>Mona Lisa</u>

School subjects are capitalized if they name a specific course.
My favorite course is Literature and Poetry.
Do not capitalize the names of general subjects.
My math teacher is also my baseball coach.
Exception: Language subjects are all proper nouns, so they should all be capitalized.
I am studying my French homework.

Write what your favorite movie is:_____

Write what your favorite song is: _____

Write the name of a book: _____

What is the name of a poem you learned last year: _____

Your other task for the day is to read. You can look online at www.plainandnotsoplain.com for book recommendations that we enjoyed reading or do an online search to find something that you are interested in. You should read for a minimum of one hour per day.

Write down the title of the book you are reading and how long you read for today.

_____

_____

Quiz

lets do it again☺

2 | 630   6 | 642   5 | 625

7 | 4977   5 | 25575

Jen bought a bike tire for $2.98. She paid for it with a $5 bill. How much should she get back?

Mom sent me with 3 dozen muffins. How many did she send?

Sayings---what does this really mean

1. Time heals all wounds.

_____

_____

2. She invited Tom, Dick , and Harry to the party.

_____

_____

3. We will be eating this pot of soup till the cows come home.

_____

_____

4. Out of the frying pan and into the fire.

_____

_____

5. A penny saved is a penny earned.

_____

_____

List your favorite Netflix movie:

_____

List your favorite book:

_____

List your favorite two songs:

_____

_____

What is your favorite subject in school:

_____

What are the names of the seven continents:

_____

_____

_____

_____

_____

_____

_____

Name two cities close to us:_____ _____

_____

Your other task for the day is to read. You can look online at www.plainandnotsoplain.com for book recommendations that we enjoyed reading or do an online search to find something that you are interested in. You should read for a minimum of one hour per day.

Write down the title of the book you are reading and how long you read for today.

_____

_____

week 22 spelling words

calves

echoes

elves

geese

halves

handkerchiefs

heroes

leaves

moose

potatoes

scarves

shelves

thieves

tomatoes

wives

wolves

women

yourselves

mental math:
- how many months are in 2 years
- how many months are in 3 years
- how many days are in 2 weeks
- ½ of 100 cents
- ¾ of 100 cents

Draw a horizontal number line from 0 to 500 with only zero and hundreds marked and labeled

Is the point 276 closer to 200 or 300?

On the Clarks road trip, they drove 408 miles on day one, 324 on day two, and 211 on day thre. Altogether, how many did they drive total?

Evan is 5 feet tall. One foot is equal to 12 inches. How many inches is Evan?

Brooklyn sold 9 cups of lemonade for $0.15 each. How much much did she make?

864÷5= $2.72÷4= remember to put the decimal point up in the answer

The number 78 is between which of these number pairs
60 and 70   70 and 80   80 and 90   0 and 10

Write the factors of 30

Which digit in 537 shows the number of hundreds?

Quotation Marks

Quotation marks show the beginning and ending of the words someone says. The speaker's name and words such as said or asked are not inside the quotation marks. ***only the actual words they say.

*capitalize the beginning words of the quote as you do a sentence. It will be the first letter after your first quotation. The punctuation is to be put inside the quotation marks as well.

"Can we come over today?" asked Shelly.
Lauren said, "Let's go play at the Maryon's."

Add quotation marks to each sentence. Make sure to put the comma before the ending quotations.

1. I like to go to church, said Amy.

2. My favorite song is Give us Clean Hands, said Jadyn.

3. Collin asked, When is it time for lunch?

4. Evan replied, After the service is over.

5. What are we going to eat? asked Brooklyn.

6. We are going to have spaghetti, said Dad.

7. Will you come over? said Jentzen.

8. The mountains are awesome! said Molly.

9. Austin replies, I am coming next month.

10. Lauren responds, I won't be there.

Your other task for the day is to read. You can look online at www.plainandnotsoplain.com for book recommendations that we enjoyed reading or do an online search to find something that you are interested in. You should read for a minimum of one hour per day.

Write down the title of the book you are reading and how long you read for today.

_____

_____

```
Y  D  M  G  A  Y  I  O  R  Q  S  C  L  N  S
J  W  O  V  E  B  T  H  I  E  V  E  S  E  D
X  I  O  A  J  E  D  U  V  D  C  O  V  N  L
I  V  S  F  Q  N  S  L  W  O  Y  L  G  D  X
E  E  E  U  P  O  A  E  K  H  O  Z  L  L  G
X  S  S  B  T  C  P  M  B  W  U  I  Y  W  J
N  C  Z  C  T  O  K  A  B  X  R  C  K  O  R
A  U  S  E  A  L  M  S  F  E  S  H  S  M  B
C  U  H  O  L  R  E  A  M  T  E  E  H  E  X
Y  Q  E  R  Z  V  V  A  T  B  L  R  A  N  D
V  N  L  K  P  N  E  E  V  O  V  O  L  E  X
C  C  V  X  J  G  C  S  S  E  E  E  V  L  J
I  J  E  P  O  T  A  T  O  E  S  S  E  H  R
B  O  S  S  E  C  H  O  E  S  J  C  S  C  N
J  S  H  A  N  D  K  E  R  C  H  I  E  F  S
```

CALVES	ECHOES	ELVES
GEESE	HALVES	
HEROES	LEAVES	MOOSE
POTATOES	SCARVES	SHELVES
THIEVES	TOMATOES	WIVES
WOLVES	WOMEN	YOURSELVES

We measure the passage of time by the movement of Earth. A day is the length of time it takes Earth to spin around on its axis once. We divide a day into 24 hours. Each hour is divided into 60 equal lengths called minutes. Then each minute is divided into 60 seconds.

Besides spinning on its axis, the Earth also moves on a long journey around the sun. The time it takes to travel around the sun is a year. It takes the Earth 365 ¼ days to travel once around the sun. To make the number of days in every year a whole number, we have three years of 365 days and then one year we have 366 days. A year with 366 is called a leap year.

A year is divided into 12 months. Learn the poem to figure out how many months have how many days. "Thirty days…etc"
A decade is ten years. Century is 100 years. Millennium is 1000 years.

A century is how many decades?

A leap year has how many days?

Four centuries is how many years?

4387+2965+4943= $3.56x8=

4010-r=563

What is the largest 3 digit even number that has the digits 5,6,7

Proofreading
Today you will do something different. You will go through and find all of the mistakes in the following letter. I then want you to rewrite the letter. correctly. There are 4 spelling mistakes, 1 contraction mistake, 4 punctuation mistakes, 5 capitalization mistakes.

June 4, 2015

Der sarah,

 my summer vacation was awesome? I got to work at a horse camp all summur long. my jobs were to brush the horses, feed them, and clean up after them? i didnt get to ride them much, but it was still fun?

I'm looking forward to you cominge to visit me. when wil you get here.

Your friend,
Judy

Your other task for the day is to read. You can look online at www.plainandnotsoplain.com for book recommendations that we enjoyed reading or do an online search to find something that you are interested in. You should read for a minimum of one hour per day.

Write down the title of the book you are reading and how long you read for today.

_____

_____

write sentences for your words

A clock can be either digital or analog. Analog clocks show time with hands that point to places in a circular motion. A quarter of an hour is 15 minutes. A quarter after 2 is 2:15. A quarter to 4 is 3:45. Half past 7 is 7:30.

Elapsed time is the amount of time between a starting time and an ending time. For example, if you start your homework at 4:00pm and finish at 5:15pm, then 1 hour and 15 minutes elapsed between the time you started and time you ended.

Write the time that is a quarter to nine in the morning

Write the time that is 30 minutes after midnight

Write the time that is quarter after 3 in the afternoon

The movie started at 3:15pm and ended at 5:00pm. How long was the movie?

$528 \div (12-7)$ $6.00/8$ * this means divide

Show how to check the division answers for this. Remember multiplication is the opposite of division. Ask your teacher.

$$\begin{array}{r} 22R2 \\ 9\overline{)200} \end{array}$$

What are the next three terms in this sequence
....400,500,600,700,_____,_____,_____

How many quarter circles equal a whole circle

A personal letter has 5 parts. The heading, greeting, body, closing and signature.

Begin by putting the date in the right hand corner at top. After the day put a comma.--heading

Use hand motions to explain this----

Then you have the greeting—Dear Tony,----put a comma after the persons name.
Then the body—your letter
The closing----your friend,----put a comma after the persons name.
The signature Amy

January 4, 2015

Dear Jan,

I am planning on coming for a visit this summer to Michigan. I can't wait until we can spend a whole week together. We will have so much fun. I would like to go swimming at the lake. Can we go to the zoo? I look forward to visiting.

Your friend,
Amy

Write your own letter to your friend about coming for the summer.

_____

_____

_____
_____
_____
_____
_____
_____

_____
_____

Your other task for the day is to read. You can look online at www.plainandnotsoplain.com for book recommendations that we enjoyed reading or do an online search to find something that you are interested in. You should read for a minimum of one hour per day.

Write down the title of the book you are reading and how long you read for today.

_____

_____

Quiz

The multiples of a number are the answer we get when we multiply the number by 1,2,3,4,and so on. Multiples of 10 all end in zero. 10,20,30,40,...

Any multiple of 10 can be written as a number times 10.
20= 2 x 10
30=3x10

Multiples of 100 all end with at least two zeros
100,200,300,400.....
Any multiple of 100 can be written as a number times 100.
200=2x100
300=3x100

When we multiply by a multiple of ten or hundreds, we can just multiple the whole numbers and then add the number of zeros (1 for ten, 2 for hundreds, 3 for thousands,etc)

11 x 20= we take 11 x2=22 and add a zero 220 is answer

33x 300= take 33 x 3=99 and add two zeros 9900

Your turn:

34x200   500x36

400x37 $1.25 x 30
            **when you multiply with decimals, count over the number it is over in this case it is 2 times and multiply normally and move over your decimal two times in your answer.

$1.43x200   24x1000

Laura, Lesley, and Sarah equally shared a box of 1 dozen pencils. How many pencils did each girl get?

Write the factors of 60

Show how to check this division answer, is the answer correct?

300÷7=43R1

Grab a book. Copy a paragraph that has dialogue between two people. Pay attention to how you copy and do punctuation. Double check for mistakes and show your teacher.

Your other task for the day is to read. You can look online at www.plainandnotsoplain.com for book recommendations that we enjoyed reading or do an online search to find something that you are interested in. You should read for a minimum of one hour per day.

Write down the title of the book you are reading and how long you read for today.

_____

_____

week 23 spelling list

conserve

constructed

impatient

imperfect

impersonate

impractical

impure

prearrange

prepaid

preview

react

recall

recharge

reclaim

redecorate

redeem

relate

retain

Rounding numbers

The attendance of the game was 614. 614 is rounded to about 600 people who attended the game.
The price of the shoes was $48.97. The shoes cost about $50.

Numbers that have been rounded usually end in one or more zeros. When we round a number, we find another number to which the number is near. When you are rounding a number, underline the place value you are rounding and then look to the right. If that number is 5 or more(which is halfway) your number goes up. If it is less than 5 you go back to the nearest rounding number.

For example 67 , rounded to the nearest tens. Underline the 6 and look at the 7. The seven is more than 5, so we round 67 up to 70. 67 is in between 60 and 70.

For example 43, rounded to the nearest tens. Underline the 4 and look at the 3. Since it is less than five, we go down to the nearest tens, which is 40. 43 is in between 40-50.

You try, round to the nearest hundred 523. It is in between 500 and 600. So underline the 5 and look at the 2. Since it is less than 5, we go down to 500.

Your turn:

Round to the nearest ten:

72   87   49   95

Round to the nearest hundred:

685   420   776   450

10 | 2735   563x90=

Write the time that is a quarter after one in the afternoon?

From March 1 to December 1 is how many months?

Plural review

Write the singular form of the following words:

Accounts _____

Adventures_____

Arches_____

Blouses_____

Classes_____

Compasses_____

Couches_____

Decisions_____

Dresses_____

Erasers_____

eyelashes_____

Inches_____

Indexes_____

Larynxes_____

Syllables_____

Telescopes_____

Toothbrushes_____

Walruses _____

Oxen_____

Geese_____

Teeth_____

Strawberries_____

moose_____

Women_____

Children_____

Wolves_____

Bodies_____

Families_____

Butterflies_____

Your other task for the day is to read. You can look online at www.plainandnotsoplain.com for book recommendations that we enjoyed reading or do an online search to find something that you are interested in. You should read for a minimum of one hour per day.

Write down the title of the book you are reading and how long you read for today.

_____

_____

```
I   G   R   U   R   W   C   V   Z   R   C   M   C   P   W
M   Q   E   Z   I   E   P   O   T   W   T   X   E   R   R
P   C   C   D   I   M   L   L   N   C   V   G   K   E   E
E   Q   H   Q   L   M   P   A   A   S   N   J   G   V   D
R   P   A   G   D   C   P   E   T   A   E   L   L   I   E
F   R   R   S   K   T   R   R   R   E   M   R   L   E   C
E   E   G   P   O   F   J   R   A   S   J   F   V   W   O
C   C   E   D   R   U   A   Q   L   C   O   G   C   E   R
T   L   V   S   W   E   G   I   J   R   T   N   G   I   A
F   A   U   J   R   O   P   D   M   U   E   I   A   S   T
N   I   X   P   S   U   K   A   I   P   L   D   C   T   E
G   M   Y   O   F   O   W   N   I   X   U   U   E   A   E
I   M   P   A   T   I   E   N   T   D   Z   R   U   E   L
E   Q   W   R   E   T   A   I   N   H   A   M   E   E   M
C   L   I   C   C   O   N   S   T   R   U   C   T   E   D
```

CONSERVE	CONSTRUCTED	IMPATIENT
IMPERFECT	IMPERSONATE	IMPRACTICAL
IMPURE	PREARRANGE	PREPAID
PREVIEW	REACT	RECHARGE
RECLAIM	REDECORATE	REDEEM
RELATE	RETAIN	

Recall that the answer to a division problem is called a quotient. Sometimes when we divide, one or more of the digits in the quotient is a zero. When this happens, we continue to follow the four steps in the division algorithm: divide, multiply, subtract, and bring down.

Divide

$$10\overline{)6503}$$

$$6\overline{)\$6.36}$$

95x100

43x200

How many years were there from 1492 to 1620

What is the product of nine hundred nineteen and ninety

Let me teach you how to calculate an equivalent fractions by doing the Z method.   This is helpful in finding equivalent fractions. For the first one you say, 4 goes into 20 how many times? 5, then 5 x1=5 Answer is 5/20

$$\frac{1}{4} \qquad \frac{}{20}$$

$$\frac{2}{3} = \frac{}{15}$$

$$\frac{3}{5} = \frac{}{25}$$

$$\frac{5}{9} = \frac{}{45}$$

$$\frac{1}{2} = \frac{}{8}$$

$$\frac{3}{4} = \frac{}{12}$$

The period is used in more than just sentences. Periods are used in abbreviations, initials, and titles before names.
Use a period after each part of an abbreviation. Do not leave a space between the period and the following letter.
B.C.   A.D.
Use a period after each letter of an initial.
Michael J. Fox
Use a period with abbreviated titles before names.
Mr.   Mrs.   Dr.
Do not use periods if the abbreviation is an acronym. Acronyms are words formed from the first letters of words in a phrase. NATO (North Atlantic Treaty Organization)

Match up the following abbreviations

Column A   Column B
B.S.   Public Broadcasting System
DJ   United Nations International Children's Educational Fund
PBS   District Attorney
D.A.   Disc Jockey
SCUBA   Mister
D.V.M   Doctor of Veterinary Medicine
UNICEF   Bachelor of Science
Mr.   Self-contained underwater breathing apparatus
M.D.   Bachelor of Arts
B.A.   Medical Doctor

Write your mother's name using Misses and initial for middle name._
_____
Write your father's name using Mister and initial for middle name.

_____
What are your initials

_____
What is your doctors name using title

_____
What is your dentist name using title

_____

Your other task for the day is to read. You can look online at www.plainandnotsoplain.com for book recommendations that we enjoyed reading or do an online search to find something that you are interested in. You should read for a minimum of one hour per day.

Write down the title of the book you are reading and how long you read for today.

_____

_____

write sentences for your words

```
  23,456          6,876,999        ⌐5  25670
- 7,789          +543,865
```

```
4 | 23456          2 | 58023
```

Question marks –periods--exclamation review
Put appropriate punctuation marks. Remember within the quotations.

1. Did you hear back from the doctor's office
2. Collin said he saw the movie 21 times
3. My mom asked, "How much candy do you have left"
4. Did your pastor say, "Are you coming to youth group"
5. I asked Lauren if she had a good day
6. The hiker asked, "Is this as far as the trail goes"
7. Are you going to the play with your brother
8. My brother asked, "Are we all going to town"
9. Did the coach say, "Run three more laps"
10. Watch out   The stove is hot
11. Thank you for the coffee
12. Ouch   My fingers got burned
13. Wait I forgot the keys
14. The ice is melting
15. My favorite color is brown
16. I won the race
17. Are we going to the park
18. Collin yelled, "Hey"
19. Ugh   More homework
20. Are we there yet

Commas have a variety of uses. One of them is used in a series of at least three items. Commas are used to separate them.
I must clean the kitchen, bathroom, and the living room.
Put commas in the appropriate places.

1. I like apples oranges and bananas.
2. The soft sweet loving cat purred.
3. The sweet juicy ripe peaches were perfect.
4. The pickle was slender green and sour.
5. Write a sentence describing three or more things you like about summer.

_____

_____

Your other task for the day is to read. You can look online at
www.plainandnotsoplain.com for book recommendations that we
enjoyed reading or do an online search to find something that you
are interested in. You should read for a minimum of one hour per
day.

Write down the title of the book you are reading and how long you
read for today.

_____

_____

Quiz

When you add and subtract fractions, as long as the denominators are the same, you add the numerators. When you have $\frac{3}{4} + \frac{1}{4} = $ What you are saying is that you have 3 parts of the pie cut into 4 pieces plus 1 part of the pie cut in 4 pieces. How many do you have altogether? 3 plus 1 equals 4 parts of the pie cut into 4 pieces. Which equals 1 whole pie.

Remember to reduce down your answer to lowest terms if the fraction can be divided by a number or if the top is bigger (improper)

$$\frac{1}{5} \quad + \quad \frac{4}{5} = \qquad\qquad \frac{5}{8} \quad + \quad \frac{6}{8} = \qquad\qquad \frac{5}{9} \quad + \quad \frac{4}{9} =$$

Subtract the same way:

$$\frac{5}{7} \quad - \quad \frac{4}{7} = \qquad\qquad \frac{13}{6} \quad - \quad \frac{5}{6} = \qquad\qquad \frac{8}{3} \quad - \quad \frac{3}{3} =$$

Circle the ODD numbers

432,234,123   543,879,900   543,876,999   543,876,567

The bus started with 6 ½ gallons of gas. When the driver add 9 ½ more gallons of gasoline, how much gasoline was in the bus?_____

The leader cut a watermelon in 16 slices. The girls at 8 of the slices. What fraction of the watermelon did they eat?_____

Commas used in direct address and multiple adjectives
When the name of a person spoken to is used in a sentence, it is called direct address. A comma is used to separate the name of the person from the rest of the sentence.
Mindy, after our school is done, we can go swimming.

When more than one adjectives is used to describe a noun, they are separated by a comma.
The sweet, cool apple pie tasted good on the hot day.

Put comma's in the appropriate places.

1. They stayed out of the biting cold water.
2. Jentzen please answer the phone.
3. I worked out on the treadmill bike and elliptical cycle.
4. The sizzling hot sauce was too hot to eat.
5. Mady please pass the bread.
6. The students grabbed their books papers and pencils.
7. John would you please come here.
8. Brooklyn after we finish eating, we can have dessert.
9. The sweltering hot sun was unbearable.
10. Please pick up the shirts shorts and pants.
11. Grab out some strawberries apples and bananas.
12. Want to go play at the park pool or beach?
13. The new red car was his favorite.
14. I checked in on the slowly boiling water.
15. Evan had to eat dinner pick up his room and walk the cat.

Write your own sentence describing your three favorite desserts.

_____

_____

Write your own sentence describing your three favorite activities.

_____

_____

Write your own sentence describing where you like to take the cat.

_____

_____

Your other task for the day is to read. You can look online at www.plainandnotsoplain.com for book recommendations that we enjoyed reading or do an online search to find something that you are interested in. You should read for a minimum of one hour per day.

Write down the title of the book you are reading and how long you read for today.

_____

_____

week 24 spelling words

administer

advantage

adventure

defog

dehumidify

depart

derail

disagree

disappeared

dishonest

disinterested

explode

external

extricate

unequal

unprepared

untrue

Remember how to multiply by a power of ten? Just add up the number of zeros and add them to your multiplicand. 43x10,000= We know that 43 times 1 is just 43, then we add four zeros 430,000 this is your answer.

32 x 10,000=_____ 456 x 100=_____

29 x 100=_____ 343 x 10,000=_____

Draw me a rectangle and divide it into 3 sections. Shade1 of the boxes. What fraction is shaded?

If an octagon is separated into 8 sections and three of them are shaded, What is the fraction of shaded sections?

Round 615 to the nearest hundred

Round 48 to the nearest tens

342
X 11

32,621
+32,873

98,765
-11,399

8 | 356

If one pizza is shared equally by 6 people, then each person will get what fraction of the pizza?

Use a comma to combine two independent clauses with a coordinate conjunction.
The players must be well trained, and they must train for at least six weeks.

If a sentence begins with a prepositional phrase, set it off with a comma.
After he finishes his homework, he can talk with his friends.

Commas are also used when setting off dialogue from the rest of the sentence.
The tour guide said, "Today's walking tour will take us past several museums."
"Then, we will eat in a café," promised the tour guide.

Add commas where necessary.
1.	The Teton Mountain Range is a beautiful sight and it is challenging for rock climbers.
2.	The Teton Mountain Range is located in Wyoming and the range is in part of the Grand Teton National Park.
3.	Because of its beauty more than 3 million people visit each year.
4.	Visitors have been known to say "This is one of the most inspiring places I've seen."
5.	Millions of people gaze at the peaks yet it remains peaceful.
6.	The range not only has more than 100 lakes but also 200 miles of trails.
7.	Rock climbers come from all over the world to climb Grand Teton.
8.	"The view from the mountains is breathtaking" said one climber.
9.	While Grand Teton's highest peak is 13, 700 feet other peaks attract climbers.
10.	"Wildlife viewing is amazing here" said another tourist.

Write a personal letter thanking your mother for dinner last evening.

_____

_____

_____

_____

_____

_____

_____

_____

_____

_____

Your other task for the day is to read. You can look online at www.plainandnotsoplain.com for book recommendations that we enjoyed reading or do an online search to find something that you are interested in. You should read for a minimum of one hour per day.

Write down the title of the book you are reading and how long you read for today.

_____

_____

```
H  J  U  H  U  Z  S  R  W  S  E  G  H  L  B
D  I  X  C  N  Y  E  C  V  A  X  D  B  E  M
I  A  D  D  P  A  X  G  D  D  T  I  R  K  A
S  D  I  E  R  D  P  J  I  D  R  S  V  U  D
I  E  S  P  E  M  O  U  S  E  I  A  U  T  V
N  F  H  A  P  I  R  N  A  H  C  P  N  C  A
T  O  O  R  A  N  T  T  G  U  A  P  E  H  N
E  G  N  T  R  I  I  R  R  M  T  E  Q  Y  T
R  W  E  K  E  S  L  U  E  I  E  A  U  E  A
E  W  S  F  D  T  K  E  E  D  F  R  A  D  G
S  L  T  W  V  E  U  K  T  I  E  E  L  E  E
T  R  E  N  A  R  S  U  E  F  A  D  C  R  D
E  X  T  E  R  N  A  L  S  Y  U  L  Z  A  G
D  V  R  I  A  D  V  E  N  T  U  R  E  I  H
P  I  B  A  E  X  P  L  O  D  E  L  A  L  J
```

ADMINISTER	ADVANTAGE	ADVENTURE
DEFOG	DEHUMIDIFY	DEPART
DERAIL	DISAGREE	DISAPPEARED
DISHONEST	DISINTERESTED	EXPLODE
EXPORT	EXTERNAL	EXTRICATE
UNEQUAL	UNPREPARED	UNTRUE

mental math
- One week is how many hours
- The ceiling is 280 cm high. Round it to the nearest hundred centimeters
- 8 x800
- 10 cents x 25

Greg estimates that it will take 2 ½ hours to finish reading a book and 1 ½ hours to write a book report. To find the amount of time he needs to finish the assignment, add them. Line them up vertically like before

What year was two centuries after 1492

3106-528= $80.00-$77.56

804x700   4228÷7

A rattlesnakes rattle shakes about 50 times each second. At that rate, how many times would it shake in 1 minute?

Round 151 to the nearest hundred

The local pizzeria, will donate 14 pizzas to the 6^(th) grade picnic. How many pizzas will there be for each of the three classes of sixth graders

The sides of a triangle are 3cm, 4cm, and 5cm long. What is the distance around the triangle?

Contractions

Let us= let's
Write the contraction for these words

Are not_____

Can not_____

Could not_____

Did not_____

Does not_____

Do not_____

Have not_____

Is not_____

Should not_____

Will not_____

Would not_____

I am _____

He will_____

It is_____

She is_____

She would_____

They are_____

If you are writing about more than one letter of the alphabet or number, only add s to form the plural.

My name has two Bs in it.

I have two page 4s in my book.

How many letters are in your name? Write your full name=first, middle, and last
Lee ==1 L and 2 Es

_____

Has how many letters=_____

Your other task for the day is to read. You can look online at
www.plainandnotsoplain.com for book recommendations that we
enjoyed reading or do an online search to find something that you
are interested in. You should read for a minimum of one hour per
day.

Write down the title of the book you are reading and how long you
read for today.

_____

_____

write sentences for your words

Grab a ruler that has centimeters and inches.. Length is the measure of the distance between two points.

The words centimeter and millimeter are abbreviated cm and mm. The centimeter scale is divided into segments 1 centimeter long and may be further divided into millimeters. 10 millimeters equals 1 centimeter.

The distance across a nickel is about 2 centimeters. Two centimeters is how many millimeters?

What is the length of this rectangle in centimeters

Measure the length of your math page to the nearest centimeter

How many millimeters is your pencil

3 ¾ -1 2/4 =   33 1/3 +33 1/3=

One bag of apple chips costs $.75 Ten bags cost how much?

What is ½ of 51

Jadyn is 5 feet 4 inches tall. How many inches tall is Jadyn?

A noun that shows ownership is a possessive noun. Add an apostrophe (') and –s to a singular noun to make it possessive.

Flower===flower's center

Add an apostrophe (') to a plural noun that ends in –s, -es, or –ies to make it show ownership.

Ships===ships' sails   strawberries===strawberries' color

Some irregular(means different) plural nouns do not end in –s. To make these nouns possessive, add an apostrophe (") and –s.

Women===women's skirts   children===children's books

Circle the nouns showing possession.

1. The insect's legs are long and sticky.
2. The students' job is to finish their homework.
3. The dirt's layers are packed down.
4. The children's teacher will give them a treat.
5. Our cat's house is green.

Add an (') or an (' and –s) to the underlined word in each phrase to form the possessive. Write the phrase. The first one is done for you.

6. the water of the <u>ocean</u>   **the ocean's water**
7. the work of the <u>doctors</u> _____
8. the ears of the <u>rabbit.</u> _____
9. the bananas of the <u>monkeys</u> _____
10. the phone of my <u>brother</u> _____
11. the cheers of the <u>insects</u> _____

Write with the correct answer:

12. The _____ meowing was loud!
     cats   cat's   cats'
13. The _____sweet smell fills the air.
     flower   flower's   flowers'   flowers's

Your other task for the day is to read. You can look online at www.plainandnotsoplain.com for book recommendations that we enjoyed reading or do an online search to find something that you are interested in. You should read for a minimum of one hour per day.

Write down the title of the book you are reading and how long you read for today.

_____

_____

Quiz

Carl ran a quarter mile in 1 minute 15 seconds. What was his time in seconds?

The pumpkin weighed 3 pounds 8 ounces. How many ounces did the melon weigh?

The 7 of 374,021 means what of the following?

7   70   700   70,000

Use a ruler and measure in inches

$\longrightarrow$

(20x25) + (5x25)   1405÷7=

If each side of a pentagon is 45 millimeters long, what is the distance around the pentagon?

Lauren could type 90 words per minute. At that rate, how many words could she type in 6 minutes?

Draw a square. Make each side 1 ½ inches long

Ada is 6 years older than Mike. If Ada is 21, then how old is Mike?

Commas

Commas are used in addresses: 42 Stick Lane, Tuxedo, NC 24389
Commas are used in dates: January 21, 2011
Commas are used to start letters: Dear Sarah,
Commas are used to separate 3 or more things: I like to play soccer, baseball, and football.
Commas are used to end a letter: Love, Dad

Add commas where they are needed.

1. I am going to begin school on September 22 2014
2. We will learn reading writing and arithmetic.
3. The school is in Hendersonville North Carolina.

Write your address correctly as you are supposed to for an envelope

_____
_____
_____
_____

Write today's date

_____

Write your birthday

_____

Use commas between the day of the week and the date: Sunday, April 21
Use commas when joining two complete sentences with a connecting word such as and, or, but: I like to eat bananas, but apples are my favorite.

Add commas where they are needed.

1. I practice piano but my sister practices guitar.
2. I like to eat apples oranges and bananas.
3. My birthday is on Sunday February 12.
4. Were you born on December 22 1992?
5. I have one boy and she has two girls.

Your other task for the day is to read. You can look online at www.plainandnotsoplain.com for book recommendations that we enjoyed reading or do an online search to find something that you are interested in. You should read for a minimum of one hour per day.

Write down the title of the book you are reading and how long you read for today.

_____

_____

week 25 spelling words

arrange

bore

capture

compare

create

crowd

dance

divide

explore

give

mend

promise

reduce

shake

strange

surprise

tame

write

Average

To find the average of numbers, you add up all the numbers and divide by the number of numbers you are adding.

Mike was swimming laps. His sister recorded the following times for him:
80,85,90,85,90
What is the average?
Add them all up===430
Then divide by 5 the number your adding up. 430÷5=86

Your turn:

Our bowling scores were 112,126,98, and 118. What is Ned's average score?

My kids are ages: 21,18,11,7, and 5. What is the average age of my kids?

Change the following mixed numbers into improper fractions.

1 ¼ =_____   3 ½=_____6 ½ =_____

2 ¾ =_____ $5\frac{1}{3}$=_____$3\frac{4}{5}$=_____

Change the following into a mixed number

$\frac{14}{3}$=_____ $\frac{22}{5}$=_____ $\frac{11}{5}$=_____

$\frac{11}{4}$=_____ $\frac{9}{2}$=_____ $\frac{32}{9}$=_____

Rewrite the following words correctly. Use capitalization, spelling, and commas.

march 22 2012 _____

septomber 22 1998 _____

sonday janary 12 _____

tuesday april 16_____

june 11 1876 _____

july 7 1998 _____

detroit michigan_____

raleigh north carolina_____

greenville south carolina _____

miami florida _____

hendersonville north carolina _____

deer michael_____

your daughter amy_____

february 10 1976_____

Colon (:)
- Use a colon to separate the hour from the minute 7:20 am
- Use a colon to punctuate the greeting of a business letter Dear Nabisco foods:
- Use a colon to introduce a list. This list will include the words….following or these….Please find the following: car, boat, truck, and train.

   Hyphen (-)
- Use a hyphen to join words that are thought of as one: well-cooked, twenty-one.
Semi colon (;)
- Use a semicolon to join two clearly related, short sentences when a conjunction is not used: I have one goal; to find her.
Examples:
One of the most violent storms occurs primarily in the United States: tornadoes.
You can prepare by doing the following: have a safety plan, practice home drills, and listen to weather reports.

Fill in where colons are needed:

1. Included with this letter are the following my resume, references, and a photo.
2. You can reach me anytime between 7 00 am and 5 00 pm.

Your other task for the day is to read. You can look online at www.plainandnotsoplain.com for book recommendations that we enjoyed reading or do an online search to find something that you are interested in. You should read for a minimum of one hour per day.

Write down the title of the book you are reading and how long you read for today.

_____

_____

```
E  H  J  G  S  T  M  F  D  I  V  I  D  E  F
T  X  X  S  X  I  T  A  M  E  V  G  R  Z  R
H  Q  P  P  Q  U  S  E  G  Y  X  U  X  C  G
W  H  W  L  J  Z  P  U  I  W  T  E  H  W  P
M  W  G  A  O  G  Y  A  R  P  K  B  O  R  E
D  H  B  B  K  R  G  G  A  P  D  H  R  I  G
A  T  J  A  B  A  E  C  Q  P  R  R  I  T  B
C  R  E  A  T  E  C  P  R  O  M  I  S  E  R
Z  T  R  S  V  D  S  O  Z  S  X  X  S  G  G
S  T  R  A  N  G  E  Z  M  D  A  N  C  E  I
N  V  D  E  N  L  W  Y  B  P  P  N  Z  V  V
C  V  M  D  T  G  G  M  S  H  A  K  E  U  E
W  R  E  D  U  C  E  U  N  V  C  R  O  W  D
W  P  O  B  T  W  E  E  T  L  O  O  E  O  R
V  K  V  M  G  O  G  F  N  D  Q  Q  I  Z  H
```

ARRANGE	BORE	CAPTURE
COMPARE	CREATE	CROWD
DANCE	DIVIDE	EXPLORE
GIVE	MEND	PROMISE
REDUCE	SHAKE	STRANGE
SURPRISE	TAME	WRITE

389

count aloud: count by 12's from 12 to 120
mental math:
- 2feet 2 inches is how many inches
- Amy has traveled to 5/10 of the 50 states how many states is that
- 3 ¼ - 1 ¼ =
- How many years is a ¼ of a century
- What is 25% of 24
- What is 10% of 20
- 2 minutes 10 seconds is how many seconds

Billions			billions comma	millions			millions comma	thousands			thousands comma	ones (units)		
hundreds	tens	ones		hundreds	tens	ones		hundreds	tens	ones		hundreds	tens	ones

We see that the pattern of ones, tens, hundreds repeats itself through the thousands, millions, and billions.

Which digit shows the number of hundred billions in 987,654,321,100
Moving from right to left, the digit in the hundred billions place is 9

What is the value of the 2 in the number 12,345,455,377
2,000,000,000   2000   2   20,000
The value depends upon its place in the number. Here the 2 means "two million"

Use digits to write one hundred thirty-four billion, six hundred fifty-two million, seven hundred thousand.
134,652,700,000

Write 2,500,000 in expanded notation
We write 2 times its place value plus 5 times its place value
(2x1,000,000) + (5x100,000)

Your turn:
Name the value of the place held by the zero in each number

345,052   20,434,677

1,056,888,976   405,632,777

Use words to write the value of the 1 in 321,987,987

Use words to name the number 174000000000

Use digits to write the number: two hundred six million, seven hundred twelve thousand, nine hundred thirty-four

Write 7,500,000 in expanded notation *use parentheses

periods	question	exclamation	commas	quotation
apostrophes	colons	semicolons	hyphens	parenthesis
abbreviations	letters			

```
n  c  b  w  n  z  w  f  s  p  r  s  k  s  w  s
j  o  x  x  m  l  e  t  t  e  r  s  n  a  n  r
y  h  i  y  u  e  j  i  w  y  q  o  n  o  r  d
r  p  c  t  w  o  j  l  n  u  l  u  i  l  p  s
p  m  o  z  a  g  j  o  o  o  x  t  m  a  v  h
c  c  l  s  p  m  i  t  c  h  a  n  r  k  w  p
t  x  o  y  i  t  a  i  s  i  y  e  u  p  y  q
h  a  n  f  s  t  m  l  v  a  n  p  e  p  g  b
o  c  s  e  i  e  a  e  c  t  m  r  h  x  v  f
p  q  u  o  s  n  r  h  h  x  i  m  y  e  q  v
q  q  n  g  j  b  l  e  g  o  e  p  o  v  n  q
q  d  l  p  b  j  s  x  d  s  k  w  u  c  n  s
o  q  h  a  e  i  h  s  z  t  r  f  b  d  t  u
f  s  w  q  s  z  t  o  y  n  n  t  t  o  v  z
f  x  b  q  a  p  o  s  t  r  o  p  h  e  s  q
v  g  p  c  t  r  q  a  y  g  j  f  e  o  b  i
```

Your other task for the day is to read. You can look online at www.plainandnotsoplain.com for book recommendations that we enjoyed reading or do an online search to find something that you are interested in. You should read for a minimum of one hour per day.

Write down the title of the book you are reading and how long you read for today.

_____

_____

write sentences for your words

Jadyn made 5 dozen baked cookies and gave 24 to her friend Autumn. How many cookies did she have left?

Collin weighs 120 pounds. His younger brother, Evan weighs one half as much. How much does his brother weigh?

Write (1x100)+ (4x10)+(8x1) in standard form

Draw a rectangle that is 2 inches long and 1 inch wide. Shade all but 3/8 of it.

Use words to name the number 250,000

Which digit in 789,453,210 shows the number of hundred millions?

Write 1236 to the nearest hundred

27x22=   167x89=

4328÷4   5670÷10

Out of the following numbers what is the average? 2,9,2,5,4,1,4,7,4,2

Parentheses

Parentheses are used to enclose numbers in a series.
I do not want to go to the movie because (1) it is too late, (2) it is all the way across town, and (3) it is too scary.

Supplementary material is a word or phrase that gives additional information.
Those apples (the ones in the basket) are good for eating.

REVIEW
The following sentences are missing punctuation. Add periods, question marks, and exclamation points were needed.

1. Don't forget to stop by the store and pick up milk on your way home from school
2. What time is Gary stopping by
3. Jadyn said, "Those chickens are eating my lettuce"
4. Look out
5. T R Banks is my favorite author.
6. My doctor is Dr Smith
7. September 11 2001
8. Bloomfield Michigan
9. 7 00 am
10. Monday January 21 2001

What are the 4 types of sentences:

_____,_____

_____

What is the name of a book you have read this week:

_____

Write the name of a show you watched:

_____

Write today's date:

_____

Write your name with proper title:

_____

Your other task for the day is to read. You can look online at www.plainandnotsoplain.com for book recommendations that we enjoyed reading or do an online search to find something that you are interested in. You should read for a minimum of one hour per day.

Write down the title of the book you are reading and how long you read for today.

_____

_____

Quiz

Perimeter

We know to find the distance around a square or rectangle, we add up all the sides.
If a rectangle's sides measure 3 cm long and 2 cm wide, its perimeter is 10 cm.

How do we find the perimeter of a circle? The distance around a circle is called circumference. The center of the circle is the middle point. The radius is the distance from the center to the curve. The diameter is the distance across the circle through its center. Thus, the diameter is twice the radius.

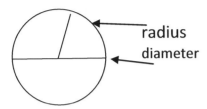

radius

diameter

If I were to say the diameter is 4 inches long, the radius would be? 2 inches long

Your turn:

What is the diameter of a circle whose radius is 10 cm?_____

11 ft

5ft   What is the perimeter of the rectangle?_____

6cm   6cm   What is the perimeter of the triangle?_____

6cm

8in   what is the perimeter of the square?_____

In the number 123,456,789,000 the 2 means, which of the following?

2 billion   20 billion   200 billion   2000billion

Use digits to write nineteen million, four hundred ninety thousand

300x200   800x70   5t=500 what is t

Today I want you to write a dialogue about a visit to the underground caves. Have two people in it. One that is hesitant to go and one that is excited to go.
Look in a chapter book so that you can see how it is written. Each time a new person talks you indent the quote. Place quotes around what is said.

_____
_____
_____
_____
_____
_____
_____
_____
_____
_____
_____
_____
_____
_____
_____
_____
_____
_____
_____
_____
_____
_____
_____
_____
_____

Your other task for the day is to read. You can look online at www.plainandnotsoplain.com for book recommendations that we enjoyed reading or do an online search to find something that you are interested in. You should read for a minimum of one hour per day.

Write down the title of the book you are reading and how long you read for today.

_____

_____

week 26 spelling words

attached

attended

avoiding

builder

catcher

concerned

drawing

enjoying

escorted

established

poster

prisoner

repeated

scalding

scooter

seller

spelling

younger

Dividing 2 digit numbers that are multiples of ten. Multiples of ten are 10,20,30,40, ...We will continue to follow the four steps of the division algorithm: divide, multiple, subtract, and bring down. The divide step is more difficult when dividing by two-digit numbers because we may not quickly recall two digit multiplication facts. To help us divide by a 2-digit number, we may think of dividing by the first digit only.

To help us divide this:

$$30 \overline{)75}$$

We may think $3 \overline{)7}$

We use the answer to the easier division for the answer to the more difficult division. Since 7÷3 is 2, we use 2 in the division answer. We complete the division by doing the multiplication and subtraction steps.

Notice where we placed the 2 above the box. Since we are dividing 75 by 30, we place the 2 above the 5 of 75 and not above the 7.

```
      2R15
30 | 75          The 2 above the 5 means there are two 30s in 75. This is correct place.
   -60
    15
```

Your turn:

The staff arranged 454 chairs in the school gymnasium. Each row contained 30 chairs, except the last row. How many complete rows are in the arrangement? How many chairs in the last row? Divide this out

Divide $60 \overline{)725}$ $50 \overline{)610}$

$20 \overline{)\$3.20}$ $40 \overline{)\$4.80}$ *put the decimals up in the dividend

Comparative and Superlative

When comparing 2 or more things add –er ----comparative

When comparing 3 or more things add –est----superlative

Write the base word and than write the other 2 forms of the adjective

Base word	comparative	superlative
Large	larger	largest
Strong		
Fierce		
Small		
Long		
Dark		
Pretty		
Big		
Tall		
Quiet		
Loud		
Light		
Weak		
Sad		
happy		

Sometimes you use the words more or most when comparing (hint usually it is when it is a two-syllable word)

Beautiful	more beautiful	most beautiful
Important		
joyful		
careful		

As with all English we have the irregulars that don't follow any rules ☺

Good	better	best
Bad	worse	worst
Little	less	least
Many	more	most

Your other task for the day is to read. You can look online at www.plainandnotsoplain.com for book recommendations that we enjoyed reading or do an online search to find something that you are interested in. You should read for a minimum of one hour per day.

Write down the title of the book you are reading and how long you read for today.

_____

_____

```
G  H  F  W  I  A  E  N  E  B  S  B  C  A  B
S  E  L  L  E  R  G  L  S  F  C  A  A  T  L
B  D  R  Y  O  S  Z  C  T  Q  O  N  T  T  S
W  V  I  K  K  C  E  S  A  R  O  F  C  A  P
A  X  H  Q  U  A  T  U  B  E  T  E  H  C  E
T  B  Y  F  R  L  M  G  L  P  E  S  E  H  L
T  F  F  O  Z  D  N  N  I  E  R  C  R  E  L
E  W  Y  F  U  I  E  E  S  A  A  O  S  D  I
N  D  P  W  Y  N  X  P  H  T  T  R  K  Q  N
D  G  I  O  G  G  G  E  E  Z  T  H  O  G
E  I  J  P  M  G  V  E  D  D  E  U  P  D
D  N  B  U  I  L  D  E  R  F  Z  D  S  V  X
E  M  A  B  X  O  C  P  R  I  S  O  N  E  R
Q  A  V  O  I  D  I  N  G  P  O  S  T  E  R
A  P  N  R  C  O  N  C  E  R  N  E  D  Y  B
```

ATTACHED	ATTENDED	AVOIDING
BUILDER	CATCHER	CONCERNED
ENJOYING	ESCORTED	ESTABLISHED
POSTER	PRISONER	REPEATED
SCALDING	SCOOTER	SELLER
SPELLING	YOUNGER	

Multiplying by larger numbers.
When we multiply larger numbers, we continue the same method as we do when we do smaller. Make your turtle head on the ones, drop a zero, make another turtle head on the tens, drop a zero, and make the last turtle head on the hundreds. **look this up online to explain it further.

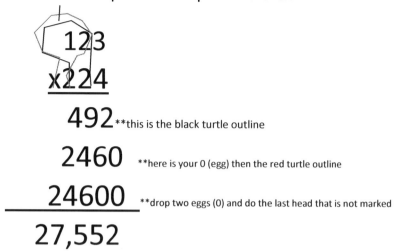

123
x224
_____
492 **this is the black turtle outline

2460 **here is your 0 (egg) then the red turtle outline

24600 **drop two eggs (0) and do the last head that is not marked
_____
27,552

Your turn:

342
x121

675
x253

Which digit in 98,765,432 is in the ten millions place?

Use digits to write six hundred seventy-nine million, five hundred forty-one thousand, two hundred.

The side of the square measured 10cm long. What is the perimeter?

406

We did some comparative and superlative words yesterday. Let's see if we can fill in the chart again.

Base	comparative	superlative
Pretty		
Good		
Bad		
Loud		
Quiet		
Beautiful		
Little—(You have little money)		
Many		
Light		
Strong		
Small		
Joyful		
Careful		

Write the contractions for the following words:

Did not
Do not
Will not
Is not
We will
I am
It is
Have not
Has not
We have

Your other task for the day is to read. You can look online at www.plainandnotsoplain.com for book recommendations that we enjoyed reading or do an online search to find something that you are interested in. You should read for a minimum of one hour per day.

Write down the title of the book you are reading and how long you read for today.

_____

_____

Write sentences for your words

Multiply the following:

```
 243              243
x102             x120
```

What is 600x400   234x100

Three weeks and three days is how many days?

Draw me a number line with even numbers from -4 to 4

What coin is 10% of a dollar

Sarah's younger brother is 2 years 8 months old. How many months old is her brother?

$(10 \times 10 \div 2)-(7 \div 1)-(1 \times 6)=$

Circle the correct word in parentheses.

1. Of the three bats, Sam's is the (light, lightest)
2. Lauren has a very (cute, cuter) kitten.
3. My notebook is (bigger, biggest) than yours.
4. (Light, lightest) rain fell on the roof.
5. Every mother thinks her child is the (cute, cutest) in the class.
6. After playing soccer, Aaron has a (big, bigger) appetite.
7. I think the cartoon at 9:00 is (cuter, cutest) than the cartoon at 9:30.
8. Adam has a (bigger, biggest) lead in the race than Samuel.
9. Of all the boxes, Joe picked the (lighter, lightest) to carry.

Fill in the blanks with correct word: more, most, good, better, best, bad, worse, worst.

1. I like my ice cream cone _____than your ice cream cone.
2. This is the _____banana in the bunch.
3. That was a _____book.
4. Paula has _____pencils than Sam.
5. Alicia has a _____cold.

MORE	MOST	GOOD	BETTER	BEST
BAD	WORSE	WORST		

```
M X Q U W D O O G Q
M B E S T E N T O C
N O W O N P S W Y N
D V R L K O O Z V Q
E B Y E M R P F W I
S A Q S S H B E O L
R D Z T B E T T E R
O P Q V T Q X F T B
W C E H P I Y R U S
U F Q Q N O I Z I T
```

Your other task for the day is to read. You can look online at www.plainandnotsoplain.com for book recommendations that we enjoyed reading or do an online search to find something that you are interested in. You should read for a minimum of one hour per day.

Write down the title of the book you are reading and how long you read for today.

_____

_____

Quiz

A foot equals 12 inches. A person who is 5 feet 4 inches tall is how many inches tall?

How many years is 10 centuries

What word is used to name the perimeter of a circle

Use words to name the mixed number $10 \frac{7}{10}$

what is the value of the place held by the zero in 321,098,333

What are the factors of 20

$43.15-$28.79=   423 x 302=   99+36+42=

Prefixes

A prefix is a word part that is added to the beginning of a root word to make a new word. Every prefix has a meaning and alters the meaning of the root word.

Pre-before   **con-with, together**   **im-not**   **re-again, back**

Conserve	constructed	impatient	imperfect	impersonate
Impractical	impure	prearrange	prepaid	preview
React	recall	recharge	reclaim	redecorate
Redeem	relate	retain		

1. Be careful! Don't drink that _____water.(not pure)
2. It is _____to own five automobiles.(not practical)
3. Don't be so _____-this takes time to complete.(not patient)
4. The comedian will _____the president.(make fun of)
5. It was not a very good mold; it was _____. (not perfect)

Match each clue with a word containing the prefix re

1. Call again _____
2. Energize the battery_____
3. To pay off, buy back _____
4. To decorate again_____
5. To tell or narrate_____
6. To respond _____
7. Win in competition after losing title _____
8. To hold onto_____

Your other task for the day is to read. You can look online at www.plainandnotsoplain.com for book recommendations that we enjoyed reading or do an online search to find something that you are interested in. You should read for a minimum of one hour per day.

Write down the title of the book you are reading and how long you read for today.

_____

_____

week 27 spelling words

apply

boundary

canary

century

city

company

country

dairy

enemy

factory

grocery

hobby

lily

marry

memory

pity

reply

worry

We know in a division problem, the leftover amount is called the remainder. Sometimes we need to write it as a mixed number. Here is how it is done.

If two children share 5 cookies, equally how many cookies will each receive?

We divide 5 into 2 equal parts. We find that the quotient is 2 and the remainder is 1. Each child will receive two cookies and there will be an extra cookie. We can take the extra and divide it in half. Then each will receive ½ . To write a remainder as a fraction, we simply make the remainder the numerator of the fraction and make the divisior the denominator of the fraction.

Your turn:

A 15-foot long board is cut into 4 equal lengths. How long is each length?

Divide 17 by 4 with a mixed number remainder

Divide 49 by 10 with a mixed number remainder

Divide 77 by 6 with a mixed number remainder

Prefixes

Ex=out of, from   de=down, away from   dis, un=not, opposite of   Ad=to, at, toward

Administer	advantage	adventure	defog	dehumidify	depart
Derail	disagree	disappeared	dishonest	disinterested	explode
Export	external	extricate	unequal	unprepared	untrue

Words with the prefix un

1. _____

2. _____

3. _____

Words with the prefix dis

1. _____

2. _____

3. _____

4. _____

Words with the prefix ad

1. _____

2. _____

3. _____

Words with the prefix ex

1. _____

2. _____

3. _____

4. _____

Add the prefix de- to each of these root words. Say each word to yourself as you write it on the line.

Humidity _____

Part _____

Fog _____

Rail _____

Write a sentence with a contraction in it.

_____

_____

Your other task for the day is to read. You can look online at www.plainandnotsoplain.com for book recommendations that we enjoyed reading or do an online search to find something that you are interested in. You should read for a minimum of one hour per day.

Write down the title of the book you are reading and how long you read for today.

_____

_____

```
D  L  O  V  B  T  P  I  T  Y  X  O  L  S  Z
M  S  K  A  B  B  D  D  A  I  R  Y  L  V  C
N  O  H  L  P  K  T  X  P  B  C  U  D  J  D
C  C  Y  H  O  B  B  Y  P  V  X  Z  L  H  H
A  L  Y  K  B  G  V  M  L  D  F  L  U  F  C
N  A  E  M  A  R  R  Y  Y  E  Y  X  E  M  E
A  J  F  A  C  T  O  R  Y  N  X  C  C  A  L
R  O  N  T  J  B  Y  V  A  E  X  E  O  G  X
Y  Y  M  T  B  R  O  P  V  M  P  N  U  Q  V
S  M  E  A  E  H  M  U  A  Y  T  T  N  P  N
P  F  M  C  V  O  B  V  N  N  D  U  T  V  R
N  V  O  H  C  L  I  L  Y  D  J  R  R  J  P
T  R  R  E  L  W  O  R  R  Y  A  Y  Y  Z  Q
G  T  Y  D  K  M  T  F  F  W  M  R  E  G  H
F  C  I  T  Y  T  A  G  R  E  P  L  Y  C  C
```

ATTACHED	APPLY	BOUNDARY
CANARY	CENTURY	CITY
COMPANY	COUNTRY	DAIRY
ENEMY	FACTORY	GROCERY
HOBBY	LILY	MARRY
MEMORY	PITY	REPLY
WORRY		

Evan baked a pie. After dinner, he and his family ate 1/3 of the pie for dessert. What fraction was not eaten?

If we have 1 whole pie and take away 1/3 of that, what is the answer?

1 whole pie is cut into 3 pieces so $1=\frac{3}{3}$ then we subtract from $\frac{1}{3}$

Answer is $\frac{2}{3}$

Your turn: Subtract 1- ¼=

1- 2/3=

$2\frac{5}{8}+\frac{3}{8}=$

$2\frac{7}{8}-\frac{3}{8}=$

364

x211

Use words to name the mixed number **8** 9/10

Divide 15/4. write the quotient as a mixed number.

Divide 687/40 and write as a remainder

Adverbs modify verbs, adjectives, and other adverbs. Some are easily confused with adjectives.

Bad is an adjective and badly is an adverb. Determine what you are modifying before using bad and badly.

A bad storm is heading our way.—Bad is used as ad adjective modifying the noun storm.

Cami sings badly.—Badly is used as an adverb modifying the verb sings.

Good is an adjective and well is an adverb.

Claudia is a good cook and bakes well, too.---the adverb well modifies the verb bakes. The adjective good modifies the noun cook.

The words very and really are both adverbs.

Please talk very softly in the library. The adverb very modifies the adverb softly that modifies the verb talk.

Complete the following sentences by circling the correct adverb. Circle the word it modifies.

1. Jim was sick and so ran (bad, badly) during the race.
2. Amy had a great day and ran (well, good) in her race.
3. The day I lost the race was a (bad, badly) day for me.
4. I was a (bad, badly) beaten runner.
5. But it was a (good, well) day for my friend.
6. She accepted her praises (good, well).
7. I will train harder so I do (good, well) in my next race.
8. That will be a (good, well) day for the whole team.

Homophones

Circle the letter of the definition of the underline homophone that fits the sentence.

1. Jadyn will have many books to <u>buy</u> when she starts college.
    a. To purchase
    b. To be near
2. The horse's <u>mane</u> glistened in the morning sunshine.
    a. The most important
    b. Hair
3. My father said we weren't <u>allowed </u>to see that movie.
    a. To be permitted
    b. To be audible
4. Susan lives <u>by</u> the pond with the ducks and geese.
    a. To purchase
    b. To be near

Your other task for the day is to read. You can look online at www.plainandnotsoplain.com for book recommendations that we enjoyed reading or do an online search to find something that you are interested in. You should read for a minimum of one hour per day.

Write down the title of the book you are reading and how long you read for today.

_____

_____

write sentences for your words

½ plus what fraction equals 1
1/3 plus what fraction equals 1
¼ plus what fraction equals 1
1/8 plus what fraction equals 1

Sarah has read one fourth of her book. What fraction of her book is left unread?

5/8 of the girls could do cartwheels. What fraction of the girls could not do them?

In the class there are three more girls than boys. There are 14 boys. How many STUDENTS are in the class?

The diameter of the bike tire is 24 inches. What is the radius?

Round 487 and 326 to he nearest hundred. Then add the rounded numbers. What is the sum?

374x360=   1340÷20

100÷10=   100÷20=

1- 1/3=   1-1/4=

Write a descriptive paragraph describing what the day is like today. Topic sentence, lots of vivid words, supporting details, and then sum it all up.

_____
_____
_____
_____
_____
_____
_____
_____
_____
_____
_____
_____
_____
_____
_____
_____
_____
_____
_____
_____
_____
_____

Your other task for the day is to read. You can look online at www.plainandnotsoplain.com for book recommendations that we enjoyed reading or do an online search to find something that you are interested in. You should read for a minimum of one hour per day.

Write down the title of the book you are reading and how long you read for today.

_____

_____

Quiz

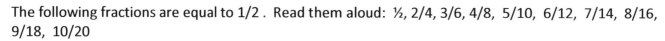

The following fractions are equal to 1/2 . Read them aloud: ½, 2/4, 3/6, 4/8, 5/10, 6/12, 7/14, 8/16, 9/18, 10/20

How much is half of 5? half of 9? half of 15?

$2\frac{1}{2}$ = half of 5 | $4\frac{1}{2}$ is half of 9 | $7\frac{1}{2}$ = half of 15

Write the standard form for (7x1000) + (4x10)

7,000 + 40 = 7,040

Round 56 and 23 to the nearest ten. Multiply the rounded numbers. What is their product?

60
x 20
00
1200
1200

1200

Which of these does not equal ½ ?

6/12   12/24   24/48   48/98

Divide and write the quotient with a fraction: 25/6

What month is 15 months after November?

MARCh

1000÷2= 500   1000÷4= 250

1- 1/5= 0.5   1-4/5= 2

I have completed 50% of my 400 mile trip. How far have I gone?

8 miles

Write two different sentences uses the homophones below:

Ad/add

1. _I hate when there are Ads on YouTube._
2. _Add 20+20._

Bail/bale

3. _I bailed him out of Jail._
4. _I bale of stra is being brought today_

Board/bored

5. _I have a board outside to make a_
6. _Seesal_

Capital/capitol

7. _The capital of OHio._
8. _capitol letters For a Sentieel_

Do/dew/due

9. _____

10. _____

11. _____

Knight/night

12. _____

13. _____

Flew/flu

14. _____

15. _____

Feat/feet

16. _____

17. _____

Your other task for the day is to read. You can look online at www.plainandnotsoplain.com for book recommendations that we enjoyed reading or do an online search to find something that you are interested in. You should read for a minimum of one hour per day.

Write down the title of the book you are reading and how long you read for today.

_____

_____

week 28 spelling words

approach

beaten

blueprint

boasted

bread

breath

disagreement

easel

eastern

feelings

flue

glued

groan

increase

leather

needless

peek

reason

Subtract fraction from whole numbers greater than one.

Imagine we have 4 whole pies on a shelf. If someone asks for half a pie, we would have to cut one of the whole pies into 2 halves. Before removing half of a pie from the pan, we would have 4 pies, but we could call those pies $3\frac{2}{2}$

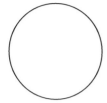 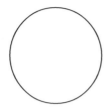 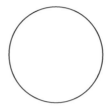 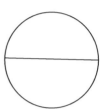

We use this idea to subtract a fraction from a whole number. We take 1 from the whole number and write it as a fraction with the same denominator as the fraction being subtracted. We will answer the problem 4- ½ It becomes $3\frac{2}{2}$ - ½ = 3 ½

Your turn:
There were 5 pies on the shelf. The server gave 1/3 of the pie to the customers. How many pies remained on the shelf?

Subtract 3- ¾ =   6- 1 2/3=

A 100 centimeter stick broke into 3 pieces. One piece was 7 cm long and another was 34 cm long. How long was the third piece?

What is the sum of five million, two hundred eighty-four thousand and six million, nine hundred eighteen thousand, five hundred?

Divide 20÷9, write the quotient with a fraction

What is the perimeter of an equilateral triangle whose sides are 20mm each?
Suffixes ******(This week order a biography and start reading it—lesson to follow)

A suffix is a group of letters added to the end of the root word to form a new word. When the root words ends in silent e, you usually drop the final e before adding the suffix.

Ex: trade + ed= traded move + er= mover

arrange	bore	capture	compare	create	dance
divide	explore	give	promise	reduce	shake
strange	surprise	tame	write		

Write the correct root word of the following:

1. comparing _____

2. surprising _____

3. promised _____

4. captured _____

5. dancer_____

6. writing _____

7. stranger _____

8. creating _____

9. shaker _____

10. taming _____

11. arranged _____

12. giving _____

13. bored _____

14. reducing _____

15. divided _____

16. exploring _____

Add the apostrophe were it is needed in each contraction. Then write the words it stands for.

1. Hes_____   5. Youre_____

2. Werent_____   6. shouldve_____

3. Im_____   7.youll_____

4. Lets_____   8.cant_____

Your other task for the day is to read. You can look online at www.plainandnotsoplain.com for book recommendations that we enjoyed reading or do an online search to find something that you are interested in. You should read for a minimum of one hour per day.

Write down the title of the book you are reading and how long you read for today.

_____

_____

```
T  E  Y  L  A  W  M  B  U  G  Q  A  Q  Y  U
Y  A  I  J  P  O  T  J  R  M  I  M  B  A  M
M  S  P  V  K  F  B  L  U  E  P  R  I  N  T
D  T  K  P  W  F  Q  F  Q  P  A  M  A  U  B
Y  E  X  E  Z  E  I  I  L  F  F  D  L  N  B
F  R  F  E  O  G  E  N  E  U  F  Z  O  B  B
E  N  K  K  L  X  S  Y  C  Q  E  P  S  Y  E
E  A  P  P  R  O  A  C  H  R  Z  S  H  W  A
L  B  I  D  I  S  A  G  R  E  E  M  E  N  T
I  L  B  W  E  A  S  E  L  T  A  J  X  E
N  X  E  P  G  L  U  E  D  I  E  Y  S  E  N
G  A  A  N  B  F  L  E  A  T  H  E  R  E  A
S  B  O  A  S  T  E  D  X  W  H  B  V  O  I
R  E  A  S  O  N  M  B  R  L  R  T  J  A  G
G  R  O  A  N  N  E  Z  U  B  R  E  A  T  H
```

APPROACH	BEATEN	BLUEPRINT
BOASTED	BREAD	BREATH
DISAGREEMENT	EASEL	EASTERN
FEELINGS	FLUE	GLUED
GROAN	INCREASE	LEATHER
NEEDLESS	PEEK	REASON

What are the equivalent fractions of ½ ? 2/4 …etc

Place value with money chart

hundreds	tens	ones	decimal point	tenths	hundredths
$4	3	2	.	3	2
$100bills	$10 bills	$1 bills		dimes	pennies

What is the place value of the 4 in $6.24?

The 4 is in the second place to the right of the decimal point, which is the hundredths place. This is reasonable because 4 shows the number of pennies, and a penny is a hundredth of a dollar.

Is $3.67 closer to $3.60 or $3.70?
We round $3.67 to the nearest ten cents, that is the tenths place. Since 7 cents is more than half of a dime, it rounds up to $3.70

Your turn:
What is the place value of the 5 in each of these numbers

$25.60_____ $54.32_____ $12.75_____ $21.50_____

Is $6.08 closer to $6.00 or $6.10?

Divide 25 by 8. Write the quotient with a fraction.

360-a=153   5m=875

1586÷60=   5x4x3x2x1x0=

Suffix

When adding a suffix beginning with a vowel to a word that ends in a consonant + y, change the y to i before adding the suffix. An exception to this rule occurs when adding the suffix ing.

Worry + es=worries   copy +ed=copied   dry +ing=drying   fry+ing=frying

Apply	boundary	canary	century	city	company	country
Dairy	enemy	factory	grocery	lily	hobby	marry
Memory	pity	reply	worry			

Write the correct word with an appropriate suffix on each line.

1. People work for these_____

2. Borders_____

3. Recollections_____

4. Urban areas _____

5. Little yellow birds_____

6. Milk processors _____

7. Fun things done in free time _____

8. Easter flowers _____

9. More than one period of 100 years_____

10. Petitioned _____

11. Places of manufacturing _____

12. One's adversaries_____

13. To be concerned _____

14. Food purchases _____

15. Answering _____

16. Felt sorry for _____

17. USA and Mexico are examples of these _____

18. Joined in matrimony _____

Your other task for the day is to read. You can look online at www.plainandnotsoplain.com for book recommendations that we enjoyed reading or do an online search to find something that you are interested in. You should read for a minimum of one hour per day.

Write down the title of the book you are reading and how long you read for today.

_____

_____

write sentences for your words

Writing fractions with denominators of 10 or 100 as decimal numbers. A common fraction with a denominator of 10 can be written as a decimal number with one decimal place. The numerator of the common fraction is written in the tenths place of the decimal number. For example:

$\frac{1}{10}$ can be written as 0.1

These are both named "one tenth"

Write three tenths as a fraction and a decimal number

$\frac{3}{10}$ 0.3

Write twelve hundredths as a common fraction

$\frac{12}{100}$ 0.12

Write $4\frac{9}{100}$ as a decimal number: 4.09

Your turn:

Write each fraction or mixed number as a decimal

9/10   39/100   2 99/100

10- (3 +1 1/3)   24x8x50=

The cake was cut into 12 slices, and 5 slices have been eaten. What fraction of the cake remains?

10x10=   10x10x10=

442

Abbreviations

Match the initials with the words they represent.

NBA	ABC	VCR	FDR	GE	CPA	USA
SEC	BLT	FBI	NAFTA	PO	YMCA	CNN
FDA	GM	NAACP	RSVP	VFW	BBC	CD
UN	NFL	FCC				

1. _____National Basketball Association
2. _____Federal Communications Commission
3. _____American Broadcasting Companies
4. _____National Football League
5. _____videocassette recorder
6. _____United Nations
7. _____Franklin Delano Roosevelt
8. ____compact disc
9. _____General Electric
10._____Bachelor of Arts
11._____Certified Public Accountant
12._____United States of America
13._____British Broadcasting Company
14._____Veterans of Foreign Wars
15._____repondez s'il vous plait
16.____National Association for the Advancement of Colored People
17.____General Motors
18.____Food and Drug Administration
19.____Cable News Network
20._____Young Men's Christian Association
21._____post office
22._____North American Free Trade Alliance
23.____Federal Bureau of Investigation
24.____bacon, lettuce, and tomato
25.____Securities and Exchange Commission

Your other task for the day is to read. You can look online at
www.plainandnotsoplain.com for book recommendations that we
enjoyed reading or do an online search to find something that
you are interested in. You should read for a minimum of one
hour per day.

Write down the title of the book you are reading and how long
you read for today.

_____

_____

Quiz

Place value	hundreds	tens	ones	decimal point	tenths	hundredths	thousandths
	4	3	2	.	4	2	1

Decimal values, go beyond just money. They keep going to the right just as they keep going to the left. Learn the place value.

Use words to name the decimal number 12.25
twelve AND twenty-five hundredths

Use digits to write the decimal number ten and twelve hundredths

10.12

Use digits to write the decimal number two and thirty-two thousandths
2.032 **put a place holder of zero to move the number over to the thousandths place

For example. Once slice of pizza that is cut into ten pieces can be represented as $\frac{1}{10}$. This same quantity can be represented in decimal form as 0.1 (read one tenth). Five slices of the same pieces can be written as $\frac{5}{10}$ or 0.5 (read as five tenths).

Fractions with 100 parts such as pennies are written with a denominator of 100. Seventy five pennies is $\frac{75}{100}$ of a dollar in fraction form and 0.75 in decimal form. Eight pennies can be written as $\frac{8}{100}$ or 0.08. The placement of the 8 is very important. A misplaced decimal point can change . 08 to 0.8

Always read a decimal as a fraction. Read 3.14 as (three and fourteen hundredths) not as three point fourteen or three point one four. The word "and" is used to separate the whole number from the decimal fraction. Read 214.37 as "two hundred fourteen and thirty seven hundredths"

Color in the base ten square to represent a decimal fraction.

0.3 (three tenths)

0.63 (sixty-three hundredths)

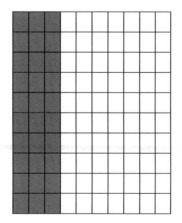

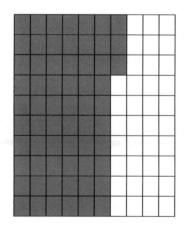

446

Write a synonym for the following:

To chastise _____ faithful_____

A prize _____delusional _____

Write the homonym that will complete each pair

plane _____paws _____

symbol _____counsel_____

Write ten sets of homonyms:

1._____ _____ 2. _____ _____

3._____ _____ 4._____ _____

5._____ _____ 6. _____ _____

7._____ _____8._____ _____

9. _____ _____ 10_____ _____

Antonyms for the following:

accidental _____ active _____

to add _____ to admit _____

modern _____ noisy _____

exactly _____ absence _____

amateur _____ departure _____

asleep _____ beauty _____

blunt _____ bitter _____

calm_____certainly _____

cellar _____ceiling _____

Your other task for the day is to read. You can look online at www.plainandnotsoplain.com for book recommendations that we enjoyed reading or do an online search to find something that you are interested in. You should read for a minimum of one hour per day.

Write down the title of the book you are reading and how long you read for today.

_____

_____

week 29 spelling words

believe

brief

died

eight

freight

leisure

lie

perceive

piece

pies

receive

reign

retrieve

shield

shriek

siege

sleigh

vein

Try shading in the following base ten charts with the correct numbers 0.4   0.11   0.59

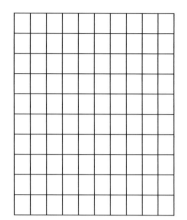

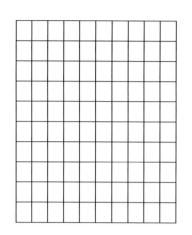

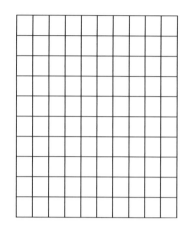

Shade 0.37   shade 0.04   shade 0.7

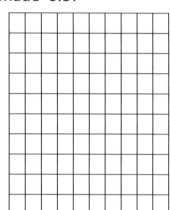

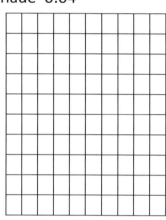

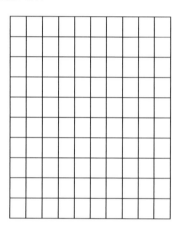

The decimals 0.3, 0.30, and 0.300 each represent three tenths.

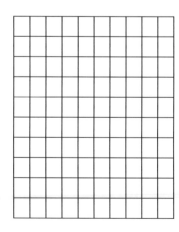

Shade 0.3.

Now shade 0.300 what happens?

$\frac{3}{10}$ is the same as $\frac{3}{100}$. One is just simplified or reduced down. Can you see that?

Lets write equivalent fractions for the following given decimals.

Example $0.45 = \frac{45}{100}$ or $\frac{450}{1000}$ or $\frac{9}{20}$

0.5_____   0.9_____   0.7_____

0.1_____   0.57_____   0.012_____

Negatives and Double negatives

A negative sentence states the opposite. Negative words include: not, no, never, nobody, nowhere, nothing, barely, hardly, scarcely, and contractions containing the word not.

Double negatives occur when two negative words are used in the same sentence. Don't use double negatives; it will make your sentence positive again and it is poor grammar.

Negative: We do not have any soup in the pantry
Double negative: We do not have no soup in the pantry.

Negative: I have nothing to wear to the party.
Double negative: I don't have nothing to wear to the party.

Identify which of the following has a double negative. Put a big X on the line.

1. _____Mary hasn't done nothing to make him angry.
2. _____It makes no difference to me.
3. _____I went back to get more soup, but there wasn't none.
4. _____I haven't ever seen no peacocks.
5. _____We looked for gold, but there was none.
6. _____We looked for gold, but there wasn't any.
7. _____We looked for gold, but there wasn't none.

Prepositions
Remember all of these? See if you can fill in the blanks of the missing ones.

about	before	down	like	_____	until
_____	_____	_____	near	_____	_____
_____	below	except	_____	through	_____
after	beneath	_____	_____	___	_____
_____	_____	_____	_____	_____	_____
along	_____	in	onto	under	without
_____	_____	inside	_____	underneath	
at	but	into	over		
	_____				
	concerning				

list the 8 linking verbs:

_____,_____,_____,_____,_____,_____,_____,_____

List the 21 helping verbs-linking plus more:

_____,_____,_____,_____,_____,_____,_____,_____,_____,_____,_____,_____,_____,_____

_____,_____,_____,_____,_____,_____,_____

Your other task for the day is to read. You can look online at www.plainandnotsoplain.com for book recommendations that we enjoyed reading or do an online search to find something that you are interested in. You should read for a minimum of one hour per day.

Write down the title of the book you are reading and how long you read for today.

_____

_____

```
Q   U   O   W   V   V   G   B   S   F   J   U   W   P   Q
G   W   N   S   H   R   I   E   K   R   B   J   V   R   X
T   E   Q   G   C   Z   I   L   V   E   I   N   G   Y   E
W   V   L   P   N   P   Z   I   S   H   I   E   L   D   O
L   S   D   F   C   P   E   E   W   D   X   A   Q   O   R
C   J   K   R   H   E   U   V   R   U   W   G   I   V   E
Z   M   R   E   T   R   I   E   V   E   K   D   U   S   I
V   G   Z   I   C   C   R   D   D   Q   C   G   C   D   G
W   M   S   G   V   E   E   F   B   R   I   E   F   K   N
Y   W   L   H   T   I   Y   A   B   I   B   S   I   I   P
Z   L   E   T   D   V   A   M   E   T   X   M   L   V   I
S   W   I   G   D   E   B   K   H   P   U   U   A   F   E
O   Y   G   M   K   I   L   G   P   P   L   H   T   N   C
K   B   H   T   L   E   I   S   U   R   E   K   L   I   E
K   D   V   N   U   E   M   S   U   S   I   E   G   E   T
```

BELIEVE	BRIEF	DIED
EIGHT	FREIGHT	LEISURE
LIE	PERCEIVE	PIECE
PIES	RECEIVE	REIGN
RETRIEVE	SHIELD	SHRIEK
SIEGE	SLEIGH	VEIN

To compare decimal fractions look at one digit at a time.
   a) Start with the whole number. The decimal with the larger whole number is greater number. 3.87 > 1.87. if the whole numbers are the same, move right to the tenths place.
   b) Compare the tenths. The decimal with the larger number in the tenths place is greater number. 5.6> 5.59. If tenths are equal move to the hundredths place.
   c) Compare the hundredths. The decimal with the larger number in the hundredths place is greatest. 6.37>6.368
   d) Keep going

Write < > or =

0.31_____0.20   0.090_____0.09   0.33_____0.3

2.001_____2.01   0.03_____0.3   6.02_____602

When adding or subtracting decimals, just make sure to line up the numbers. If you need to add some zeros as place holder you can.

24.523   45.98   765.7645
+5.754   - 9.65   -456.8751

Add the following numbers: line up the decimals 43.20 + .04 + 2.876=_____

Subtract the following numbers, add zeros if needed: 42.87- 4.769=_____

A business letter is written the same way as a friendly letter except that you put the business address you are sending it to above the greeting. Fill in the letter to a business and tell them how much you appreciate their products. Use a colon after the greeting as well. Sometimes you do not know who you are sending it to, so you can address the greeting with "to whom it may concern:"

_____

_____

_____

_____

_____

_____:

_____

_____

_____

_____

_____

_____

_____

_____

_____

_____

Your other task for the day is to read. You can look online at
<u>www.plainandnotsoplain.com</u> for book recommendations that we
enjoyed reading or do an online search to find something that you
are interested in. You should read for a minimum of one hour per
day.

Write down the title of the book you are reading and how long you
read for today.

_____

_____

write sentences for your words

Reading and writing decimals and Decimals as fractions

Practice writing decimals in words. 0.29 is twenty-nine hundredths : 4.7 is four and seven tenths; Notice that you do not reduce the fractions in decimals. All decimals have a denominator of 10,100, 1000, 10,000, etc.

Practice writing decimals as fractions and fractions as decimals. $\frac{23}{100}$ is 0.23, and 0.03 is $\frac{3}{100}$

Write the following decimals in digits:

Twenty-three hundredths_____forty-one hundredths_____

Five and three tenths_____ Five hundred twenty-three thousandths_____

Write the following as fractions:

0.45_____   0.87_____   0.4_____

0.654_____   0.8_____   0.76_____

Write the following as decimals:

$\frac{29}{100}$_____ $5\frac{5}{10}$_____ $\frac{234}{1000}$_____

$3\frac{23}{100}$_____ $4\frac{9}{1000}$_____ $245\frac{23}{100}$_____

Add or subtract
43.76+2.07+0.04=_____   56.87-5.321=_____

Write me a one page descriptive about your favorite month of the year and tell me why. Put a title for your paragraph on the top line.

_____

Your other task for the day is to read. You can look online at www.plainandnotsoplain.com for book recommendations that we enjoyed reading or do an online search to find something that you are interested in. You should read for a minimum of one hour per day.

Write down the title of the book you are reading and how long you read for today.

_____

_____

Quiz

Because the decimal point shows you the value of each digit in a decimal, you can add zeros after the last digit of a decimal without changing its value. You can add zeros before the decimal point. All the decimals below are equal.

0.5   =0.50   =00.50   =00.500   =.5

No matter how many zeros are added after the decimal point, the decimal point shows that 4 is in the one's place

        4=4.0=4.00=4.000

Learn to simplify decimals that have extra zeros

        0.240= .24
        38.00= 38

If you have 38.01 you cannot simplify that, ONLY if the zeros are to the right after the numbers

Reading decimals on a number line

        5.0   6.0

Can you find on the line where 5.3 would be? How about 5.2?
Since it is divided into 10 parts, each part is 1/10 of a mark. 5.1 then 5.2 then 5.3 etc

    Comparing decimals
Remember when you compare numbers, you start with the greatest place value.
Compare 8.82 and 8.98   compare the ones place 8=8
                                   Compare the tenth's   .8< .9
                                   Then 8.82<8.98

7.77____8.98   7.07_____7.77   4.99_____4.999

3.343____3.043   58.765____58.766   .878_____.888

54.87____5.487   84.88____8.855   432.876____876.9

462

Write me a paragraph persuading me to read a book that you have read lately. Use good persuasion techniques.

_____

_____

_____

_____

_____

_____

_____

_____

_____

_____

_____

_____

_____

_____

_____

_____

_____

_____

_____

_____

_____

_____

Your other task for the day is to read. You can look online at www.plainandnotsoplain.com for book recommendations that we enjoyed reading or do an online search to find something that you are interested in. You should read for a minimum of one hour per day.

Write down the title of the book you are reading and how long you read for today.

_____

_____

week 30 spelling words

auction

audience

autumn

awkward

caught

cause

dawn

fawns

flaunt

haunt

jaw

lawful

raw

scrawl

shawl

taught

yawn

Here are some problems. Write them out and line up the decimals. If you need to add some zeros.

432.8 +32.005 +1.001=   32.001+2.4+27.24=

34.87-4.49=   34.00-24.64=

To convert a decimal to a fraction, remove the decimal point and write the decimal over a power of ten. If the decimal goes to the tenths place, place it over ten; if the decimal goes to the thousandths place, place it over 1000. Reduce the fraction to lowest terms.

Examples: $0.45 = \dfrac{45}{100} = \dfrac{9}{20}$ $0.007 = \dfrac{7}{1000}$

Convert the following decimals into fractions.

0.23=_____   0.11=_____0.87=_____

4.2=_____   5.22=_____   8.25=_____

89.50=_____   76.454=_____126.777=_____

REVIEW

Choose the correct verb tense in parentheses.

1. Jim (saw, see) three snakes in his backyard.

2. The cook yelled, "(Come,Came) and get it!"

3. Sarah liked to (ran, run) and swim for exercise.

4. Mike (go, went) on a river kayaking trip last year.

5. Did you (saw, see) the baseball games on TV last night?

6. Do you remember the last time we (do, did) this hike?

7. Evan cannot get his cat to (run, ran).

8. Bill (sat, sit) and waited patiently for the interview to start.

9. Mr. Maryon (do, has done) that kind of work for years.

10. Brooklyn wanted Jadyn to (sat, sit) with her.

11. After she had left, Sam (come, had come) back to pick up her bag.

12. Jim and Tom like to (go, went) to the football games every weekend.

13. Mr. Smith (run, had run) the lawn mower many times before it stopped.

14. Noah (go, went) with his mother to the store.

15. My sister and brother (came, come) to my party this past weekend.

16. Members of the track team had (ran, run) home from school instead of walking.

17. Greg (did, do) his homework before he ate dinner.

18. They (go, have gone) to the festival since they were children.

19. I (do, have done)my chores when I first get home from school.

20. The rain (come, had come)in downpours throughout the night.

Your other task for the day is to read. You can look online at www.plainandnotsoplain.com for book recommendations that we enjoyed reading or do an online search to find something that you are interested in. You should read for a minimum of one hour per day.

Write down the title of the book you are reading and how long you read for today.

_____

_____

```
E  A  U  C  T  I  O  N  K  P  E  W  V  J  S
N  L  S  F  L  A  U  N  T  M  G  C  Y  V  Z
L  K  F  Z  P  Z  Y  F  I  Q  Z  X  A  B  A
D  Q  K  O  P  H  F  F  L  Y  I  O  W  E  W
B  L  D  C  E  O  B  I  F  F  A  W  N  S  K
Z  T  J  A  I  G  G  R  L  A  W  F  U  L  W
O  C  D  U  H  X  L  E  M  E  K  W  P  Q  A
N  T  M  G  T  K  C  X  S  L  K  B  V  E  R
A  Q  G  H  O  N  U  T  L  Q  S  I  N  H  D
X  E  W  T  E  Z  C  W  A  T  H  P  S  P  A
I  S  D  I  M  R  A  W  U  Q  A  A  J  A  W
S  H  D  O  B  R  U  X  T  J  W  U  U  S  N
Q  U  I  B  C  H  S  Q  U  A  L  J  G  N  H
A  N  B  S  T  Y  E  N  M  W  Z  B  E  H  T
C  Y  K  J  K  W  F  F  N  C  O  D  C  V  T
```

AUCTION	AUDIENCE	AUTUMN
AWKWARD	CAUGHT	CAUSE
DAWN	FAWNS	FLAUNT
HAUNT	JAW	LAWFUL
RAW	SCRAWL	SHAWL
TAUGHT	YAWN	

Write out 36.125 in words:_____

_____

Write two hundred thirty-seven and twenty-one hundredths in numerals

_____

Use < > to indicate which decimal fraction is greater

3.147_____3.205   3.06_____3.059

Round 87.658 to the nearest whole number _____
Round 87.658 to the nearest tenth._____
Round 87.658 to the nearest hundredth _____

Write 0.5 as a fraction in lowest terms _____
Write 0.67 as a fraction in lowest terms_____
Write 7.85 as a fraction in lowest terms_____

Fill in 0.37

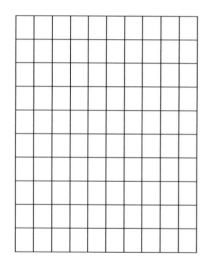

8.276-0.228=_____   465.52-104.1=_____

1. Jamie thought the play was the (cute, cutest) she had ever seen.
2. We have to climb over one (big, biggest) rock in order to pass the test.
3. That is the (bigger, biggest) mountain I have ever seen.
4. Cliff makes (more, most) money mowing lawns than Jim does.
5. The ice storm we had last night was (worse, worst) than the one we had last year.
6. Going to the beach for a vacation is a (good, better) idea than going to the mountains.
7. The blizzard brought the (more, most) snow I had ever seen.
8. Flat Rock is a (good, well) park for hiking and biking.

Rewrite the following sentences fixing any errors:

9. Susan plans to by earrings but she may get a necklace instead.

_____

_____

10. Amy wanted to go to the game, to.

_____

11. Whats the best way to get there

_____

12 My legs are longest than Katie's

_____

13. Wow The ball blue past my face

_____

14. That is the bigger plain I have ever scene in the sky

_____

Your other task for the day is to read. You can look online at www.plainandnotsoplain.com for book recommendations that we enjoyed reading or do an online search to find something that you are interested in. You should read for a minimum of one hour per day.

Write down the title of the book you are reading and how long you read for today.

_____

_____

write sentences for your words

We multiplied money before, remember I said to count over how many decimal places there was in your numbers and that is how many you move over in your answer. The same is true for decimals.

```
   4.3
 X1.2
   8 6
 4 3 0
 5 .1 6
```

Do the following problems and put the decimal point in the proper place.

```
  2.21            2.5            3.1
 x.15            x2.1            3.1
```

```
 6.6432          4368.3216       0.87
 X   0.3         x       0.2     x .04
```

Add commas to the sentences where they are needed.

1. Rebecca the new girl in school is a very good cook.
2. My favorite snacks are red apples carrots and cheese.
3. Thomas Edison an inventor had failures before each success.
4. No I won't be seeing the movie.
5. The coating on the pecans was sweet sugary and crisp.
6. Sam would you please pass me my pen?

Possessive pronouns can show who or what owns, or possesses, something.
Singular possessive pronouns----singular=one, possessive=possesses, pronoun=takes place of a noun
My/mine   her/hers   your/yours   his   its
Sam and I both have MP3 players.
His is black. Mine is pink.

Plural possessive pronouns- plural=more than one, possessive=possesses, pronoun=takes place of a noun
Our/ours   your/yours   their/theirs
My shoes are wet.
Their sides are muddy. Are those shoes yours?

Write the possessive pronoun in each sentence.

1. _____The sea thrashed the fisherman with its huge waves.
2. _____Their clothing was soaking wet.
3. _____Yours would have been as well!
4. _____My family lives in the mountains of North Carolina.
5. _____Our area gets no snow.
6. _____Betty house is next to mine.
7. _____Sam brings his bike over to our yard.
8. _____Ours has a steep hill for riding on.

Write the possessive pronoun that takes the place of each underlined word/words.

1. _____Mom was sick so we did <u>Mom's</u> chores.
1. _____ <u>Fred's and my</u> house is next to each other.
2. _____ The <u>yard's</u> fence is broken down.
3. _____Dad had to fix <u>Mom's and Dad's</u> fence.
4. _____Lauren and Jadyn were glad that cutting the grass was not <u>Lauren's and Jadyn's</u> job!

Your other task for the day is to read. You can look online at www.plainandnotsoplain.com for book recommendations that we enjoyed reading or do an online search to find something that you are interested in. You should read for a minimum of one hour per day.

Write down the title of the book you are reading and how long you read for today.

_____

_____

Quiz

Decimal division

You divide decimals by whole numbers the same way you divide whole numbers by whole numbers. You put the decimal point in the quotient above the decimal point in the dividend. Answers can go to the right 3,4 places unless noted. Add zeros to the dividend—ask your teacher

$$\begin{array}{r} 3.2 \\ 6\overline{)\ 18.6} \end{array}$$

Practice

$$4\overline{)\ 12.\ 8}$$

$$5\overline{)\ 20.55}$$

$$2\overline{)\ 84.12}$$

$$3\overline{)\ 12.24}$$

$$8\overline{)\ .860}$$

$$6\overline{)\ 4.56}$$

This week you will read a biography about a famous person and write about them. Draft your information about what you will write on them. This is just a draft, no complete sentences, just information for you to write with tomorrow.

Who is the book about?_____

What are 4 main points in their life?

1. _____

2. _____

3. _____

4. _____

Think of a topic sentence that will grab your readers attention. What is something great that your person has done that you will be telling us about.

_____

_____

Your conclusion is going to sum up everything that your person is about. What is it

?_____

_____

Any important dates you want to remember, that pertains to what you are going to write about?

_____

_____

Save this paper for tomorrow.

Your other task for the day is to read. You can look online at www.plainandnotsoplain.com for book recommendations that we enjoyed reading or do an online search to find something that you are interested in. You should read for a minimum of one hour per day.

Write down the title of the book you are reading and how long you read for today.

_____

_____

week 31 spelling words

appointed

boiling

county

destroying

disloyal

employ

eyebrow

fowl

joyous

mountain

noises

pronounce

power

shower

spoiled

stout

surround

thousand

In decimal division, the divisor must be a whole number. The decimal point must be moved to the right until the divisor is a whole number, but you cannot make a change in the decimal divisor without making the same change to the dividend. If you moved the decimal one place to the right, you have multiplied the divisor and the dividend by 10. Place the decimal point in the quotient directly above the newly placed decimal point in the dividend. Think of the division problem $3.4 \div 1.2$ as a fraction $\frac{3.4}{1.2}$ multiply both the numerator and the denominator by 10 to make an equivalent fraction. The new (equivalent) division problem is $34 \div 12$

$$1.1 \overline{)12} \qquad = \qquad 11 \overline{)120}$$

8. $4 \div 2.1 = $ _____ $1.872 \div 0.36 = $ _____

$0.4712 \div 1.24 = $ _____ $1.12 \div 8.0 = $ _____

Now take your four main points about your person and expand them.

Give me some information that supports those main points:

Main point 1 _____

1. _____
2. _____
3. _____
4. _____

Check---do all those correspond with your main point #1?

Main point 2 _____

1. _____
2. _____
3. _____
4. _____

Check ===do all those correspond with your main point #2?

Main point 3 _____

1. _____
2. _____
3. _____
4. _____

Check ===do all those correspond with your main point #3?

Main point 4 _____

1. _____
2. _____
3. _____
4. _____

Check ==do all those correspond with your main point #4? **save these sheets

Your other task for the day is to read. You can look online at www.plainandnotsoplain.com for book recommendations that we enjoyed reading or do an online search to find something that you are interested in. You should read for a minimum of one hour per day.

Write down the title of the book you are reading and how long you read for today.

_____

_____

```
P  M  N  D  E  S  T  R  O  Y  I  N  G  N  M
K  J  M  B  F  D  E  M  P  L  O  Y  L  H  L
C  K  Q  D  F  O  Y  S  U  R  R  O  U  N  D
D  G  Q  B  C  O  W  J  O  Y  O  U  S  F  V
P  I  A  K  K  L  W  L  X  M  Z  X  V  H  S
C  R  S  A  M  O  U  N  T  A  I  N  B  S  P
X  H  O  L  P  O  W  E  R  Y  S  E  A  S  O
C  V  S  N  O  P  T  C  J  O  T  Y  Z  T  I
O  B  H  J  O  Y  O  O  Z  U  O  E  B  H  L
U  O  O  I  Q  U  A  I  M  S  U  B  N  O  E
N  M  W  L  Z  V  N  L  N  M  T  R  O  U  D
T  R  E  L  J  F  A  C  Q  T  C  O  I  S  B
Y  K  R  F  X  M  S  M  E  X  E  W  S  A  K
T  C  H  R  B  O  I  L  I  N  G  D  E  N  S
Q  F  S  I  X  J  T  S  T  Q  H  K  S  D  O
```

APPOINTED	BOILING	COUNTY
DESTROYING	DISLOYAL	EMPLOY
EYEBROW	FOWL	JOYOUS
MOUNTAIN	NOISES	PRONOUNCE
POWER	SHOWER	SPOILED
STOUT	SURROUND	THOUSAND

Remember when we learned how easy it was to multiply by 10,100,1000, etc? Just add the same amount of zeros right?

In decimals and multiplying by 10, 100, 1000 etc, you move the decimal to the right the amount of zeros. If you need to add more zeros do so.

In dividing by 10,100,1000 you move the decimal to the left the same amount of zeros. If you need to add more zeros do so.

Ex. 34.87 x 100= 3487   0.67 x 1000= 670

93.79 ÷ 100= 0.9379   643 ÷ 10000= 0.0643

4.2876 x 100=_____   0.65 x 1000=_____

654.875 x 10000=_____   0.654 x 10=_____

65.87 ÷ 1000=_____   7.643 ÷ 10000=_____

9.98 ÷ 10000=_____   8.065 ÷ 100=_____

Write the following in digits:

Forty-three and seven tenths _____

One hundred twenty seven and thirteen thousandths._____

Begin writing your draft.

- Write an introduction with a topic sentence. Explain the purpose of your writing.
- Write the body of your paper. Use the organizer of information that we wrote out yesterday. Remember each new main idea is a new paragraph.
- Write your conclusion. It will summarize your paper.

Edit your paper

- Add or change words
- Delete unnecessary words or phrases
- Move text around
- Repeat run on sentences.
- Check for over usage of words and change them.

Save your paper

Your other task for the day is to read. You can look online at www.plainandnotsoplain.com for book recommendations that we enjoyed reading or do an online search to find something that you are interested in. You should read for a minimum of one hour per day.

Write down the title of the book you are reading and how long you read for today.

_____

_____

write sentences for your words

REVIEW

Write 207.426 in words

_____

_____

Write forty-seven and thirteen thousandths in numerals _____

Use < > to indicate which decimal fraction is greater   17.35 _____17.295

Round 12.769 to nearest whole number _____
Round 12.769 to nearest tenth _____
Round 12.769 to nearest hundredth _____

Write 0.36 as a fraction in lowest terms_____

Write 0.25 as a fraction in lowest terms _____

Write ¾ as a decimal number _____

Solve
36.2 + 27.325=_____

87.36-84.95=_____

4.6 x1.2=_____

3.46 x 10=_____

11.55 ÷ 7=_____

Proofread your paper.

- Check spelling
- Check punctuation
- Check grammar.

Write your final copy of your paper. This will be nice and neat. No mistakes at all. Hand it in when finished.

Your other task for the day is to read. You can look online at www.plainandnotsoplain.com for book recommendations that we enjoyed reading or do an online search to find something that you are interested in. You should read for a minimum of one hour per day.

Write down the title of the book you are reading and how long you read for today.

_____

_____

Quiz

Positive and Negative numbers

On a Celsius thermometer, zero degrees is the temperature at which water freezers. A common room temperature is +20 and -10 is the outdoor temperature of a very cold winter day.

The number +20 or 20 is a positive number. You read it as positive 20 or just 20.
The number -10 is a negative number. You read it as negative ten.

You can write positive numbers with or without a + sign. BUT you MUST always write a negative sign with a negative number.

We can show positive and negative numbers on a number line.

Numbers to the left of 0 on the number line are negative. Numbers on the right of 0 are positive. The number 0 is neither positive or negative.

Whole numbers are called integers. The positive integers are +1,+2,+3... the negative integers are -1,-2,-3.....

We use integers in everyday life. For instance the ten dollars you earn for doing a job is an example of a positive integer. When you spend the money on treats. That number is the negative amount you spend.

To mark the sea floor 300 meters below sea level, we can use the negative integer -300 to mark it. To mark a mountain 3,200 feet above sea level, we use +3200.

Comparing integers
An integer on the number line is greater than those to its left and less than those to its right.
-6 < -3 < 3
A positive integer is always greater than a negative integer. The farther to the left of a negative integer is from zero, the smaller its value.

Practice

-3_____-2   4_____-4   -6_____-5   +3_____+6

+2_____-2   -8_____-6   +10_____8   -5_____-10

Review

1. Sarah has (all ready, already) handed in her paper.
2. (All right, alright) I'll mow the lawn now.
3. What was the coach's (advice, advise) to you players at half time?
4. Are you taking a (course, coarse) in sewing?
5. This poison is supposed to have a deadly (affect, effect).
6. Last night we (choose, chose) our leader.
7. He did not, of (course, coarse), remember me.
8. The mechanic adjusted the (brakes, breaks).
9. You can (choose, chose) your own music.
10. The were (all together, altogether) at Thanksgiving.
11. The newspaper strike seriously (affected, effected) sales in stores.
12. I'm sure that the baby will be (all right, alright).
13. A fragile piece of china (brakes, breaks) easily.
14. Are they (all ready, already) to go now?
15. Congress appropriated funds for a new irrigation project in the (desert, dessert).
16. The new hat will (compliment, complement) my fall outfit.
17. With my brother away at college, the house seems (deserted, desserted).
18. Sitting in the back row, we could hardly (here, hear) the speaker.
19. The class is proud of (its, it's) progress.
20. It is already (passed, past) 9:00.
21. Facing defeat, he did not (loose, lose) courage.
22. Mother told us to stay (hear, here).
23. (It's Its) too late to catch the early train.
24. Everyone was (formally, formerly) dressed at the dance.
25. Mrs. Stuart just (past, passed) me in the hall.

Your other task for the day is to read. You can look online at www.plainandnotsoplain.com for book recommendations that we enjoyed reading or do an online search to find something that you are interested in. You should read for a minimum of one hour per day.

Write down the title of the book you are reading and how long you read for today.

_____

_____

week 32 spelling words

answer

broad

combine

council

cymbal

downstairs

false

freeze

narrow

pause

plain

punish

question

reward

separate

thaw

true

upstairs

Underline the number you are rounding to help you:

Round the following to the nearest tens

328_____   543_____

Nearest hundred

432_____   655_____

Nearest thousand

34532_____   6543_____

Nearest ten thousand

43233_____   56555_____

Nearest tenth

63.87_____   8.057_____

Nearest hundredth

654.754_____876.5328_____

Nearest thousandths
0.6547_____34.7623_____

$$20 \overline{)56740}$$ $$3 \overline{)3.246}$$

REVIEW

1. This (piece, peace) of chicken is bony.
2. Please be as (quiet, quite) as possible in the church.
3. Mr. Carver is the (principal, principle) of our school.
4. The bleachers did not seem very (stationary, stationery).
5. That night the big moon (shown, shone) brightly.
6. Joe knows how to use a (plane, plain) in his shop.
7. What did you do (then, than)?
8. Do you still live (their, there, they're)?
9. Do you drink your coffee (plain, plane) or with cream and sugar?
10. All of the student's invited (their, there, they're) parents to the play.
11. (Their, There, They're) coming here tomorrow.
12. This summer my mother has decided that I am going to improve myself rather (than, then) enjoy myself.
13. (their, there, they're) books are still here.
14. The (weather, whether) in Florida was pleasant.
15. Dad (threw, through) the skates in my closet.
16. Sally is going to the concert. Are you going (to, too, two)?
17. Next (weak, week) the Bears will play the Packers.
18. The ball crashed (threw, through) the window.
19. (your, you're) trying too hard, Ben.
20. I don't remember (weather, whether) I bought milk or not.
21. The water seeped (threw, through) the basement window.
22. (Whose, Who's) going to be first?
23. You should not consider this a (waist, waste) of time.
24. I forgot (to, two, too) address the envelope.
25. Grab me some (stationary, stationery) at the store to write to my Mom.

Your other task for the day is to read. You can look online at
www.plainandnotsoplain.com for book recommendations that we
enjoyed reading or do an online search to find something that you
are interested in. You should read for a minimum of one hour per
day.

Write down the title of the book you are reading and how long you
read for today.

_____

_____

```
K  L  K  V  F  R  E  E  Z  E  W  S  B  E  A
O  I  C  Y  M  B  A  L  D  D  Y  C  S  P  U
F  P  O  B  U  J  B  R  O  A  D  U  Z  F  Z
A  T  U  T  S  L  A  S  W  E  A  Y  T  K  O
L  P  N  P  I  H  E  V  N  P  N  P  H  N  Y
S  U  C  N  S  G  L  O  S  J  S  K  A  A  B
E  N  I  P  T  T  I  X  T  W  W  B  W  R  B
N  I  L  C  L  T  A  U  A  R  E  R  C  R  J
X  S  C  P  S  A  F  I  I  S  R  E  O  O  Y
W  H  Y  E  A  Y  I  K  R  T  C  W  M  W  Y
O  X  U  Q  W  P  R  N  S  S  H  A  B  F  C
S  Q  S  E  P  A  R  A  T  E  T  R  I  D  D
P  A  Y  K  Y  E  X  P  K  E  W  D  N  M  J
O  S  W  U  Y  M  H  H  H  F  T  P  E  J  R
J  T  D  J  Q  T  P  B  D  L  T  R  U  E  X
```

ANSWER	BROAD	COMBINE
COUNCIL	CYMBAL	DOWNSTAIRS
FALSE	FREEZE	NARROW
PAUSE	PLAIN	PUNISH
QUESTION	REWARD	SEPARATE
THAW	TRUE	UPSTAIRS

Put these decimals in order from largest to smallest:

32.45   33.4   31.55   78.1   32.09

_78.1, 33.45, 32.45, 32.09, 31.55_

Put these in order from smallest to largest:

3.45   76.88   2.001   3.03   3.43   .03451

_____

Add these decimals. Fill in the zeros:

32.32+43.001+54.01=

$$32.320$$
$$43.001$$
$$\overline{75.321}$$

Subtract
432.98-32.021=

75.32 x2.1=

Write me a paper comparing the summer to the winter. What are the good and bad points to them.

Begin with a topic sentence and end with a conclusion. Put a title on top line.

_____

_____

_____

_____

_____

_____

_____

_____

_____

_____

_____

_____

_____

_____

_____

_____

_____

_____

_____

_____

_____

_____

_____

_____

Your other task for the day is to read. You can look online at www.plainandnotsoplain.com for book recommendations that we enjoyed reading or do an online search to find something that you are interested in. You should read for a minimum of one hour per day.

Write down the title of the book you are reading and how long you read for today.

_____

_____

write sentences for your words

Compare < > = **start on the left and see which one is larger

43.76_____43.99   323.876_____654.98   32.04_____32.40

678.890____678.891   432.55_____432.55   432.8_____432.0

-43_____43   -876_____-976   -876_____-887

What digit in 67.89 is in the hundredths place_____

Use digits to write the decimal number fifteen and twelve hundredths

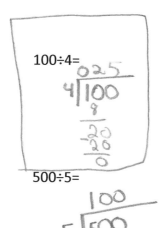

100÷4=
          025
4|100
      8
    ‾‾
    20
    20
    ‾‾
     0

200÷4=   050
        4|200
          20
          ‾‾
           0
           0
           ‾

500÷5=
        100
5|500
   5
   ‾
   0
   0

32x100=   003
        32|100

Write the decimal 12.6 with three decimal places: 12.600 *remember you can add zeros to the end and it does not affect the amount 12.6 is the same as 12.600

Your turn:
Write the decimal 7.8 with four decimal places:_____

Which is bigger: 12.6 or 12.600

What is something that someone does for you that you appreciate? It can be anyone. Write them a
letter telling them why you are thankful for what they do.

_____

_____

_____

_____

_____

_____

_____

_____

_____

_____

_____

_____

_____

_____

_____

_____

Your other task for the day is to read. You can look online at www.plainandnotsoplain.com for book recommendations that we enjoyed reading or do an online search to find something that you are interested in. You should read for a minimum of one hour per day.

Write down the title of the book you are reading and how long you read for today.

_____

_____

Quiz

Fractions, decimals, and percents are three ways to name parts of a whole

Percent

The term percent means "per hundred". A percent compares a number to 100. For example 30 percent means 30 out of 100 or $\frac{30}{100}$. The symbol % stands for a percent. You write 21 out of 100 as 21%.

To write a percent as a decimal, remember that a percent is always in the hundredths. 35 percent is the same as 35 hundredths.

$$35\% = \frac{35}{100} = 0.35$$

To write a decimal as a percent, think of the decimal in hundredths. Then you can write it as a percent. 7 tenths (0.7) is the same as 70 hundredths (0.70), which is the same as 70%

$$.7 = 0.70 = \frac{70}{100} = 70\%$$

A quick way to write a decimal as a percent is to multiply the decimal by 100. This method words because percents are already in hundredths.

.40 = 40 %

Write the following as a percent:

.30_____   .25_____   .77_____

.98_____   .43_____   .80_____

What is the total cost of a $7.98 book that has $.49 tax?

In room 9 there are 6 rows of desks with 5 desks in each row. There are 4 books in each desk. How many books are in all the desks?

In 1.234 which digit is in the thousandths place?_____

Compare 12.2_____12.20

510

Writing letters to your friends. When you write letters to people, you want to begin the letter with something positive. A bible verse or a positive greeting is a great way to begin. In your letter you want to share something that has happened in your life. Keep it positive, this is not the time to bring negative information. Inform them of something and let it put a smile on their face. No need to puff yourself up, but share what you are learning, maybe a new skill or something that has encouraged you lately. Ask only a few questions, as you don't want them to feel they have to respond to empty ended questions. Include something small in the letter a trinket, piece of candy, or perhaps a sticker. End it with a positive note and let them know you miss them.

Your other task for the day is to read. You can look online at www.plainandnotsoplain.com for book recommendations that we enjoyed reading or do an online search to find something that you are interested in. You should read for a minimum of one hour per day.

Write down the title of the book you are reading and how long you read for today.

_____

_____

Week 33

Circle the word in each row that are spelled correctly.

ilegible	illegable	illegible	illeegible
misspell	mispell	misespell	misspel
inpolite	impolit	inplolit	impolite
inproper	improper	impropeer	inpropr
misguide	missguide	misguid	misgyde
imaction	inacshun	inaction	inaktion
incorect	incorrect	imcorrect	incorret
ilegal	illegal	illegul	illeagal

Circle the misspelled word in the sentences below. Spell it correctly on the line.

It was inconvenent for me to pick up Sarah from school.

_____

Sometimes I am inpatient as I am waiting for the school bus to arrive in the mornings.

_____

It was inconsiderate of Sam to missuse her new calculator.

_____

It was inpossible to make a good grade on the difficult science test.

_____

A quick way to write percent as a decimal is to divide by 100.

40%= .40   remember how to move the decimal to the left. Since it is already at the end of the whole number you move it to the left two places for the 2 zeros.

Write the following as a decimal

60%_____   3%_____   22%_____

32%_____   7%_____   88%_____

Write these fractions as decimal:

30/100 _____   45/100_____

Write these decimals as percents:

0.45=_____   .75=_____

How many minutes is 2 ½ hours?

How much is ½ of 12

452.23x1000=   436.23÷100=

Put all of your family in ABC order by first name:

1. _____
2. _____
3. _____
4. _____
5. _____
6. _____
7. _____
8. _____
9. _____
10. _____
11. _____
12. _____

What are the linking verbs(8)

_____,_____,_____,_____,_____,_____,_____,_____

Helping verbs (21)

___=___=___=___=___=___=___=___=___=___

___=___=___=___=___=___=___=___=___=___

Words that describe the sky right now:

1. _____
2. _____
3. _____
4. _____
5. _____

Your other task for the day is to read. You can look online at www.plainandnotsoplain.com for book recommendations that we enjoyed reading or do an online search to find something that you are interested in. You should read for a minimum of one hour per day.

Write down the title of the book you are reading and how long you read for today.

_____

_____

In the following group of words circle the one that is not a synonym for the others.

happy	thrilled	sad	excited
fearful	bold	brave	fearless
swift	stern	fast	rapid
gaze	observe	look	pitch
eat	chew	dine	starve
health	illness	sickness	disease
hop	jump	tardy	leap
rip	ripe	tear	split

Circle the word that is an antonym for the underlined word.

The lion in the story was very <u>timid.</u>

1. shy
2. courageous
3. careful

The hurricane in the Pacific Ocean was a <u>gentle</u> storm.

1. kind
2. huge
3. violent

The last way is to change them to fractions.
We are going to memorize the common ones.

25% = ¼   50%= ½   75%= ¾

10%=1/10   20%=2/10   30%=3/10   etc.

20%= 1/5   40%=2/5   60%=3/5   80%=4/5

How you would solve these is to take the percentage number or the decimal number and put it over 100. Then reduce down.   25/100= ¼ = 25%

Let's fill in the blanks for the fractions:

20%=_____   25%=_____   30%=_____

75%=_____   50%=_____   60%=_____

10%=_____   70%+_____   90%=_____

What is the area of a rectangle whose sides measure 3 cm and 4 cm?

What is the area of a rectangle whose sides measure 5 inch and 2 inch?

Lori's bedroom is 10 feet wide by 12 feet long, how much carpet will she need to cover the area of the floor?

What comes next in 4,5,8,9,12,13,____,_____,____

Rewrite the passage correctly fixing the capitalization mistakes.

mary leston takes home a runaway Cat. It seems to mary as though
the cat has been mistreated by her Owner, mindy smith. Mrs. smith has the
reputation of being mean and nasty.
mr. and mrs. leston, Mary's Parents, know that their daughter has grown fond
of the cat, whom she has named fluffy. mary takes the Cat to the Animal
Doctor, doc murphy. mindy smith is angry when she finds out that the Cat has
been injured. mr. lester says that his daughter will pay for the Animal Doctor.

_____

_____

_____

_____

_____

_____

_____

_____

_____

_____

_____

_____

_____

_____

_____

_____

_____

_____

Your other task for the day is to read. You can look online at www.plainandnotsoplain.com for book recommendations that we enjoyed reading or do an online search to find something that you are interested in. You should read for a minimum of one hour per day.

Write down the title of the book you are reading and how long you read for today.

_____

_____

Circle the answer that is an antonym to the underlined word.

1. What was your <u>response</u> to the teacher?
   a. answer
   b. joke
   c. question

2. The <u>clear</u> glass bottle once held medicine used during Colonial times.
   a. opaque
   b. brown
   c. clean

3. The ambulance paramedics <u>leisurely</u> worked at the car accident.
   a. urgently
   b. carefully
   c. slowly

4. Max is very <u>vain</u> about his acting accomplishments.
   a. happy
   b. excited
   c. modest

5. Addison <u>carelessly</u> put all the books on the shelf.
   a. carefully
   b. quickly
   c. swiftly

6. Marie <u>collected</u> the food in the dog's pen.
   a. planted
   b. scattered
   c. watered.

7. The photographer asked the children to <u>grimace</u> for the camera.
   a. smile
   b. frown
   c. scowl

Name the decimal number 12.25 in words

Write a fraction that shows how many twelfths equal one half

Write the factors of 16

What digit in 436.2 is in the ones place

30m=6000 what is m $80-$72.07=

375x548= $40.53÷7=

Add 3.4+6.7+11.3=   0.436-0.2=

4.2+2.65=   6.75-4.5=

In each group of words, circle the plural noun that is NOT correct.

hawks
rattlers
skys
enemies

crashes
creatures
wetlands
searchies

discoveries
hikers
branchies
targets

seconds
mountains
gullys
days

emergencyes
births
delays
reptiles

snakes
edges
rescues
foxs

coyotes
ashes
medicines
decoyes

masses
splashs
places
temperatures

scents
predators
gulchs
classes

memorys
tracks
mammals
diamondbacks

Your other task for the day is to read. You can look online at www.plainandnotsoplain.com for book recommendations that we enjoyed reading or do an online search to find something that you are interested in. You should read for a minimum of one hour per day.

Write down the title of the book you are reading and how long you read for today.

_____

_____

Circle the word that is an antonym for the word underlined.

1. The <u>ferocious</u> dog went to sleep.
    a. mean
    b. angry
    c. calm

2. It was a <u>normal</u> day when the clown walked into the classroom.
    a. regular
    b. strange
    c. sunny

3. Who understands how to answer the <u>difficult</u> math question?
    a. hard
    b. funny
    c. simple

4. Pete and John <u>angrily</u> carried the books for their teacher.
    a. happily
    b. sullenly
    c. quickly

5. Collin sat <u>cheerfully</u> outside the principal's office.
    a. laughingly
    b. suddently
    c. sullenly

6. My mother always tells me to wear <u>foolish</u> shoes.
    a. new
    b. white
    c. sensible

7. The girls were very <u>friendly</u> when we first met them.
    a. helpful
    b. closely
    c. rude

Situation	Fraction	percent
30 marbles out of 100 marbles are red	$\dfrac{30}{100}$	30%
29 people out of 100 voted		
10 fish out of 100 fish are tropical		
7 cats out of 100 cats live indoors		
4 turtles out of 100 turtles lay eggs		
7 out of 10 puppies had spots		
17 out of 25 rules are blue		
18 out of 20 goldfish are orange		
The dress was reduced from $5 to $20		

To find the average of a set of numbers, you add up all the numbers and then divide by the number of addends. This is helpful in finding out averages of your tests. If I had 5 tests and I want to know what the average score was , I would add them all up and divide by 5.

Find the average of the following numbers:

5   3   6   8   3   2

_____

Now if you want to find out what the **mean** of your numbers is---the middle number you line up your numbers and get the middle number.

The range is the difference between the highest and lowest number is

Find me the following:

2   1   3   6   12   7   9

Mean_____   Average_____Range_____

In each group of words circle the plural noun that is NOT correct

selves
scarfs
igloos
deer

heroes
leafs
wolves
feet

people
pianos
knives
discoverys

stereoes
themselves
women
banjos

mice
chieves
patios
gentlemen

wives
videos
tooths
oxen

roofs
series
childrens
radios

studioes
species
aircraft
autos

lifes
predators
yourselves
tomatoes

shelves
men
calfs
thieves

Your other task for the day is to read. You can look online at www.plainandnotsoplain.com for book recommendations that we enjoyed reading or do an online search to find something that you are interested in. You should read for a minimum of one hour per day.

Write down the title of the book you are reading and how long you read for today.

_____

_____

week 34

Circle the word that is spelled incorrectly in each sentence. Write the correct spelling on the line.

We had to say the Pledje of Allegiance to the Flag every morning after the announcements.

_____

The jentle lady bug landed on the soft leaf.

_____

Disney World is the most majical place in the world in my opinion.

_____

The agent called an emerjency while we were at the football game.

_____

It is danjerous to play near the water.

_____

Please sing directly into the mikrofone.

_____.

Answer the telefone.

_____

You told a pretty grafic story with lots of vivid details.

_____

Review from yesterday and solve:

1   1   2   3   4   3   5

Mean_____   Average_____Range_____

Finding a percent of a number

There are 432 people in our church. 45% of them are boys. How many people are boys.
To solve this we find a percent of a number. What is 45% of 432?
Let me share something with you. The word "is" means = and the word "of" means multiply(x)
When we solve these, we changed the percentage to a decimal. 45% becomes .45.
Then let's rewrite the formula.   432 x .45= Now we can solve it. 195 people are boys

Solve:
What is 32% of 21?   _____   What is 11% of 15?_____

Draw	Fraction	Percent	decimal
			0.25
	$\dfrac{37}{100}$		
		18%	
	$\dfrac{7}{10}$		
		4%	

Do you remember possessive nouns?

It shows who or what owns something. A singular possessive noun is formed by adding an 's to the noun.

A plural possessive that ends in s, add an apostrophe.

A plural possessive that does not end in s, add an ' and s.

Write the correct possessive of the bold noun on line.

1.   Marie found the three **girls** note in the basket. _____
2.   All the **houses** balconies had beautiful railings._____
3.   Both **door** hinges squeaked._____
4.   **Grandmas** frown made them feel a little scared._____
5.   Jim called his **sister**s names to get their attention._____
6.   The girls smelled the **pies** aroma, so they stayed longer._____
7.   When the **girls** got home, Moms face showed that she was upset._____
8.   The **childrens** trip to the beach was special because Jim joined them. _____

Write correct form of possessive:

The islands people _____

the girls box_____

the familys trip _____

citizens language_____

streets color _____

the forts walls _____

the horses dark eyes_____

Your other task for the day is to read. You can look online at www.plainandnotsoplain.com for book recommendations that we enjoyed reading or do an online search to find something that you are interested in. You should read for a minimum of one hour per day.

Write down the title of the book you are reading and how long you read for today.

_____

_____

Read each sentence. Find the correct spelling of the word that fits.

1. How is _____ these days?
   a. business
   b. busyness
   c. bisiness

2. The _____scampered up the tree.
   a. squirell
   b. scwirral
   c. squirrel

3. Have a glass of _____.
   a. juice
   b. juce
   c. jiiuce

4. _____comes before Wednesday.
   a. Teusday
   b. Tuesday
   c. Tuseday

5. You have nothing to _____!
   a. lose
   b. loose
   c. loze

6. Jim did a lot of _____for his project.
   a. reserch
   b. research
   c. reasearch

7. Don't_____-be hopeful instead!
   a. despare
   b. dispair
   c. despair

Area of a triangle
To find the area of a triangle, you need to multiple the base times the height and divide by 2
Area of triangle=(b x h) ÷ 2

7in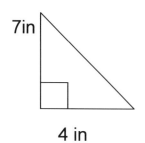

4 in

A=_____in^2

9ft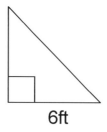

6ft

A=_____

10cm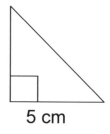

5 cm

A=_____

3in

12 ft.

A=_____in^2

7ft

15 cm

A=_____

9cm

8 in

A=_____

Add correct punctuation to each sentence: quotation and comma and exclamation point

1. People always say The desert is no place for the thirsty dog.
2. My grandmother said, It's important to have more than one means to get water.
3. Hurray the people cheered.
4. To survive in the desert, one must be sharp as a cactus said my uncle.
5. My neighbor asked How long do you plan on using the water pump?

Correct each sentence and rewrite them.

1. paul smith learned about healing plants in the rainforest.

    _____

2. mr. andrews teaches at jones lane elementary.

    _____

3. lewis and clark wanted to reach the pacific ocean.

    _____

4. last tuesday we visited henderson county.

    _____

5. many people travel on wednesday to visit family at thanksgiving.

    _____

6. he said that uncle bob knows how to fly a plane.

    _____

Your other task for the day is to read. You can look online at www.plainandnotsoplain.com for book recommendations that we enjoyed reading or do an online search to find something that you are interested in. You should read for a minimum of one hour per day.

Write down the title of the book you are reading and how long you read for today.

_____

_____

Circle the word that is spelled correctly in each row.

breathe	brethe	breithe
explaned	explened	explained
particulor	particuler	particular
rescue	reskue	rescu
meanwhile	meanwile	mean while
advertisement	advertisment	advertizement
parashute	parachute	perachute
notice	nottice	notise
advantage	advandage	advandedge
anshient	ancient	ankshent
shirt	shert	shiert
yeers	years	yeares

Measure in inches.

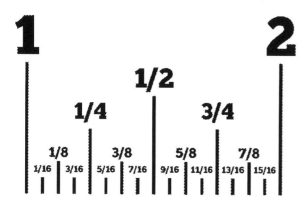

Here is the break down of an inch ruler. Measure the following to the exact sizes. Use the above chart to help you.

Measure in inches _____

Measure in inches _____

A garden that is 18 feet wide and 22 feet long needs to be fenced. Will 25 yards of fencing be enough to go around the entire garden? *change feet to yards.Explain_____

_____

Adding adverbs. Rewrite each sentence. Add two adverbs that tell when, where, or how.

1.   The Golden mare ran.

_____

2.   Alex hunted.

_____

3.   The president gave orders.

_____

4.   The Firebird flew.

_____

5.   The dog walked.

_____

6.   Lauren drove.

_____

Write good or well.

7.   The president did not rule _____.

8.   The teacher advised Alex _____.

9.   The crab was a _____ swimmer.

10.   Lauren has a _____ heart.

11.   The beautiful bird flew _____ after it had been set free.

Your other task for the day is to read. You can look online at www.plainandnotsoplain.com for book recommendations that we enjoyed reading or do an online search to find something that you are interested in. You should read for a minimum of one hour per day.

Write down the title of the book you are reading and how long you read for today.

_____

_____

Circle the word that is spelled incorrectly in each row

cirses	knives	media	roofs
pianos	waves	wishes	armys
brieves	videos	heroes	data
tomatos	tomatoes	oxen	ox
loafs	loaves	messages	canoes
lives	bacteria	bakteria	carry
illigal	illegal	garden	plant
believes	belief	bilieves	score
smoke	smoak	smote	telling
nature	hike	advinture	adventure
scene	sene	screen	seem
silence	silens	band	practice
realized	moveing	table	surprise

Adding and Subtracting Fractions

Step 1 – Find a common denominator (a number that both denominators will go into)
Step 2 – Raise each fraction to higher terms as needed
Step 3 – Add or subtract the numerators only as shown
Step 4 – Carry denominator over
Step 5 – Change the answer to lowest terms

Example #1: $\dfrac{1}{2} + \dfrac{7}{8} =$ Common denominator is 8 because both 2 and

8 will go into 8

$$\dfrac{1}{2} \searrow \dfrac{4}{8}$$

$$+ \ \dfrac{7}{8} \searrow \dfrac{7}{8}$$

$$\dfrac{11}{8} \quad \text{which simplifies to} \quad 1\dfrac{3}{8}$$

Example #2: $4\dfrac{3}{5} - \dfrac{1}{4} =$ Common denominator is 20 because both 4

and 5 will go into 20

$$4\dfrac{3}{5} \searrow 4\dfrac{12}{20}$$

$$- \ \dfrac{1}{4} \searrow \dfrac{5}{20}$$

$$4\dfrac{7}{20}$$

Write in lowest terms. Do you remember how to reduce down? Think what is the largest number that will go into both of them.   This is like making equivalent fractions, but going down instead of up☺

1. $\dfrac{5}{30}$ _____   2. $\dfrac{21}{35}$ _____   3. $\dfrac{18}{27}$ _____   4. $\dfrac{12}{15}$ _____

542

Combine the following sentences. Leave out words that repeat.

1.   Dennis went fishing. His dad went fishing.

_____

2.   It was fun looking at creatures. The creatures were tiny.

_____

3.   Dennis studied plants. Dennis studied insects.

_____

4. Dennis used microscopes. He used them to help other scientists.

_____

5. He observed nature. He observed it every day.

_____

6.   Scientists ask questions. They look for answers.

_____

7.   Frogs returned to the lakes. Fish returned to the lakes.

_____

8.   Tell someone that you want to learn. Tell a scientist.

_____

9.   There was a volcano blast. It was in 1980.

_____

10.   They saw dead trees. The trees were covered with ash.

_____

Your other task for the day is to read. You can look online at www.plainandnotsoplain.com for book recommendations that we enjoyed reading or do an online search to find something that you are interested in. You should read for a minimum of one hour per day.

Write down the title of the book you are reading and how long you read for today.

_____

_____

week 35

circle the word in each row that is spelled incorrectly

island	design	calm	colum
sword	half	yollk	walked
talk	chaulk	wrinkled	wrong
autum	solemn	aisle	foreign
lightning	benign	glistend	redesign
abcent	present	servant	moment
kurrent	assistant	statement	government
migrant	participlant	participant	patient
translation	lazyness	laziness	invention
generation	invention	situation	sicness
forgiveness	education	smallness	latness
federation	subtraction	polution	pollinate
column	colum	wrong	high school
asistant	assistant	already	servant
love	happy	family	sikness
autum	autumn	fall	winter

545

Adding unlike fractions—reduce down to lowest terms

Before we begin, we need to get the denominators the same. We need to decide which is the smallest number that both of these will go into. For example on the first problem, what is the smallest number that both 10 and 5 will go into? The answer is 10. Then we do that backwards z of making equivalent fractions. The top one stays the same because it doesn't change and the bottom changes to 8. Then we can add normally.

$$\frac{1}{10} \quad \frac{1}{10}$$

$$+\frac{4}{5} \quad \frac{8}{10}$$

_____

$$\frac{3}{12}$$

$$+\frac{1}{6}$$

_____

$$\frac{1}{2}$$

$$+\frac{1}{3}$$

_____

$$\frac{2}{3}$$

$$+\frac{1}{4}$$

_____

$$\frac{5}{12}$$

$$+\frac{1}{6}$$

_____

$$\frac{2}{5}$$

$$+\frac{9}{20}$$

_____

Write as a mixed number.

1. $\frac{10}{4}$ _____ 2. $\frac{19}{2}$ _____ 3. $\frac{25}{3}$ _____ 4. $\frac{9}{8}$ _____

5. $\frac{25}{16}$ _____ 6. $\frac{35}{4}$ _____ 7. $\frac{7}{3}$ _____ 8. $\frac{21}{8}$ _____

Draw a picture of a garden and what you would plant in it.

Now write a small paragraph describing your garden. Include lots of adjectives. Save it for tomorrow.

Your other task for the day is to read. You can look online at www.plainandnotsoplain.com for book recommendations that we enjoyed reading or do an online search to find something that you are interested in. You should read for a minimum of one hour per day.

Write down the title of the book you are reading and how long you read for today.

_____

_____

Choose a proper noun of your own to complete the sentence. Write the sentence.

11. I live in the state of_____.

12. We have a park called_____.

13. A lake by us is called_____.

14. My state capital is_____.

15. We hike up the mountain called_____.

16. The nearest big town is called_____.

17. My road is called_____.

18. My church is called_____.

19. Our pastor is named_____.

20. My mom's name is _____.

Fill in the following with common nouns not proper.

11. My favorite foods to eat are _____,
_____, and _____.

12. My favorite animals is _____.

13. My favorite outside activity is _____.

14. The animal I least like is _____.

15. My least favorite food is _____.

16. A sport played outdoors is _____.

17. A sport played indoors is _____

18. _____you will find in a body of water.

19. _____you will find up in the air.

20. _____you will find on the land.

Use a crayon or colored pencil and highlight all the proper nouns one color and all the common nouns another color. Notice that none of them are capitalized☺

river	mississippi river	georgia	state
oak	tree	lauren	girl
town	zirconia	doll	sarah
teacher	mr. maryon	country	ireland
mt. mitchell	restaurant	jesus	person

Subtracting unlike fractions—remember how we did this yesterday? Convert to a equivalent fraction with the lowest possible denominator. Then solve

$$\begin{array}{r} \frac{3}{5} \\ -\frac{1}{4} \\ \hline \end{array}$$

$$\begin{array}{r} \frac{5}{6} \\ -\frac{1}{3} \\ \hline \end{array}$$

$$\begin{array}{r} \frac{9}{16} \\ -\frac{1}{4} \\ \hline \end{array}$$

$$\begin{array}{r} \frac{2}{3} \\ -\frac{1}{12} \\ \hline \end{array}$$

$$\begin{array}{r} \frac{18}{25} \\ -\frac{2}{5} \\ \hline \end{array}$$

$$\begin{array}{r} \frac{1}{7} \\ -\frac{1}{14} \\ \hline \end{array}$$

Write as an improper fraction.

1. $1\frac{1}{8}$ _____ 2. $4\frac{1}{5}$ _____ 3. $1\frac{2}{3}$ _____ 4. $2\frac{3}{16}$ _____

5. $2\frac{5}{7}$ _____ 6. $2\frac{1}{16}$ _____ 7. $1\frac{5}{8}$ _____ 8. $3\frac{4}{5}$ _____

550

Take your writing from yesterday and circle five adjectives. I want you to look up synonyms for those adjectives and choose words you normally would not use. I want you to add 3 prepositional phrases to your writing. Rewrite your paragraph.

_____

_____

_____

_____

_____

_____

_____

_____

_____

_____

_____

_____

_____

_____

Your other task for the day is to read. You can look online at www.plainandnotsoplain.com for book recommendations that we enjoyed reading or do an online search to find something that you are interested in. You should read for a minimum of one hour per day.

Write down the title of the book you are reading and how long you read for today.

_____

_____

Which reference book would you use for the following:

1. Which source would you use to learn how to make pancakes?

   Dictionary   atlas   cookbook

2. Which source might show where Triple Falls is?

   Dictionary   atlas   thesaurus

3. Which source would describe the peacock?

   Book on insects   encyclopedia   newspaper

4. Which source would describe the sounds a cricket make?

   Book on insects   thesaurus   atlas

5. Which source would give the meaning of "constable"

   Newspaper   atlas   dictionary

6. Which source would describe the most recent world events?

   Newspaper   encyclopedia   thesaurus

7. Which source would tell you how to divide "accommodations" into syllables?

   Dictionary   book on insects   thesaurus

8. Which source could give a synonym for "pull"?

   Thesaurus   cookbook   encyclopedia

9. Which source might best forecast tomorrow's weather?

   Newspaper   atlas   encyclopedia

10. Which source would show you kitchen measurement equivalents?

   Cookbook   dictionary   atlas

Add

1. $\dfrac{3}{8} + \dfrac{7}{8} =$

2. $\dfrac{2}{3} + \dfrac{3}{4} =$

3. $\dfrac{3}{32} + \dfrac{1}{8} =$

4. $\dfrac{3}{5} + \dfrac{5}{6} =$

9. $1\dfrac{5}{8} + \dfrac{13}{16} =$

10. $2\dfrac{2}{3} + \dfrac{4}{9} =$

$\dfrac{7}{8} - \dfrac{1}{2} =$

$\dfrac{11}{16} - \dfrac{1}{4} =$

$5\dfrac{5}{6} - 2\dfrac{3}{9} =$

Write a paper detailing what you have learned this year in the 5th grade. Include and use all your rules to your paper. Write it today and then you will go over and see what you can change to make it more interesting and rewrite tomorrow.

_____

_____

_____

_____

_____

_____

_____

_____

_____

_____

_____

_____

_____

_____

_____

_____

_____

_____

_____

_____

_____

_____

_____

_____

Your other task for the day is to read. You can look online at www.plainandnotsoplain.com for book recommendations that we enjoyed reading or do an online search to find something that you are interested in. You should read for a minimum of one hour per day.

Write down the title of the book you are reading and how long you read for today.

_____

_____

Circle the word that is spelled correctly in each row

capable	capabel	capeable
carless	careless	kareles
desireable	desirable	dessireable
restless	reslecs	resttless
helpless	helples	help less
undeniable	undeniabel	undenible
reliable	relble	realiable
tastless	tasteless	tastlss
enginner	enginear	engineer
pionear	pioneer	pionner
commandr	commander	commandar

Factors---remember when we did the factors of a number? The factors of 10 are: 1,2,5,10. Those are all the numbers that can divide into ten. Finding the GCF greatest common factor of numbers is helpful in reducing fractions.

Find the GCF of 6 and 9.

The Factors of 6: 1,2,3,6

the factors of 9: 1,3,9

The biggest factor that is common is 3

Find the GCF of:

6 and 10

12 and 15

When sixty-five and fourteen hundredths is subtracted from eighty and forty-eight hundredths, what is the difference?

Use the GCF of 20 and 30 to reduce 20/30

If one side of a regular octagon is 12 inches long, what is the perimeter?

Can you hold your hand one foot apart? _____ Hold them one yard apart? _____

One miles is how many feet?

One foot is how many inches?

How many feet in one yard?

Subtract and reduce $5 \ 5/6 - 2 \ 1/6 =$

Find the average of Eva's bowling score: 109,98, and 135

If the width of a rectangle is half its length, the length is 20mm, what is the perimeter?

What is eighty-seven dollars divided by 6 equal?

Read your paragraph out loud to yourself from yesterday and see if there is something that you can do to make it better. Circle your mistakes and improve them here.

_____

_____

_____

_____

_____

_____

_____

_____

_____

_____

_____

_____

_____

_____

_____

_____

_____

_____

_____

_____

Your other task for the day is to read. You can look online at www.plainandnotsoplain.com for book recommendations that we enjoyed reading or do an online search to find something that you are interested in. You should read for a minimum of one hour per day.

Write down the title of the book you are reading and how long you read for today.

_____

_____

Solve

1,035 ÷23

492 x 832

x- 56,409= 240,021   solve for x

Y÷7200= 900 solve for Y

N ÷14=236

List the factors for

26:

40:

59:

Write the numbers

70 million 16 thousand 90

32 billion 232 thousand

five hundred twenty-one thousand, four hundred nine

four million, two hundred fifty one thousand, seventeen

eight hundred million, nineteen

Use the following number to answer the questions below

1,234,567,890

What is the VALUE of the 2?

What is the Value of the 9?

What is the value of the 3?

What place value is the 7 in?

What place value is the 1 in?

432 x 25   827x 233

873÷22   923÷3

Your other task for the day is to read. You can look online at www.plainandnotsoplain.com for book recommendations that we enjoyed reading or do an online search to find something that you are interested in. You should read for a minimum of one hour per day.

Write down the title of the book you are reading and how long you read for today.

_____

_____

100 Multiplication facts

9 x1	2 x2	5 x1	4 x3	0 x0	9 x9	3 x5	8 x5	2 x6	4 x7
5 x6	7 x5	3 x0	8 x8	1 x3	3 x4	5 x9	0 x2	7 x3	4 x 1
2 x3	8 x6	0 x5	6 x1	3 x8	1 x 1	9 x0	2 x8	6 x4	0 x7
7 x7	1 x4	6 x2	4 x5	2 x4	4 x 9	7 x0	1 x2	8 x4	6 x5
3 x2	4 x6	1 x9	5 x7	8 x2	0 x8	4 x2	9 x8	3 x6	5 x5
8 x9	3 x7	9 x7	1 x7	6 x0	0 x3	7 x2	1 x5	7 x8	4 x0
8 x3	5 x2	0 x4	9 x5	6 x7	2 x7	6 x3	5 x4	1 x0	9 x 2
7 x 6	1 x 8	9 x6	4 x 4	5 x3	8 x1	3 x3	4 x8	9 x3	2 x0
8 x0	3 x1	6 x8	0 x9	8 x7	2 x 9	9 x4	0 x1	7 x4	5 x8
0 x6	7 x1	2 x5	6 x9	3 x9	1 x6	5 x0	6 x6	2 x1	7 x9

564

Circle the word in the row that is spelled incorrectly

walker	calk	laws	stalk
bald	drawn	cawght	halt
strawberry	fought	caler	half
straw	small	tought	talking
awe	shawl	fallse	squall
south	porch	annoi	wallpaper
awkward	saved	hooge	cookie
worried	families	cawt	storm
funnier	huge	groop	clowns
food	shold	tasted	better
woried	ripped	huge	hole
group	caring	families	hert
discussing	laws	criminals	cawf
anoi	south	trip	caught
thaught	saved	cookie	south

Which of these letters has no lines of symmetry?

M I C K E Y

47x 26   82x 14

$5-$4.25   156 +29

284÷2   369÷3

READING

Your other task for the day is to read a book. Write the title of the book you are reading and how long you have read for.

_____

_____

Division Facts 0-9

56÷7=	15÷3=	12÷6=	8÷2=	63÷7=	0÷4=
14÷2=	42÷6=	6÷1=	16÷8=	20÷5=	49÷7=
36÷4=	64÷8=	0÷3=	54÷9=	4÷2=	48÷8=
18÷9=	3÷1=	35÷5=	8÷4=	72÷8=	6÷6=
0÷5=	42÷7=	2÷2=	36÷9=	7÷1=	12÷3=
16÷2=	30÷5=	0÷1=	28÷7=	4÷4=	40÷8=
3÷3=	32÷8=	45÷5=	4÷1=	20÷4=	15÷5=
56÷8=	5÷1=	0÷8=	6÷2=	45÷9=	0÷6=
6÷3=	21÷7=	0÷9=	7÷7=	12÷4=	18÷6=
63÷9=	18÷3=	27÷9=	24÷3=	0÷2=	28÷4=
21÷3=	16÷4=	24÷8=	10÷5=	30÷6=	1÷1=
18÷2=	27÷3=	32÷4=	9÷1=	35÷7=	40÷5=
10÷2=	8÷8=	48÷6=	5÷5=	8÷1=	24÷6=
25÷5=	9÷3=	81÷9=	24÷4=	14÷7=	12÷2=
9÷9=	54÷6=	72÷9=	0÷7=	2÷1=	36÷6=

Write a descriptive paragraph describing a place you would like to go on vacation.

Give me 10 adjectives that describe YOU:

1. _____
2. _____
3. _____
4. _____
5. _____
6. _____
7. _____
8. _____
9. _____
10. _____

What do you think you improved upon the most this year?_____

_____

What class did you enjoy the most this year?_____

_____

What is something you want to learn new next year?

_____

What is something you "wish" you didn't have to do?_____

_____

100 Multiplication facts

9 x1	2 x2	5 x1	4 x3	0 x0	9 x9	3 x5	8 x5	2 x6	4 x7
5 x6	7 x5	3 x0	8 x8	1 x3	3 x4	5 x9	0 x2	7 x3	4 x 1
2 x3	8 x6	0 x5	6 x1	3 x8	1 x 1	9 x0	2 x8	6 x4	0 x7
7 x7	1 x4	6 x2	4 x5	2 x4	4 x 9	7 x0	1 x2	8 x4	6 x5
3 x2	4 x6	1 x9	5 x7	8 x2	0 x8	4 x2	9 x8	3 x6	5 x5
8 x9	3 x7	9 x7	1 x7	6 x0	0 x3	7 x2	1 x5	7 x8	4 x0
8 x3	5 x2	0 x4	9 x5	6 x7	2 x7	6 x3	5 x4	1 x0	9 x 2
7 x 6	1 x 8	9 x6	4 x 4	5 x3	8 x1	3 x3	4 x8	9 x3	2 x0
8 x0	3 x1	6 x8	0 x9	8 x7	2 x 9	9 x4	0 x1	7 x4	5 x8
0 x6	7 x1	2 x5	6 x9	3 x9	1 x6	5 x0	6 x6	2 x1	7 x9

Write a descriptive paragraph describing how you feel about your family.

_____

_____

_____

_____

_____

_____

_____

_____

_____

_____

_____

_____

_____

_____

_____

_____

_____

READING

Your other task for the day is to read a book. Write the title of the book you are reading and how long you have read for.

_____

_____

Use words to write 356,320

9.36 – (4.37-3.8)

24.32- (8.61+12.5)

723x231   899x1000

76x1000   765432x1000

How do we find out how much will fill a container? We need to find the volume of an object. That sort of object needs to be 3d. Imagine a cube, how much could we fit inside of it? We figure that out by using this formula Volume= length x width x height

The height inside is 3

Length 2 inches   width 3 inches   To find the volume we take 3x3x2=18 inches cubed or 18 in^3

Remember V=l x w x h
What is the volume of a cube with dimensions 4 ft, 2 ft, 3 ft=_____

The dimensions are 13 in length,   9 in. width, and 2 in height. What is volume_____

The dimensions are 8 ft in length, 4 ft in width, and 3 ft in width. What is the volume_____

Write the following as a percent

.21_____   .89_____   32.39_____   31.98_____

Write the following as a decimal

75%_____   23%_____   125%_____   1/5_____

$\frac{3}{4}$_____   2/5_____ $\frac{1}{4}$_____   1/10_____

Write as a fraction

75%_____   5%_____   20%_____   25%_____

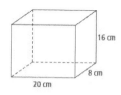 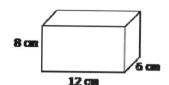 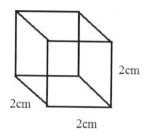

V=_____cm3   V=_____   V=_____

What is the volume of a cube with sides: 4cm,3cm, and 2cm?

5(30+4)=   5(34)=

How many dimes equal $1? and $5?

Reciprocal

If we switch the numerator and denominator in a fraction, the new fraction is the reciprocal of the first fraction. The reciprocal has the same term, but their positions are reversed. When we switch the position of the numerator and the denominator, we invert the fraction.

The reciprocal of 2/3 is 3/2

Whole numbers have reciprocals. Remember that a whole number may be written as a fraction over 1. So the whole number 2 may be written as 2/1. The reciprocal is ½

Your turn: What is the reciprocal of 1/3   Of 3?

A quarter is what fraction of a dollar?   How many quarters equal $1?

Which of the following means "How many 25s are there in 500?"
25÷500   500÷25   25x500   500x25

($20-$4.72)÷8   160x$1.42

Reduce 15/25   27x=567

Draw two circles. Shade ½ of one circle and 2/3 of the other

Use digits to write number: ninety-three million, eight hundred fourteen thousand, two hundred

9 x1	2 x2	5 x1	4 x3	0 x0	9 x9	3 x5	8 x5	2 x6	4 x7
5 x6	7 x5	3 x0	8 x8	1 x3	3 x4	5 x9	0 x2	7 x3	4 x 1
2 x3	8 x6	0 x5	6 x1	3 x8	1 x 1	9 x0	2 x8	6 x4	0 x7
7 x7	1 x4	6 x2	4 x5	2 x4	4 x 9	7 x0	1 x2	8 x4	6 x5
3 x2	4 x6	1 x9	5 x7	8 x2	0 x8	4 x2	9 x8	3 x6	5 x5
8 x9	3 x7	9 x7	1 x7	6 x0	0 x3	7 x2	1 x5	7 x8	4 x0
8 x3	5 x2	0 x4	9 x5	6 x7	2 x7	6 x3	5 x4	1 x0	9 x 2
7 x 6	1 x 8	9 x6	4 x 4	5 x3	8 x1	3 x3	4 x8	9 x3	2 x0
8 x0	3 x1	6 x8	0 x9	8 x7	2 x 9	9 x4	0 x1	7 x4	5 x8
0 x6	7 x1	2 x5	6 x9	3 x9	1 x6	5 x0	6 x6	2 x1	7 x9

READING

Your other task for the day is to read a book. Write the title of the book you are reading and how long you have read for.

_____

_____

Also including extra speed math test for practice. Copy as needed.

100 addition practice

4 +4	7 +5	0 +1	8 +7	3 +4	3 +2	8 +3	2 +1	5 +6	2 +9
0 +9	8 +9	7 +6	1 +3	6 +8	7 +3	1 +6	4 +7	0 +3	6 +4
9 +3	2 +6	3 +0	6 +1	3 +6	4 +0	5 +7	1 +1	5 +4	2 +8
4 +3	0 +9	0 +7	9 +4	7 +7	8 +6	0 +4	5 +8	7 +4	1 +7
9 +5	1 +5	9 +0	3 +8	1 +9	9 +1	8 +8	2 +2	4 +5	6 +2
7 +9	1 +2	6 +7	0 +8	9 +2	4 +8	8 +0	3 +9	1 +0	6 +3
2 +0	8 +4	3 +5	9 +8	5 +0	5 +5	3 +1	7 +2	8 +5	2 +5
5 +2	0 +5	6 +9	1 +8	9 +6	7 +1	4 +6	0 +2	6 +5	4 +9
1 +4	3 +7	7 +0	2 +3	5 +1	6 +6	4 +1	8 +2	2 +4	6 +0
5 +3	4 +2	9 +7	0 +6	7 +8	0 +0	5 +9	3 +3	8 +1	2 +7

577

100 subtraction

7 -0	10 -8	6 -3	14 -5	3 -1	16 -9	7 -1	18 -9	11 -3	13 -7
13 -8	7 -4	10 -7	0 -0	12 -8	10 -9	6 -2	13 -4	4 -0	10 -5
5 -3	7 -5	2 -1	6 -6	8 -4	7 -2	14 -7	8 -1	11 -6	3 -3
1 -1	11 -9	10 -4	9 -2	14 -6	17 -8	6 -0	10 -6	4 -1	9 -5
7 -7	14 -8	12 -9	9 -8	12 -7	12 -3	16 -8	9 -1	15 -6	11 -4
8 -6	15 -9	11 -8	3 -2	4 -4	8 -2	11 -5	5 -0	17 -9	6 -1
5 -5	4 -3	8 -7	7 -3	7 -6	5 -1	10 -3	12 -6	10 -1	6 -4
2 -2	13 -6	15 -8	2 -0	13 -9	16 -7	5 -2	12 -4	3 -0	11 -7
8 -0	9 -4	10 -2	6 -5	8 -3	9 -0	5 -4	12 -5	4 -2	9 -3
9 -9	15 -7	8 -8	14 -9	9 -7	13 -5	1 -0	8 -5	9 -6	11 -2

4 +4	7 +5	0 +1	8 +7	3 +4	3 +2	8 +3	2 +1	5 +6	2 +9
0 +9	8 +9	7 +6	1 +3	6 +8	7 +3	1 +6	4 +7	0 +3	6 +4
9 +3	2 +6	3 +0	6 +1	3 +6	4 +0	5 +7	1 +1	5 +4	2 +8
4 +3	0 +9	0 +7	9 +4	7 +7	8 +6	0 +4	5 +8	7 +4	1 +7
9 +5	1 +5	9 +0	3 +8	1 +9	9 +1	8 +8	2 +2	4 +5	6 +2
7 +9	1 +2	6 +7	0 +8	9 +2	4 +8	8 +0	3 +9	1 +0	6 +3
2 +0	8 +4	3 +5	9 +8	5 +0	5 +5	3 +1	7 +2	8 +5	2 +5
5 +2	0 +5	6 +9	1 +8	9 +6	7 +1	4 +6	0 +2	6 +5	4 +9
1 +4	3 +7	7 +0	2 +3	5 +1	6 +6	4 +1	8 +2	2 +4	6 +0
5 +3	4 +2	9 +7	0 +6	7 +8	0 +0	5 +9	3 +3	8 +1	2 +7

100 subtraction

7 -0	10 -8	6 -3	14 -5	3 -1	16 -9	7 -1	18 -9	11 -3	13 -7
13 -8	7 -4	10 -7	0 -0	12 -8	10 -9	6 -2	13 -4	4 -0	10 -5
5 -3	7 -5	2 -1	6 -6	8 -4	7 -2	14 -7	8 -1	11 -6	3 -3
1 -1	11 -9	10 -4	9 -2	14 -6	17 -8	6 -0	10 -6	4 -1	9 -5
7 -7	14 -8	12 -9	9 -8	12 -7	12 -3	16 -8	9 -1	15 -6	11 -4
8 -6	15 -9	11 -8	3 -2	4 -4	8 -2	11 -5	5 -0	17 -9	6 -1
5 -5	4 -3	8 -7	7 -3	7 -6	5 -1	10 -3	12 -6	10 -1	6 -4
2 -2	13 -6	15 -8	2 -0	13 -9	16 -7	5 -2	12 -4	3 -0	11 -7
8 -0	9 -4	10 -2	6 -5	8 -3	9 -0	5 -4	12 -5	4 -2	9 -3
9 -9	15 -7	8 -8	14 -9	9 -7	13 -5	1 -0	8 -5	9 -6	11 -2

100 multiplication facts

9 x1	2 x2	5 x1	4 x3	0 x0	9 x9	3 x5	8 x5	2 x6	4 x7
5 x6	7 x5	3 x0	8 x8	1 x3	3 x4	5 x9	0 x2	7 x3	4 x 1
2 x3	8 x6	0 x5	6 x1	3 x8	1 x 1	9 x0	2 x8	6 x4	0 x7
7 x7	1 x4	6 x2	4 x5	2 x4	4 x 9	7 x0	1 x2	8 x4	6 x5
3 x2	4 x6	1 x9	5 x7	8 x2	0 x8	4 x2	9 x8	3 x6	5 x5
8 x9	3 x7	9 x7	1 x7	6 x0	0 x3	7 x2	1 x5	7 x8	4 x0
8 x3	5 x2	0 x4	9 x5	6 x7	2 x7	6 x3	5 x4	1 x0	9 x 2
7 x 6	1 x 8	9 x6	4 x 4	5 x3	8 x1	3 x3	4 x8	9 x3	2 x0
8 x0	3 x1	6 x8	0 x9	8 x7	2 x 9	9 x4	0 x1	7 x4	5 x8
0 x6	7 x1	2 x5	6 x9	3 x9	1 x6	5 x0	6 x6	2 x1	7 x9

100 division facts

56÷7=	15÷3=	12÷6=	8÷2=	63÷7=	0÷4=
14÷2=	42÷6=	6÷1=	16÷8=	20÷5=	49÷7=
36÷4=	64÷8=	0÷3=	54÷9=	4÷2=	48÷8=
18÷9=	3÷1=	35÷5=	8÷4=	72÷8=	6÷6=
0÷5=	42÷7=	2÷2=	36÷9=	7÷1=	12÷3=
16÷2=	30÷5=	0÷1=	28÷7=	4÷4=	40÷8=
3÷3=	32÷8=	45÷5=	4÷1=	20÷4=	15÷5=
56÷8=	5÷1=	0÷8=	6÷2=	45÷9=	0÷6=
6÷3=	21÷7=	0÷9=	7÷7=	12÷4=	18÷6=
63÷9=	18÷3=	27÷9=	24÷3=	0÷2=	28÷4=
21÷3=	16÷4=	24÷8=	10÷5=	30÷6=	1÷1=
18÷2=	27÷3=	32÷4=	9÷1=	35÷7=	40÷5=
10÷2=	8÷8=	48÷6=	5÷5=	8÷1=	24÷6=
25÷5=	9÷3=	81÷9=	24÷4=	14÷7=	12÷2=
9÷9=	54÷6=	72÷9=	0÷7=	2÷1=	36÷6=

4 +4	7 +5	0 +1	8 +7	3 +4	3 +2	8 +3	2 +1	5 +6	2 +9
0 +9	8 +9	7 +6	1 +3	6 +8	7 +3	1 +6	4 +7	0 +3	6 +4
9 +3	2 +6	3 +0	6 +1	3 +6	4 +0	5 +7	1 +1	5 +4	2 +8
4 +3	0 +9	0 +7	9 +4	7 +7	8 +6	0 +4	5 +8	7 +4	1 +7
9 +5	1 +5	9 +0	3 +8	1 +9	9 +1	8 +8	2 +2	4 +5	6 +2
7 +9	1 +2	6 +7	0 +8	9 +2	4 +8	8 +0	3 +9	1 +0	6 +3
2 +0	8 +4	3 +5	9 +8	5 +0	5 +5	3 +1	7 +2	8 +5	2 +5
5 +2	0 +5	6 +9	1 +8	9 +6	7 +1	4 +6	0 +2	6 +5	4 +9
1 +4	3 +7	7 +0	2 +3	5 +1	6 +6	4 +1	8 +2	2 +4	6 +0
5 +3	4 +2	9 +7	0 +6	7 +8	0 +0	5 +9	3 +3	8 +1	2 +7

100 subtraction

7 -0	10 -8	6 -3	14 -5	3 -1	16 -9	7 -1	18 -9	11 -3	13 -7
13 -8	7 -4	10 -7	0 -0	12 -8	10 -9	6 -2	13 -4	4 -0	10 -5
5 -3	7 -5	2 -1	6 -6	8 -4	7 -2	14 -7	8 -1	11 -6	3 -3
1 -1	11 -9	10 -4	9 -2	14 -6	17 -8	6 -0	10 -6	4 -1	9 -5
7 -7	14 -8	12 -9	9 -8	12 -7	12 -3	16 -8	9 -1	15 -6	11 -4
8 -6	15 -9	11 -8	3 -2	4 -4	8 -2	11 -5	5 -0	17 -9	6 -1
5 -5	4 -3	8 -7	7 -3	7 -6	5 -1	10 -3	12 -6	10 -1	6 -4
2 -2	13 -6	15 -8	2 -0	13 -9	16 -7	5 -2	12 -4	3 -0	11 -7
8 -0	9 -4	10 -2	6 -5	8 -3	9 -0	5 -4	12 -5	4 -2	9 -3
9 -9	15 -7	8 -8	14 -9	9 -7	13 -5	1 -0	8 -5	9 -6	11 -2

100 multiplication facts

9 ×1	2 ×2	5 ×1	4 ×3	0 ×0	9 ×9	3 ×5	8 ×5	2 ×6	4 ×7
5 ×6	7 ×5	3 ×0	8 ×8	1 ×3	3 ×4	5 ×9	0 ×2	7 ×3	4 ×1
2 ×3	8 ×6	0 ×5	6 ×1	3 ×8	1 ×1	9 ×0	2 ×8	6 ×4	0 ×7
7 ×7	1 ×4	6 ×2	4 ×5	2 ×4	4 ×9	7 ×0	1 ×2	8 ×4	6 ×5
3 ×2	4 ×6	1 ×9	5 ×7	8 ×2	0 ×8	4 ×2	9 ×8	3 ×6	5 ×5
8 ×9	3 ×7	9 ×7	1 ×7	6 ×0	0 ×3	7 ×2	1 ×5	7 ×8	4 ×0
8 ×3	5 ×2	0 ×4	9 ×5	6 ×7	2 ×7	6 ×3	5 ×4	1 ×0	9 ×2
7 ×6	1 ×8	9 ×6	4 ×4	5 ×3	8 ×1	3 ×3	4 ×8	9 ×3	2 ×0
8 ×0	3 ×1	6 ×8	0 ×9	8 ×7	2 ×9	9 ×4	0 ×1	7 ×4	5 ×8
0 ×6	7 ×1	2 ×5	6 ×9	3 ×9	1 ×6	5 ×0	6 ×6	2 ×1	7 ×9

100 division facts

56÷7=	15÷3=	12÷6=	8÷2=	63÷7=	0÷4=
14÷2=	42÷6=	6÷1=	16÷8=	20÷5=	49÷7=
36÷4=	64÷8=	0÷3=	54÷9=	4÷2=	48÷8=
18÷9=	3÷1=	35÷5=	8÷4=	72÷8=	6÷6=
0÷5=	42÷7=	2÷2=	36÷9=	7÷1=	12÷3=
16÷2=	30÷5=	0÷1=	28÷7=	4÷4=	40÷8=
3÷3=	32÷8=	45÷5=	4÷1=	20÷4=	15÷5=
56÷8=	5÷1=	0÷8=	6÷2=	45÷9=	0÷6=
6÷3=	21÷7=	0÷9=	7÷7=	12÷4=	18÷6=
63÷9=	18÷3=	27÷9=	24÷3=	0÷2=	28÷4=
21÷3=	16÷4=	24÷8=	10÷5=	30÷6=	1÷1=
18÷2=	27÷3=	32÷4=	9÷1=	35÷7=	40÷5=
10÷2=	8÷8=	48÷6=	5÷5=	8÷1=	24÷6=
25÷5=	9÷3=	81÷9=	24÷4=	14÷7=	12÷2=
9÷9=	54÷6=	72÷9=	0÷7=	2÷1=	36÷6=

4 +4	7 +5	0 +1	8 +7	3 +4	3 +2	8 +3	2 +1	5 +6	2 +9
0 +9	8 +9	7 +6	1 +3	6 +8	7 +3	1 +6	4 +7	0 +3	6 +4
9 +3	2 +6	3 +0	6 +1	3 +6	4 +0	5 +7	1 +1	5 +4	2 +8
4 +3	0 +9	0 +7	9 +4	7 +7	8 +6	0 +4	5 +8	7 +4	1 +7
9 +5	1 +5	9 +0	3 +8	1 +9	9 +1	8 +8	2 +2	4 +5	6 +2
7 +9	1 +2	6 +7	0 +8	9 +2	4 +8	8 +0	3 +9	1 +0	6 +3
2 +0	8 +4	3 +5	9 +8	5 +0	5 +5	3 +1	7 +2	8 +5	2 +5
5 +2	0 +5	6 +9	1 +8	9 +6	7 +1	4 +6	0 +2	6 +5	4 +9
1 +4	3 +7	7 +0	2 +3	5 +1	6 +6	4 +1	8 +2	2 +4	6 +0
5 +3	4 +2	9 +7	0 +6	7 +8	0 +0	5 +9	3 +3	8 +1	2 +7

100 subtraction

7 -0	10 - 8	6 -3	14 - 5	3 - 1	16 - 9	7 - 1	18 - 9	11 - 3	13 - 7
13 - 8	7 -4	10 - 7	0 -0	12 - 8	10 - 9	6 - 2	13 - 4	4 -0	10 - 5
5 -3	7 -5	2 -1	6 -6	8 -4	7 -2	14 -7	8 -1	11 - 6	3 -3
1 -1	11 -9	10 -4	9 -2	14 - 6	17 - 8	6 -0	10 -6	4 -1	9 -5
7 -7	14 - 8	12 -9	9 -8	12 -7	12 - 3	16 -8	9 -1	15 - 6	11 -4
8 -6	15 -9	11 -8	3 -2	4 -4	8 -2	11 -5	5 -0	17 -9	6 -1
5 -5	4 -3	8 -7	7 -3	7 -6	5 -1	10 -3	12 -6	10 -1	6 -4
2 -2	13 -6	15 -8	2 -0	13 -9	16 -7	5 -2	12 -4	3 -0	11 -7
8 -0	9 -4	10 -2	6 -5	8 -3	9 -0	5 -4	12 -5	4 -2	9 -3
9 -9	15 -7	8 -8	14 -9	9 -7	13 -5	1 -0	8 -5	9 -6	11 -2

590

100 multiplication facts

9 x1	2 x2	5 x1	4 x3	0 x0	9 x9	3 x5	8 x5	2 x6	4 x7
5 x6	7 x5	3 x0	8 x8	1 x3	3 x4	5 x9	0 x2	7 x3	4 x 1
2 x3	8 x6	0 x5	6 x1	3 x8	1 x 1	9 x0	2 x8	6 x4	0 x7
7 x7	1 x4	6 x2	4 x5	2 x4	4 x 9	7 x0	1 x2	8 x4	6 x5
3 x2	4 x6	1 x9	5 x7	8 x2	0 x8	4 x2	9 x8	3 x6	5 x5
8 x9	3 x7	9 x7	1 x7	6 x0	0 x3	7 x2	1 x5	7 x8	4 x0
8 x3	5 x2	0 x4	9 x5	6 x7	2 x7	6 x3	5 x4	1 x0	9 x 2
7 x 6	1 x 8	9 x6	4 x 4	5 x3	8 x1	3 x3	4 x8	9 x3	2 x0
8 x0	3 x1	6 x8	0 x9	8 x7	2 x 9	9 x4	0 x1	7 x4	5 x8
0 x6	7 x1	2 x5	6 x9	3 x9	1 x6	5 x0	6 x6	2 x1	7 x9

100 division facts

56÷7=	15÷3=	12÷6=	8÷2=	63÷7=	0÷4=
14÷2=	42÷6=	6÷1=	16÷8=	20÷5=	49÷7=
36÷4=	64÷8=	0÷3=	54÷9=	4÷2=	48÷8=
18÷9=	3÷1=	35÷5=	8÷4=	72÷8=	6÷6=
0÷5=	42÷7=	2÷2=	36÷9=	7÷1=	12÷3=
16÷2=	30÷5=	0÷1=	28÷7=	4÷4=	40÷8=
3÷3=	32÷8=	45÷5=	4÷1=	20÷4=	15÷5=
56÷8=	5÷1=	0÷8=	6÷2=	45÷9=	0÷6=
6÷3=	21÷7=	0÷9=	7÷7=	12÷4=	18÷6=
63÷9=	18÷3=	27÷9=	24÷3=	0÷2=	28÷4=
21÷3=	16÷4=	24÷8=	10÷5=	30÷6=	1÷1=
18÷2=	27÷3=	32÷4=	9÷1=	35÷7=	40÷5=
10÷2=	8÷8=	48÷6=	5÷5=	8÷1=	24÷6=
25÷5=	9÷3=	81÷9=	24÷4=	14÷7=	12÷2=
9÷9=	54÷6=	72÷9=	0÷7=	2÷1=	36÷6=

These are 25 weeks of vocabulary words that every 5th grader should know. I would suggest you copy them onto index cards at the beginning of the week and have your child practice saying them and knowing what they mean by the end of each week.

Week 1	Week 2	Week 3	Week 4	Week 5
arachnophobia	psychology	scissors	diesel	mentor
couldn't	beneath	discussed	Braille	panacea
represent	cardiologist	incision	maverick	volcano
anthropology	describe	either	valentines	electricity
whether	although	personification	embarrassed	embarrassment
cardiology	belief	mesmerize	especially	frighten
clothes	another	breathe	everywhere	height
flower	bactericide	valentine	excellent	himself
teacher	insecticide	committee	atlas	humorous
dermatology	herbicide	shrapnel	cereal	cliché
meteorology	personification	desert	enough	foreign
ethnology	onomatopoeia	vandal	hygiene	ambience

Week 6	Week7	Week 8	Week 9	Week 10
bizarre	chocolate	alcohol	usually	you're
hungry	hurricanes	magazine	elegant	your
brochure	hurricane	colonel	distinct	diminutive
entourage	tornado	incognito	rugged	colossal
impromptu	canyon	alfresco	glamorous	enormous
debris	canoe	hamburger	unsightly	weight
square	avocado	schema	shadowy	considerate
knowledge	necessary	artichokes	thought	miniature
its	neighbor	receive	through	immense
immediately	ourselves	recommend	though	voluminous
malapropos	once	separate	grotesque	microscopic
cafeteria	people	themselves	throughout	where

Week 15	Week 16	Week 17	Week 18	Week 19
seriously	favorite	because	insistently	adaptation
quiet	experience	divergent	intercom	temperature
oxymoron	tendency	Europe	vacationing	customary
applicant	ancient	ocean	preference	pentagon
employer	continual	adamantly	autobiography	ambulance
permanent	decade	eerily	combination	carpenter
familiar	intermittent	anxiously	amputation	requirement
fringe benefits	annual	cynically	believable	invisible
references	periodic	cowardly	indecision	outstanding
dependents	sporadic	cautiously	excitement	mystical
chronological	lengthy	casually	disagreeable	courteous
temporary	afternoons	brazenly	expression	dedicate

Week20	Week 21	Week 22	Week 23	Week 24
translation	demonstrate	transformation	congratulations	incubate
exceptional	generosity	migration	recently	thermostat
duplicate	tradition	endurance	confusion	tolerance
numerous	disaster	prominent	captivity	resistance
compensate	circular	exportable	maneuver	exponent
assurance	decisive	perishable	photographic	dictator
endanger	graduation	confidential	organic	conditions
intercept	destructive	guardianship	immunity	determine
mischievous	precious	contribute	intestine	indicate
biologist	attention	instantly	suspension	excellent
wilderness	prediction	inspiration	tragically	discovery
solitary	promotion	distracting	property	prevention

week 25
majority
humongous
maverick
intelligent
tactical
imagine
reviewing
motorway
subdivision
punishment
plentiful
colossal

Master Teacher Spelling List

week 1
amaze
anyway
basic
brace
braid
daisy
daydream
delay
dismay
essay
faint
hasten
matriarch
nature
place
raisin
wage
rate

week 2
breathe
breeze
crease
delight
donkey
eager
hockey
kidney
lease
plead
queen
recent
respond
screech
sleeve
squeak
steam
zebra

week 3
arrive
childhood
chime
climate
delight
digest
fighting
grind
ideal
prize
sight
silence
spying
style
thigh
timing
title
violin

week 4
arrow
buffalo
burro
chose
chrome
cloak
compose
cove
foam
gopher
gown
knowing
loan
loaves
roast
rows
soak
solo

week 5
argue
blue
confuse
due
duke
dune
excuse
include
issue
museum
plume
ruby
rude
statue
tissue
truth
tube
tulip

week 6
barnyard
blastoff
brand-new
chairperson
cupboard
hide-and-seek
homesick
ice skate
peanut butter
polar bear
post office
seagulls
snowstorm
topsy-turvy
town crier
yardstick
zip code

week 7
baseball
basketball
breakfast
classroom
driftwood
firefly
flagpole
harmless
knickknack
lifetime
motorcycle
paperback
playhouse
railway
switchboard
taxicab
textbook
tiptoe

week 8
aren't
can't
couldn't
didn't
hasn't
he's
i'd
isn't
let's
shouldn't
they're
they've
wasn't
weren't
we've
wouldn't
you'd
you're

week 9
additive
badge
chapter
daffodil
dragon
fraction
gathering
kangaroo
magazine
pasture
patches
rapid
sassafras
standard
tacks
thankful
transplant
traveler

week 10
ancestor
attempt
central
definition
enforce
festival
generally
genuine
legend
medicine
necessary
pedal
reference
residence
section
sentence
temperature
tennis

week 11
activities
citizen
difference
difficulties
exit
fiction
hippopotamus
individual
instrument
interesting
kitchen
listening
miniature
miserable
officer
principal
prisoner
shipment

week 12
blocked
bother
column
common
dodge
gossip
honor
model
monster
octopus
oxen
problem
product
promise
robberies
soccer
toboggan
wobble

week 13	week 16	week 19	week 22
diabetes	probe	interact	chemical
diabolic	produce	intercept	classical
diacritical	profane	interchange	comical
diadem	profound	intercom	cylindrical
diagnosis	progress	interest	electrical
diagonal	prohibit	interfere	identical
diagram	project	interject	medical
dialect	prolong	intermission	musical
dialogue	promise	internal	optical
dialysis	promote	interpret	practical
diameter	pronoun	interrogative	radical
diamond	pronounce	interrupt	skeptical
diaper	propel	intersect	surgical
diaphragm	proportion	interstate	technical
diaries	propose	interval	theatrical
diathermy	prosper	intervene	tropical
diatomic	protein	interview	typical
diatribe	provoke	intertwine	vertical

week 14	week 17	week 20	week 23
example	precaution	infect	aggravate
exchange	precise	inflate	appreciate
exercise	predict	inform	circulate
expense	prefer	injury	enunciate
expert	prefix	insecure	estimate
explore	prehistoric	insist	fascinate
extend	premature	inspire	graduate
extent	premeditate	install	hesitate
exterior	prepare	instant	immigrate
exterminate	prepay	instead	liberate
external	preschool	instinct	migrate
extinct	prescribe	institute	narrate
extinguish	preserve	instruct	navigate
extol	presume	insult	participate
extract	prevail	intense	populate
extraordinary	prevent	intent	rotate
extravagant	previous	intrude	terminate
extreme		invade	translate

week 15	week 18	week 21	week24
adapt	percent	auction	atrocious
address	percussion	champion	conscious
adequate	perfume	collection	curious
adhere	perhaps	companion	delicious
adjective	peril	competition	disastrous
adjust	period	cushion	enormous
admire	perish	digestion	ferocious
admit	permanent	election	furious
admonish	permit	location	generous
adopt	peroxide	mention	gracious
adorn	perpendicular	occupation	luscious
adult	perplex	onion	malicious
advance	persevere	operation	precious
advantage	persist	opinion	serious
advent	personality	portion	spacious
adventure	perspire	position	suspicious
advice	persuade	region	vicious
advise	perturb	religion	vivacious

week 25
arrange
bore
capture
compare
create
crowd
dance
divide
explore
give
mend
promise
reduce
shake
strange
surprise
tame
write

week 26
attached
attended
avoiding
builder
catcher
concerned
drawing
enjoying
escorted
established
poster
prisoner
repeated
scalding
scooter
seller
spelling
younger

week 27
apply
boundary
canary
century
city
company
country
dairy
enemy
factory
grocery
hobby
lily
marry
memory
pity
reply
worry

week 28
approach
beaten
blueprint
boasted
bread
breath
disagreement
easel
eastern
feelings
flue
glued
groan
increase
leather
needless
peek
reason

week 29
believe
brief
died
eight
freight
leisure
lie
perceive
piece
pies
receive
reign
retrieve
shield
shriek
siege
sleigh
vein

week 30
auction
audience
autumn
awkward
caught
cause
dawn
fawns
flaunt
haunt
jaw
lawful
raw
scrawl
shawl
taught
yawn

week 31
appointed
boiling
county
destroying
disloyal
employ
eyebrow
fowl
joyous
mountain
noises
pronounce
power
shower
spoiled
stout
surround
thousand

week 32
answer
broad
combine
council
cymbal
downstairs
false
freeze
narrow
pause
plain
punish
question
reward
separate
thaw
true
upstairs

Due to the size of this book, I was unable to include an answer key with it. You can goto www.plainandnotsoplain.com to download a free PDF with answers.

$32.011 \div 4$

$$\begin{array}{r} 8.0 \\ 4\overline{)32.011} \\ \underline{32} \\ 0 \\ \end{array}$$

Made in the USA
Lexington, KY
28 June 2019